THE HUNTER BECOMES THE HUNTED

We began the attack. From a distance of about twelve cable-lengths we fired a salvo of four torpedos. Within a minute and a half we clearly heard two loud bangs.

"Surface the submarine, Captain, and let's see our handiwork," I said to Malyshev.

But almost as soon as Malyshev raised the periscope and took a glance at the large, listing, eight-thousand-ton ship enveloped in steam, two deafening explosions shook our submarine. The lights went out, and cork, paint and the glass of the smashed bulbs showered down on us. Some invincible force seemed to be tearing the submarine to pieces. The hydroplanes jammed. The submarine lost its buoyancy and hit the sea floor at a depth of eighty-five metres. We had received a direct hit in the region of the engine room. There was water in the control room.

I thought that the end had come.

THE BANTAM WAR BOOK SERIES

This series of books is about a world on fire.

The carefully chosen volumes in the Bantam War Book Series cover the full dramatic sweep of World War II. Many are eyewitness accounts by the men who fought in a global conflict as the world's future hung in the balance. Fighter pilots, tank commanders and infantry captains, among many others, recount exploits of individual courage. They present vivid portraits of brave men, true stories of gallantry, moving sagas of survival and stark tragedies of untimely death.

In 1933 Nazi Germany marched to become an empire that was to last a thousand years. In only twelve years that empire was destroyed, and ever since, the country has been bisected by her conquerors. Italy relinquished her colonial lands, as did Japan. These were the losers. The winners also lost the empires they had so painfully seized over the centuries. And one, Russia, lost over twenty million dead.

Those wartime 1940s were a simple, even a hopeful time. Hats came in only two colors, white and black, and after an initial battering the Allied nations started on a long and laborious march toward victory. It was a time when sane men believed the world would evolve into a decent place, but, as with all futures, there was no one then who could really forecast the world that we know now.

There are many ways to think about war. It has always been hard to understand the motivations and braveries of Axis soldiers fighting to enslave and dominate their neighbors. Yet it is impossible to know the hammer without the anvil, and to comprehend ourselves we must know the people we once fought against.

Through these books we can discover what it was like to take part in the war that was a final experience for nearly fifty million human beings. In so doing we may discover the strength to make a world as good as the one contained in those dreams and aspirations once believed by heroic men. We must understand our past as an honor to those dead who can no longer choose. They exchanged their lives in a hope for this future that we now inhabit. Though the fight took place many years ago, each of us remains as a living part of it.

RUSSIAN SUBMARINES IN ARCTIC WATERS

I. KOLYSHKIN

BANTAM BOOKS
TORONTO • NEW YORK • LONDON • SYDNEY • AUCKLAND

I. Kolyshkin
In the depth of the Polar Seas

RUSSIAN SUBMARINES IN ARCTIC WATERS
A Bantam Book

PRINTING HISTORY
Originally published as Submarines in Arctic Waters *by
Progress Publishers, Moscow, 1966.*

Translated from the Russian by David Skvirsky

*Illustrations by Greg Beecham
Maps by Alan McKnight*

Bantam edition / April 1985

*Bantam Books are published by Bantam Books, Inc. Its trade-
mark, consisting of the words "Bantam Books" and the por-
trayal of a rooster, is Registered in U.S. Patent and Trademark
Office and in other countries. Marca Registrada. Bantam
Books, Inc., 666 Fifth Avenue, New York, New York 10103.*

PRINTED IN THE UNITED STATES OF AMERICA

O   0 9 8 7 6 5 4 3 2 1

RUSSIAN SUBMARINES IN ARCTIC WATERS

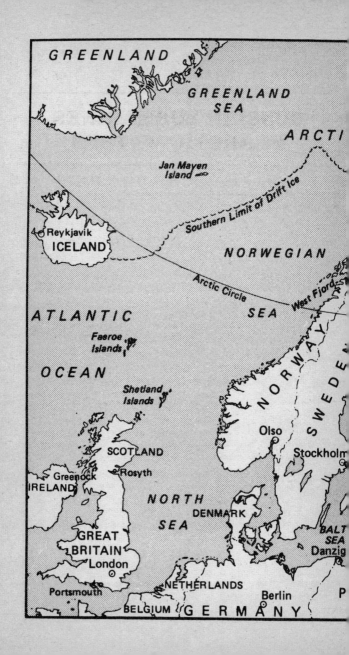

CONTENTS

PIKES SHOW THEIR TEETH

We Grapple with Our Test

It was quiet in the control room. The buzz of the main electric motors and the hum of the propellers churning the water did not reach it. The submarine was boring her way through the depths of the sea. One had only to shut one's eyes to get the impression that the submarine was motionless, that it was suspended in the water somewhere between the surface and the sea floor. But this illusion faded as soon as one glanced at the officer-of-the-watch manipulating the periscope and at the concentrated faces of the helmsmen keeping the submarine on course. Usual surroundings gave rise to usual sensations: you at once felt that the ship was alive, that she moved, obeying her well-organized crew.

The door in the watertight compartment clanged. Lieutenant-Captain Arkady Moiseyev came in dressed in a fur-lined raglan over his padded jacket and a fur-lined cap. He had just made the round of all the compartments, explaining the assignment to the men. He always made a point of talking things over with them. This, I felt, was one of the qualities that made him a fine officer.

Moiseyev had been in command of P-401 for only about six months. As Divisional Commander, I had, in that space of time, made several voyages with him. It was his first independent command and it was my job to make sure that he avoided errors that might endanger the submarine, correct him if necessary, and offer him timely advice, in short, to help him settle into his command.

I felt I knew Arkady quite well. He was no novice in the

1

submarine fleet. He had sailed as Navigator and First Lieutenant, and had a good knowledge of our difficult Northern Theater. Sailing with him as I did, I could not help noting his common sense, self-control, coolness in the face of danger, and modesty that was almost shyness. These were attractive qualities. He was simple and considerate toward his men and they quickly responded. When they spoke of him, there was genuine respect and warmth in the way they pronounced the word "skipper."

I was on board his submarine as Instructor Commander. It was the evening of June 22, 1941, a day that will always be specially marked on calendars and in the hearts of Soviet people, a day that started a significant and tragic chapter of modern history.

War creeps up stealthily and catches you unawares, even if you expect it. The clouds gather and all the ominous signs of a thunderstorm are there for all to see, but an inner voice keeps repeating: "No, no, not today, not now! Not all the crews have been made ready for combat. Not all the commanders have had the necessary training. If we could only have another six months, at least." But six months later you find the arguments against engaging in battle immediately just as weighty. That, I suppose, is how man's mind works, even if he is a soldier or a sailor. . . .

We were exceedingly anxious for a postponement. I say postponement, because nobody doubted that war would break out sooner or later. Politically, it was obvious that the conflagration, raging in Europe for two years, would inevitably leap across Soviet frontiers.

The last few weeks before the war could be compared with the lull before a storm. In May a lecturer from Moscow came to Polyarnoye, our naval base. At Naval House before an audience of officers he laid special stress on vigilance and, as though in passing, mentioned that Germany was massing troops on our frontiers.

Some days later I sailed in P-401 on patrol. The instructions from the Chief-of-Staff warned that the situation at sea was disturbing. We had information that foreign vessels were sailing near the approaches to the Kola Bay. True, they were keeping their distance, but any provocation could be expected from them.

"Your task," the Chief-of-Staff said, "is to patrol secretly, report all the vessels you see, and use your weapons only if you are attacked, in self-defense."

True, we found nothing that aroused our suspicion, and we duly reported all the ships we could not identify. We returned to our base in twelve days.

On June 18, when I was leaving the base mess, where I had had my lunch, I heard firing. It was the anti-aircraft battery near Polyarnoye. By force of habit I looked up expecting to see an aircraft towing a target. To my surprise there was no target. Dirty-gray puffs of smoke were appearing near the plane.

"What's happening?" I asked Peregudov, Brigade Artillery Flag Officer, who happened to be standing nearby.

"Haven't you heard?" came the reply. "A German plane flew over yesterday, but it was not molested. The visitor evidently liked it and came again."

I had been at sea the day before. We had come in late at night and I had heard nothing of the incident. A sinister foreboding gnawed at me.

I went out for a stroll late on a sunny Saturday evening (this does not sound outlandish to a Northerner). It was the last time that I saw Polyarnoye as a peaceful town, but already then one could feel that war was near. The streets were deserted. It was the time of year when the families of officers and re-enlisted men usually took a holiday in the warm South. A concert by Moscow entertainers was going on in Naval House, and I heard music as I passed by. Yekaterininskaya Harbor was almost empty of ships. Some were at sea, taking advantage of the weather for exercises, others had been ordered to deconcentrate in neighboring fjords.

I boarded a launch. The motor coughed and started. Soon the rocky shore screened the harbor and our new town, which had won the affection of the men of the Northern Fleet. We headed for Murmansk. I had to bring P-402, which had been undergoing repairs, back to Polyarnoye.

We entered our base in the morning and in the distance I saw the stocky figure of Brigade Commander Nikolai Vinogradov, who, for some reason, was dressed in a jacket that he usually wore on holidays. I hurried to him to report the arrival of P-402 from Murmansk. Before I could open my mouth, he said curtly: "War. Germany attacked us last night. We are in the thick of it."

Irrelevantly, the thought flashed through my mind that that

explained Vinogradov's "parade" uniform: he had not had time to change after a concert. Vinogradov added that the brigade had been ordered to prepare for combat. Our Division would consist of P-401, P-403, P-404 and P421s.

"I want you to check the preparations, and I think you ought to go out in P-401."

Things moved swiftly. The submarines took on their full quotas of food, water, fuel and ammunition. Air-raid sirens moaned their warning, and our anti-aircraft gunners repelled the first raids. I briefed the crews of the outgoing submarines and wished them luck.

P-403 and P-404 were assigned to cover the neck of the White Sea in the east. That was hardly the best way to utilize the Pikes. Our Brigade's operational zone embraced the entire Northern Theater, which stretched all the way to the Atlantic in the west, to the edge of the ice fields in the north, and to the Kara Sea in the east. The Pikes were medium-sized, seaworthy submarines with a fairly large radius of action, and under the conditions obtaining in our theater it would, of course, have been better to send them to the skerries and fjords of Norway, against the enemy's communication lines. Submarines of the Midget class, specially designed for coastal defense, could have operated successfully along our shore.

But Central Naval Headquarters evidently considered that in Moscow they knew better how to utilize our submarines. That was from where orders came to send two Pikes to the

Shchuka (Pike) Class (U.S.S.R.)

White Sea and to attach them temporarily to the White Sea Command. In the circumstances it was not only difficult but harmful to argue and try to prove your point.

P-421 put out to sea in the wake of P-403 and P-404. She was bound westward, in the direction of enemy-held shores. Brigade Commander Vinogradov and Commissar Kozlov came on board before she sailed. They made the rounds of all the compartments, shook hands with every member of the crew, and wished them success in battle and a safe return. The set of the men's faces and the flash of their eyes showed how eager they were to be off, to prove their mettle.

I appreciated their mood. I was much older than these lads and had more experience, but I was assailed by the same mingling of elation, anxiety and fear. Would we cope with the test before us? I had no combat experience. The war with Finland could not be taken into account, for our nation in that war was limited to patrols in which we did not make contact with the enemy. Now our mission was to torpedo German troop transports and warships along the Norwegian shore. The test would show our training and tenacity. Ahead of us were dangers that we now could not even imagine.

We left the Kola Bay accompanied by two MO submarine chasers and headed westward. Soon after the MOs left us, our look-out sighted enemy planes and we had to dive.

We were sailing under water. Above us, over the surface, the sun had completed its cycle and was rising again. It was the dawn of a new day—June 23. Moiseyev, who was scanning the sea through the periscope, reported:

"Horizon clear, Rybachy far astern. May we surface?"

I nodded.

We climbed to the bridge. As before, there was a dazzling sun and a keen, head-on wind. The diesel engines throbbed rhythmically.

"Smoke on the horizon, 30 to starboard!" the officer-of-the-watch suddenly bellowed with delight.

We dived at once. The forehatch heavily shut tight over us. We descended the vertical ladder.

"Battle stations!"

The bell rang for a long half-minute.

We had often heard these words and the long signal. But this time the sound was different. There was a small, but very essential difference. The order "Battle stations" was not pre-

ceded by the familiar word "exercise," and no short ring
came before the long signal. Professional hearing sharply
reacts to this difference, which meant that our lives had
changed drastically.

This time the action would involve torpedoes with live
warheads and not with red training heads filled with water.
And we would aim these torpedoes at the waterline of the
ship and not under its keel as during exercises.

The officers and men worked with swift efficiency at their
battle stations.

We closed in on our target. Moiseyev and I surveyed it by
quickly raising and then lowering the periscope. We saw the
masts and then the outline of the ship. It was a trawler. As far
as we could judge it was sailing at full speed in a southeasterly direction, and it was virtually belching smoke.

The fore compartment reported that the torpedoes were
ready. Everything was going smoothly. The only strange thing
about it was that the trawler was alone and, for some reason,
heading for our shore.

We had two minutes more in which to fire our torpedoes.
Moiseyev stood with his eye glued to the periscope. There
was a concentrated, tense look on his face and he could not
hide his agitation. I, too, was agitated, but for a different
reason: the ship looked too much like one of our fishing
trawlers.

"Take another look, Captain," I said to Moiseyev. "There's
plenty of time. We have not been discovered and, besides,
this battleship hasn't got much speed in it."

I peered into the periscope again. The trawler was quite
close. Distinctly I saw a red flag on her stern, and on her
smokestack two large letters MF, the insignia of the Murmansk
Fishing Trust.

"Give the all-clear!"

I wiped the cold sweat from my forehead. We had avoided
landing in a mess by a hair's breadth. I shivered as I thought
what would have happened if we had acted with just a little
less circumspection.

I could not help recalling a patrol in P-402 in the western
part of the Barents Sea during the war with Finland. On that
patrol, Stolbov, who had just been given command of the
submarine, suddenly discovered a coastguard battleship through
his periscope.

"It's probably the *Vianemiainen!*" he reported, his voice ringing with excitement.

"Improbable, but not to be ruled out," the Divisional Commander replied cautiously.

I thought to myself that that was all very well, but what was a Finnish battleship doing here, in the North? The battle alarm was sounded and we maneuvered for an attack. When we were about four cable-lengths away we saw hooded guns, men in black sheepskin coats, and the neutral Norwegian flag.

While we were scrutinizing the battleship, we had drawn so close that we had to dive under it. Then we surfaced on the other side and took another look at it from a distance of two cable-lengths. It bore the name *Norge*. That dispersed all doubts.

Stolboy, however, was so anxious for a kill that he clung to his doubts longer than anybody else. The attack had conformed to all the textbook rules, and the submarine had drawn so close that a bull's eye had been a dead certainty. Had it been an enemy ship he would have fired all his torpedoes into its side. . . .

Something of the sort had happened today. It was a reminder that a submariner could not afford to yield to blind excitement and forget the responsibility weighing down on him. In any case, we had avoided making a blunder.

M-176 had likewise not made a slip. She had sighted the same trawler near Rybachy and, like us, had made ready to attack it. And like us, she had identified the ship in time, and the hard worker of the sea safely returned home. . . .

We surfaced half an hour after our false alarm. By then the trawler had disappeared beyond the horizon. The sun was still shining brightly, and a fresh northwesterly had stirred up a wave with a force of three. We stood on the bridge, still discussing what had happened. Our hope of prompt success had not materialized. There was no enemy in sight and, besides, he was not so foolish as to leave himself recklessly open. We would have to look for him.

We saw the enemy shore at 12.00 hours. In the distance it resembled a black jagged line. We moved toward the area assigned to us, an area where we had to find and sink German ships. At 13.00 hours we dived, fearing discovery by the shore observation posts. At 14.30 hours we turned to starboard, steering a course along the coast, keeping at a distance of about two miles away from it.

Our periscope gave us a good view of the tiny bays, the lighthouses and solitary cottages. There was nothing to be seen on the sea around us except hungry, screaming seagulls.

Day after day we scoured the sea near the coast. A third of our time was spent going out to sea, far from inquiring eyes, in order to surface, start the diesel engines and recharge our batteries. Every time we surfaced, our wireless man tuned in to Moscow and took down the Soviet Information Bureau communique, which was passed on to all the compartments where it was read and reread.

The communiques were not comforting. On all the fronts our troops were engaged in heavy defensive fighting and retreating.

The waiting and enforced idleness was agonizing for all of us. The weather changed continuously from misty to windy and back again to misty. That was the North for you. For us the situation did not change—the sea remained deserted. We looked into the fjords, but found nothing there either. We did, however, locate several new observation posts.

On June 27, we finally made up our minds to slip into the roadstead in Bukten Bay, which was shielded by Varde Island, in the hope of striking something. We had come quite close to the bay several times and had scanned it through the periscope. From the sea, nothing could be seen except several fishing motorboats. If we entered the bay we would risk being caught by an anti-submarine net if such a net had been stretched across the entrance. That would put us in the unenviable position of a trapped fish. Besides, we had no chart either of the roadstead or of the harbor. We did not know what the depth in the harbor was—the scale of our chart was too small to show such details.

We appreciated the danger but it was becoming quite unbearable to wait for the enemy to fall into our hands. The ratings were beginning to grumble, envying the men fighting on land. However, it was not a matter of moods and emotions. If necessary, we could wait a week or a month. But the question was: should we wait? We felt this had to be an active patrol, and that implied poking our noses where the enemy was perhaps feeling secure. Moiseyev and I debated the risk: from our observations we could not infer that the bay was protected by a net. The fact that we did not know the depth

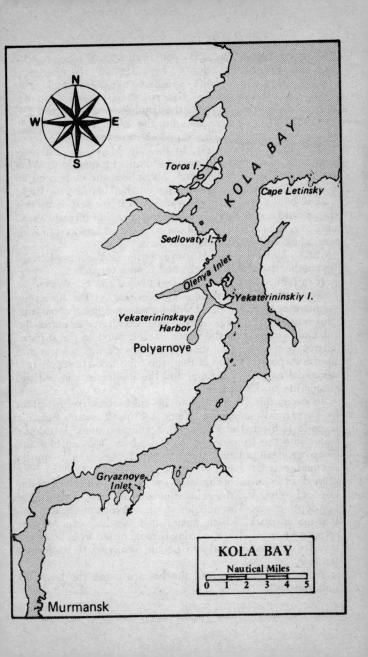

KOLA BAY

Nautical Miles

0 1 2 3 4 5

did not trouble us much. We could rely on our echo-sounder to measure it exactly under our keel. The risk, therefore, was not very great and we believed ourselves justified in taking it.

On the evening of the 27th we moved slowly into the narrow channel leading into the bay between the island and the shore. There was no sound in the submarine. Everybody was at battle stations. The torpedoes were readied in case we had to attack immediately. In the bay, Moiseyev cautiously raised the periscope and looked around. I joined him. What we saw took our breaths away. Magnified, the church on an island on our left and the houses on the shore on our right looked only a stone's throw away. And it seemed to us that they would see us just as well. Lying at anchor directly ahead of us was a small transport of some five or six hundred tons. It was about sixteen cable-lengths away.*

"Stand by for action!" Moiseyev ordered. We moved closer by another two cable-lengths and fired a torpedo.

It tore out of its tube and sped toward the transport.

. . . At this point I should mention that, at the time, our submarines were not fitted with bubble-free firing apparatus. This meant that a large bubble followed a torpedo out of the tube and churned up the water when it burst on the surface. That gave away the location of a submarine as soon as she fired a torpedo. On top of that, the tube freed of its charge, remained empty for a time, and the lighter bow forced the submarine to the surface.

To avoid this, there had to be split-second coordination between the Engineering Officer and the Coxswain. Before a torpedo is fired, the Engineering Officer usually lets some water into the trimming tank in the bow. That enables the Coxswain manipulating the horizontal planes to keep the submarine at the required depth.

In the bay such coordination was lacking. The deck under our feet rolled and the submarine shot upward. I glanced at the depth-gauge. The needle ran up and then stopped at the four-meter mark, which meant that we had exposed our conning tower. However, a string of rapid orders from Moiseyev saved the situation and the needle returned to its former position.

When we again scanned the bay we found the transport unharmed.

---

*About 2 land miles. One cable-length is equal to 608 feet.

What had gone wrong? We had not tracked the torpedo after it had left the tube. It could be that the gyroscope keeping the torpedo on course had broken down. That was possible. But something else, too, became quite obvious. Our torpedoes were set for a depth of five meters in conformity with compulsory instructions. However, only large vessels sit that deep in water. The transport we had attacked was small and empty. Its draft could not have been more than three meters. In all probability the torpedo had passed under its keel as during exercises.

As the saying goes, you must spoil before you spin. But that did not make it any easier, even if it was not our fault.

We did not fire again for fear of wasting another torpedo. Instead we swung around and left the harbor.

We Play the Role of Cart-Horses

Out in the open sea we dived to forty meters in order to feel safer and to begin the long and tedious work of resetting the firing apparatus from five to two meters. We had to take the torpedoes out of the tubes. In the cramped space of a submarine it is no simple matter to haul the eight-meter-long steel cigars out of the narrow tubes. We had no choice but to get down to the job.

A torpedo is neither a bullet nor a shell. It is a miniature submarine. A delicate and carefully tested mechanism madly drives the propellers, which give the torpedo a speed of forty knots. Clever instruments hold it on course at a preset depth while it carries its deadly charge of four hundred kilos of explosives. A lot of the people's money goes into the making of a torpedo, and to use it on the off-chance would mean going against one's conscience and sense of duty.

We set to work, now and again grumbling and aiming all sorts of uncomplimentary epithets at those who had laid down a five-meter depth for torpedoes. To their way of thinking, we had to fight only battleships and cruisers. But where were we to find these cruisers?

When we finished resetting the torpedoes we found that our batteries needed recharging. We put more distance between ourselves and the bay to get a bit of fresh air and give the batteries new strength.

In the log, the entry about the recharging of the batteries

was made under a new date—June 28. That same day we decided to try our luck again in the harbor. But when we approached it there was no sign of the transport. At the entrance buoys were bobbing up and down on the sea and there was a Coast Guard cutter. The Nazis had evidently strung an anti-submarine net across the entrance. It was a bitter pill. The Coxswain and the Engineering Officer deserved the black looks we gave them. They had taken us into the bay as though it were a joy ride. The Germans had to be real dunces not to notice the fish staring at them out of the water.

We continued our coast patrol. Everybody was in a morbid mood. I was troubled by disquieting thoughts. Were we prepared for a war against a deadly and formidable adversary like Hitler's Germany? The battle alarm had not caught us by surprise; we had put out to sea at once. That was self-evident. But preparedness to put out to sea was far from everything.

The main question was whether we would be able to fight in a manner worthy of defenders of a socialist state, of a country with the most progressive social system which had been invaded by evil forces. We had to fight savagely and show no mercy. But courage, hatred and the desire to win were not enough. To win, a submariner had to have the skill acquired by years of training and polishing. Without that skill he will, at best, die like a hero. But that was not what his country wanted of him. It was not for that that the Soviet people had denied themselves food and clothes to build up a Navy. Our motto was not to die beautifully but to destroy the enemy. How had we prepared ourselves for this? Had we at all times done what our profession and duty required of us?

When the war with Finland broke out the Northern Fleet had to get down to serious training. Things began to run more smoothly when Arseny Golovko was appointed Fleet Commander. He came to us in the summer of 1940. At the close of that year the Submarine Brigade received a new commander in Nikolai Vinogradov.

There was more artillery and torpedo practice, and the tactical background for it was given all the earmarks of a real battle. Neither poor visibility nor storms put a stop to exercises. We practised submarine maneuvers, diving under ships, secretly entering bays, breaking through enemy defenses and patrolling.

Naturally, all these years we studied and explored our stern and difficult Northern Theater. We sailed in storms and in mist and in blinding blizzards. We learned to see at night and to be invisible during the polar day. We memorized and plotted the monotonous coastline. Despite all the tangles of combat training, we felt at home in the Arctic Ocean. It became our ally. For those who failed to become its friend it was as dangerous as an enemy in a war.

Our Brigade was an active unit. It consisted of three divisions. For the time being, 1st Division had only three submarines: K-1, K-2 and D-3. But it was expecting reinforcements. D-class submarines had become obsolete. On the other hand, the Katyushas were splendid underwater cruisers any country would be proud to have. Commissioned recently, they were marvelously seaworthy and had a considerable operational range. Their armaments conformed with these tasks. They had six for'ard and four aft torpedo tubes, and two 100 mm and two 45 mm deck guns. This was formidable artillery even for a surface ship.

1st Division was commanded by Captain 2nd Rank Mahomed Gadjiev or simply Kerim as we, his friends, called him. He hailed from a mountain village in Daghestan and found his vocation at sea. A proficient submariner and tactician, he combined courage with cunning, daring with cool calculation. As a person he was charming. Generous, gay and openhearted, he had a fine sense of humor. The crews and commanders trained by him were well-drilled and morally sound.

2nd Division, which I had had under me for three years, consisted of six Pikes. They were not new boats but one could rely on them unreservedly. Their range was enough to take them to the Norwegian Sea as far as Nordkapp. They had two 45 mm guns. In short, they were battleworthy ships. And the men in them were well-trained and eager to engage the enemy.

3rd Division, consisting of six M-class submarines, was commanded by Captain 3rd Rank Nikolai Morozov, who was popularly known as "Grandfather" of Midgets for his long-standing partiality to small submarines. His entire career as a naval officer was bound up with them. The Midgets were indeed small boats, having been designed for off-shore patrol near their bases. Two torpedoes and a small-caliber anti-aircraft gun were all the armaments they carried. Frankly speaking, not everybody in the Navy believed that the Midg-

M-Class Midget (U.S.S.R.)

ets would be useful in our rugged theater. But Morozov and his crews regarded these doubts as personal insults—they were utterly devoted to their ships.

I knew these ships and the men serving in them. It was my opinion that, handled by these men, the Midgets would cope with the tasks confronting them, and maybe even more.

Had I any reason to doubt, having these ships and, principally, men like these, that our submarine fleet would withstand the enemy? No, none at all. The Germans were fighting a major war for the second year and had acquired a good deal of combat experience. We, on the other hand, were as yet inexperienced. That explained our errors, the muddles and miscalculations. But experience is something that can be marshalled. We had the training to accumulate it quickly—

the foundation was there. On this patrol, too, we learned a thing or two. . . .

These thoughts restored my mental equilibrium. Besides, I had no right to succumb to despondency. The mood of a commander is not his own business. It quickly communicates itself to the crew. With a blue mood you won't get very far in a war.

Along the Norwegian coast we saw nothing but carefree, frolicking grampuses. These younger sisters of the whale had no truck with war. We looked into a few tiny bays but the only vessels there were fishing boats.

Late on July 1, we were ordered back to our base. We turned toward our shores. I went round the compartments, talking to the men. Our bad luck had not dampened either their spirits or confidence.

"We're cart horses," said one of the men. "The Germans will never get the best of us no matter how they try."

"I'll second that," said another. "It looks as though this is going to be a long and bitter war. But we'll break the enemy's back sooner or later."

The men were unshakable in their faith that the Soviet system, the most just system the world had ever had, would not collapse no matter how strong the enemy was. . . .

We surfaced at Kildin and exchanged signals with the observation post. In Kola Bay the familiar outline of Cape Letinsky loomed to port. We sailed past the small islands of Toros, Sedlovaty and Yekaterininsky. In Yekaterininskaya Harbor we made fast at a free pier, waving greetings to Polyarnoye, the now grim-looking base of our Northern Fleet. To camouflage the houses, they had been striped and patched with paint.

On the way to Brigade Headquarters I learned that the families of officers and re-enlisted men had been evacuated. At Headquarters I picked up news that we had not heard while we were at sea: Finland was in a state of war with the Soviet Union.

I handed in a detailed report of our patrol. I said Arkady Moiseyev was an enterprising commander, a man of decision who had the knowledge and confidence to handle a submarine. He was exacting and had the respect of his subordinates. I felt he could be sent on combat patrol independently.

Our attack on the transport was analyzed comprehensively.

As it turned out, we were the first submarine in the Fleet to
have attacked the enemy. The Brigade Command and Headquarters came to the conclusion that the distance between us
and the transport had been too great and our torpedo had not
reached the target. The same opinion was offered by representatives of Naval Operations Headquarters, who were in
Polyarnoye at the time. To be quite frank, I felt this was not a
very convincing opinion. In any case, our experience was
taken into account and all submarine commanders were
ordered to reset their tubes so that their torpedoes would
strike targets at a depth of two meters.

Today, in retrospect, it is interesting to note that when
our torpedoes hit a target they worked faultlessly: their
inertia fuses were absolutely reliable. We did not have the
same trouble as German, American and Japanese submariners,
who in the early period of the war let slip quite a few kills
because of faulty fuses.

Our first patrol had not been successful, but we had
brought back observations that interested our intelligence. As
for ourselves, we now had some idea of how the Germans
protected their harbors. Incidentally, this protection was not
very zealous: evidently, they did not take Soviet submarines
seriously. Another result of our patrol was that the instructions on the depth of torpedoes were amended. Look at it
how you will, these were the first few particles of the combat
experience that we so sorely lacked at the time.

Also important was that the patrol gave an intelligent
commander like Moiseyev a start.

There was fierce fighting on land. Nazi light-infantry units
were spearheaded on Murmansk and on Rybachy and Sredny
peninsulas, which were the key to Kola Bay. They were held
back by General Frolov's 14th Army. The forces facing each
other were clearly unequal. The Nazis had numerical superiority on their side. They had more artillery and mortars, and
their aircraft had command of the sky. In spite of that, the
resistance put up by Soviet troops was not only desperate but
also successful. On some sectors of the front the Nazis were
brought to a standstill. But elsewhere the situation was bad.
To help the army the navy was hurriedly forming marine
units and throwing them into battle.

Commanders were deluged with applications for transfer to

the firing lines. All these applications could not be granted. The North needed a fleet and crews to man the ships. Still, in face of all difficulties, possibilities were found for sending men for land operations.

The naval units consisted of men from surface ships, shore bases, and submarines and training centers. Naval vessels gave these units all their rifles, submachine guns and machine guns.

The infantry units trying to break through to Rybachy and Sredny were halted on the slopes of the Musta-Tunturi Mountains. They failed to seize the peninsulas and block Kola Bay. They would continue to fail so long as even a single Soviet soldier was alive. To lose the bay would mean losing the Soviet Union's ice-free sea gates to the outside world and, together with them, the Northern Fleet.

There was fighting not only on land. Many destroyers, Coast Guard cutters, torpedo boats and MO launches had already been in action, shelling enemy troop concentrations, landing troops, providing them with artillery cover, and engaging ships and aircraft. Only the submariners had so far been left out in the cold.

Three Pikes and three Midgets returned from sea. On patrol they had not met anyone. We could not understand it. Were the German troops doing without supplies? Hardly. We could also discount any land communications having been organized across the rough, roadless terrain of Lapland. That left the sea. Why were we then not meeting heavily loaded freighters or portly, low-decked tankers? The only thing we could surmise was that we were not hunting them properly. As yet we knew nothing of the enemy's ways, his system of bases and protection, his trans-shipping points. Our intelligence had not yet been properly organized and there was little coordination with other branches of the armed forces, particularly with the Air Arm. Speaking of aircraft, when the war broke out we simply had very few of them, and those that we had were poorly equipped.

In spite of these odds, we had to strike at the enemy's communications. In war everything is interrelated. As soon as we would begin wrecking the Nazis' sea communications it would effect the combat efficiency of the infantry corps operating on land. Consequently, the navy would be able to concentrate more effort on its main tasks. Besides, successes at sea would have a telling effect on the whole Nazi Reich: the Nazis were transporting critical nickel and copper ore from ports in Finland and Norway.

After returning from my first war patrol, I stayed in Polyarnoye for only two days. On July 4, I had to sail to the Norwegian Sea in P-422, which was commanded by Lieutenant-Captain Malyshev. It took us three days to reach our patrol area. A week later our aft hydroplanes broke down and we were forced to turn back. We returned to Polyarnoye on July 12. Two days after that I was ordered back to the Norwegian Sea. This time I took my suitcase to D-3 of 1st Division.

The phrase "close-knit family" has been battered out of usage. But it would be difficult to find a better phrase to describe the relations between the men of our brigade. As a start, take the fact that almost all the older submariners were old friends. Some had met at the Frunze Academy, others had studied together at the Higher Submarine Navigation Courses. Service, too, had brought us together in different fleets and units. The Soviet submarine fleet was new, and those who had served in it for a long time had had to sail in almost all types of boats.

The middle generation, consisting of the main body of officers, had likewise gone through various Divisions. Many of the officers commanding Midgets had sailed as First Lieutenants in Pikes. Experienced commanders of Midgets were frequently given command of Pikes, and that often opened the road to command of a Katyusha.

The distinction "our" and "their" Division had been erased in our brigade. We were familiar with all the boats and not only knew the men in them but had ties of personal friendship with them.

For that reason an order to supervise the patrol of a submarine from another Division was neither unnatural nor unexpected.

To return to D-3.

I cannot help saying a few words about submarines of that class. They are a notable milestone in the history of the Soviet submarine fleet.

. . . A meeting was held in 1931 on a cold, bleak day such as we frequently get on the Baltic seaboard. It was attended by submariners, the Baltic Fleet Command, workers and engineers of a ship-building yard and representatives of Party organizations and local government bodies in Leningrad.

The heroes of the occasion were three large, new submarines, the first to be built by the Soviet ship-building industry. They were moored to the pier, shining with fresh paint and polished brass. On that day they were being turned over to the Navy and the naval ensign was hoisted on them.

A large contribution toward organizing the building of submarines had been made by Grigori Orjonikidze and Sergei Kirov. The latter had witnessed the laying down of these submarines. They were given the high-sounding, symbolic names *Decembrist*, *Narodovolets* and *Krasnogvardeyets*. Today their sides bore the submarine fleet's symbols in white letters: D-1, D-2 and D-3. *Decembrist* was regarded as the forerunner of the class and the name was given to the entire series.

The commissioning of these three submarines was a significant event. It showed that the Communist Party's policy of industrialization was beginning to yield tangible results, that the Soviet Union had begun to produce up-to-date weapons and that the beginning was being laid for a Workers' and Peasants' Navy.

When the brass band fell silent, the factory ensigns on the submarines were lowered and the officers-of-the-watch sang out:

"Up ensign, jack and dress flags!"

The brass band struck up again and the triumphant notes of

D-Class (U.S.S.R.)

The Internationale floated across the ancient harbor in Kronstadt.

The ceremony ended with a speech by Fleet Commander-in-Chief Lev Galler.

"The people have entrusted to you the fruits of their gigantic work," he said, addressing submariners. "I hope you will honorably justify this trust."

The Ds were modern submarines in their day. They differed essentially from the old, pre-Revolution Snow Leopards and AGs then in service. They were faster, had a larger range, and could dive deeper than their predecessors. They were safe in any storm and carried quite a lot of armaments: six torpedo tubes in the bow and two in the stern, and a 100 mm and a 45 mm gun on deck.

In 1933, the Ds sailed along the White Sea-Baltic Canal to the North, where a new submarine fleet was being organized. In this passage, I was Torpedo Officer in D-1. Since then I have always had a soft spot for the Ds.

Subsequently D-1 was struck off the Fleet's lists. Approximately at the same time D-2 sailed to the Baltic for an overhaul.

But D-3, despite her venerable age, remained in the ranks. She had many feats to her credit. Back in 1938, with the distinguished submariner Victor Kotelnikov as her Captain, she accomplished what for those days was an unprecedented passage to Jan Mayen Island in the Greenland Sea.

It was for many people a memorable day in February, when the Papanin ice floe was drifting along the eastern coast of Greenland and there were apprehensions that it might soon be carried to the open sea. The lives of a quartet of intrepid Arctic explorers were endangered. The Soviet Government ordered out a special expedition to take the men off their floating and now unreliable island. The expedition consisted of two Northern Fleet icebreakers and the D-3. The submarine was given the assignment of taking Papanin and his men on board from the drifting ice floe if for some reason the icebreakers failed to reach them.

The passage was accomplished in the teeth of violent storms, blizzards and fog. The submarine battled her way against huge waves. Tons of water seeped into the control room through the central hatch. But the submarine and her crew bore all the hardships of that difficult ocean voyage. D-3 reached the assigned area and safely returned. The hull and the mechanisms had stood the test well. It was the best testimony of the excellent work of the builders of the first Soviet submarines.

Filipp Konstantinov went on that voyage as Brigade Flag Navigation Officer. Now he was in command of D-3, and I was accompanying him on a war patrol.

We sailed to a neighboring harbor to await orders to proceed to our patrol area. We had hardly cast anchor than an air-raid alarm sounded. A group of Focke-Wolfs attacked the bay. The AA batteries in Polyarnoye opened up and D-3 joined in with her guns.

The shells from our guns and from the battery closest to us caught one of the raiders in a ring of explosions, and the Focke-Wolf burst into flames, sideslipped and went into a dive, leaving a trail of black smoke behind it. We saw the pilots bail out.

It was difficult to say who had scored the hit: we or the battery. But that made little difference. The main thing was that we had bagged a plane.

We pulled out of the harbor on July 15, but before we got to our area we found that the port diesel sluice valve needed repairs. It was letting through a good deal of water, so much in fact that the diesel compartment became flooded in an hour. We started the repairs several times, and it took a lot of time which might have been put to better use hunting the enemy. Besides, the weather was detestable. Dense fogs that reduced visibility to zero wrapped around us frequently.

During the patrol we had to evade aircraft several times, and once encountered a U-boat. The meeting came as a surprise to both sides. And we executed identical maneuvers: simultaneously turning away and diving.

When the throbbing of our hearts returned to normal, Konstantinov and I talked the incident over. The enemy had proved to be neither more cunning nor more resourceful than we in spite of having more combat experience. It was safe to say that novices were not sent to the North. All in all we were quite pleased that we had held our own against the enemy for it meant that we would soon be striking at him.

A mass of local news awaited us at Polyarnoye when, on July 30, we entered the base in a blinding fog. Mikhail Avgustinovich, our Brigade Chief-of-Staff, had, at his own request, been given command of K-1, a large submarine, which had had bad luck as far as commanders went. At the

outbreak of the war, one of them had been drafted out
because of illness. The same fate overtook his successor. The
job of Captain remained vacant, because no suitable candidate could be found at once. That was when Avgustinovich
stepped in, requesting an "honorable demotion." He could
not remain calmly on shore, planning operations and meeting
and seeing off ships. His application was granted.

Avgustinovich had been serving in the North since 1933.
He had commanded a Pike and a Decembrist. During the
Finnish War he was Divisional Commander, and sailed in
D-1. Now he had settled in a Katyusha with a well-trained
crew and was making preparations to go out on his first war
patrol.

Air-raid alarms became frequent in Polyarnoye. But the
base was rarely raided: most of the aircraft flew past, heading
for Murmansk.

Two submarines from my division—P-401 and P-402—
returned to Polyarnoye soon after us, bringing glad tidings.
They had been in different areas but had opened their score
on one and the same day—July 14.

P-402 was commanded by Nikolai Stolbov, a competent and
experienced submariner. By nature he was lively, energetic
and perhaps a little quick-tempered, but he could not be
accused of rashness. Restraint had become a professional
feature of his nature. He had been in command of the Pike
for nearly two years, a considerable length of time. Prior to
that he had commanded a Midget, sailing from the Baltic to
the North in her.

During the war with Finland he had sailed many hundreds
of miles in his Pike. I was with him in February 1940 on a
twenty-day patrol. Because of what I know about him I can
say definitely that his victory was not fortuitous.

On the day the war broke out, P-402 was, if the reader
remembers, transferred to Polyarnoye from Murmansk for
repairs. Some refitting work had to be completed. This job
was quickly finished by our floating workshop. The submarine's
machinery was tested before schedule and she put out to sea.
While patrolling along the enemy coast Stolbov entered one
of the fjords and discovered a transport of about five thousand
tons riding at anchor. He sank it with two torpedoes, which
he fired at close range, and safely steered his submarine out
of the fjord.

Moiseyev, however, was the hero of the day. Although his

attack had been executed later on the same day, he had had much more complicated conditions to contend with.

It was his first independent war patrol. He surfaced and was creeping up to the enemy coast when in the haze he sighted the silhouettes of two mine sweepers. Without wasting time he dived and drew closer to the ships. From eight cable-lengths, he fired two torpedoes at the nearest mine sweeper. The vessel sank rapidly after a terrific explosion. The second mine sweeper, which proved to be a fairly fast ship, gave chase eight minutes after the attack. It dropped thirty-six depth charges, putting out of commission the Pike's aft hydroplanes and the control room periscope. Despite the damage Moiseyev coolly maneuvered his submarine and escaped from his pursuer.

The Pikes thus showed that they had sharp teeth and that they could bite painfully.

"The score has been opened," said S. G. Kucherov, Fleet Chief-of-Staff, when P-401's patrol was analyzed. "The ice has been broken."

Skill Is Also a Weapon

In war one frequently re-evaluates people. One observes all sorts of metamorphoses. Besides, the yardstick one now uses is, I would say, more definite and concrete. Behavior in battle is the key criterion. Time and again, an officer who had earlier not distinguished himself in any way displays miracles of resourcefulness and courage in battle. At the other extreme, an officer with a settled reputation who walks around with head proudly uplifted suddenly shows that he is a dunderhead and a coward.

These are, of course, extremes, antipodal cases. Most commanders justified the trust placed in them. Yet we had some of these extreme cases in the worst sense, and there was no getting away from it.

Before the war we regarded Lysenko, Captain of M-172, as a skilled submariner and an exacting officer. He handled his submarine without any glaring errors, and under his command the crew worked efficiently during exercises. In short, on the surface of it, everything seemed normal.

But during his very first operational patrol he showed his true colors. Fear took possession of him almost as soon as he started out on patrol. He imagined danger all around him. Without rhyme or reason he executed strange maneuvers, "eluding" an enemy of whom there was not a sign in the vicinity. This made the crew nervous and unsure of itself. In the circumstances there could be no question of hunting enemy ships.

The worst happened on the way back to the base. Mistaking our planes for the enemy, Lysenko hastily dived near the shore. The submarine hit a submerged rock. Lysenko lost what remained of his self-control and panicked. "It's a magnet!" he screamed. "The Germans have special magnets to attract our submarines. We're trapped!"

The submarine had to be saved, but the Captain could do nothing. Had it not been for the skill and presence of mind of Engineering Officer Karatayev, M-172 would never have surfaced and returned home.

The Midget was urgently docked for repairs. Of course, Lysenko was immediately removed from his command.

Evidently he had never seriously thought of what the end purpose of a regular naval officer's job was. He had never tried to picture to himself what he would have to do if war broke out. He had never trained his mind to cope with possible combat assignments. He had made no attempt to study the possible enemy, to probe his strong and weak points. The showy side of the service, the privileges of an officer were what attracted him. That was the life he wanted.

Neither can the men who trained him be absolved of blame. The character of a commander is shaped in struggle against difficulties, in situations where a man fully feels his independence and also his responsibility for a ship and for the men in it. Lysenko had been wet-nursed too much, and he had never been put in a situation that came anywhere close to real combat conditions. Without rigorous training nobody will ever make a commander, and you'll not even make out properly if there is a foundation for the qualities that a commander needs.

Skill, too, has to be nurtured. Even good seeds require fertile soil. That soil is a person's physical and moral health, the steadiness of his nervous system. By going through the crucible of military training, talent is smelted into an alloy of intelligence, character and temperament made strong by its harmonious integrity. A submarine captain must have not only self-control, he must be not only courageous, daring and soberly calculating but also possess all these qualities in the required proportions. Once that is achieved, he will creatively show his worth with the greatest success in all fields of military activity. In battle the creative element is an indispensable part of a Captain's armaments.

The skill of a captain is, therefore, a powerful weapon that must be highly valued.

It was fortunate that Lysenko was replaced by a really skilled commander.

Lieutenant-Captain Israel Fisanovich joined the Brigade at the close of July, coming from Leningrad, where he had just completed submarine navigation classes for commanders. He was appointed First Lieutenant in a Pike.

He was no novice in the North. Prior to taking the courses in the autumn of 1939 he had been our Brigade Flag Navigator. He knew the Northern Theater like the back of his hand.

I had sailed with him on several patrols. What particularly impressed me was his efficiency and his love for his work during a long patrol in stormy weather in the autumn before the war. He made it his business to know the Pike inside out.

Fisanovich was First Lieutenant for only a few days. He was found to be the most suitable successor to Lysenko. Indeed, he knew Midgets like a book, having sailed in them since 1936, after his graduation from a naval school.

Outwardly, he was not an imposing figure of a man. Of medium height, with a clear, high forehead, grey dreamy eyes beneath thick, black eyelashes, and somewhat protruding ears, he did not impress one as a dashing sea wolf. But how erudite and charming he was. In fact, the breadth of his erudition was amazing. The history of naval tactics, technology and literature were his favorite subjects for conversation. Once started he would recite excerpts from Pushkin's *Eugene Onegin*, Mayakovsky's bracing and rhythmical *Good*, or Shevchenko's melancholy *Katerina* with great feeling for hours on end. Yet he was no soppy dreamer; he was a man of action.

His first act as captain of M-172 was to have a talk with each and every member of the crew, to get at the "innards" of each man. The submarine herself was in a dock in Murmansk, where the work on her went on day and night. Spurred on by their impatience to see action, the crew helped the dock workers.

Early in August M-172 returned to Polyarnoye. Under the

established rules in the Fleet, a new captain had to work out
several problems from the naval training course before taking
his ship out to sea to make sure he could handle the ship and
rely on his crew. That made for harmony and better
understanding. Without this preliminary training it was, to
say the least, dangerous to send a submarine out. The
accepted system of training was followed rigidly in peace time
and in war. Of course, the time given for this training was
shortened.

The course tasks were carried out under the supervision of
a senior officer. Morozov was at sea at the time and Vinogradov,
Captain 1st Rank, appointed me to act as Instructor Commander in M-172.

On the day after I joined the submarine we pulled out of
Kola Bay into a safe training area. As a matter of fact, safety
in that area was extremely relative. Enemy aircraft on their
way to bomb Murmansk or Gryaznoye Inlet kept appearing in
the sky overhead. In addition to emergency training dives,
we had to dive to save ourselves from air attack.

Training continued for fourteen and sometimes sixteen
hours at a stretch day in and day out. But nobody complained.
The crew were wonderful. They could not help feeling partly
to blame for the ill-starred patrol. Although it was obvious to
everybody that they had had nothing whatever to do with
that disaster, the men took it very close to heart. They did
everything they could to help their young captain. They hung
on his words, carrying out his orders with swift precision and
efficiency. Particularly noticeable was the help given him by
Engineering Officer Karatayev and Coxswain Tikhonenko.

Fisanovich surpassed all my expectations. He mastered his
duties three or four times quicker than anybody else I knew.
All the course assignments were fulfilled with good marks. I
reported to the Brigade Commander that the submarine was
ready for combat duty. Morozov, the "Grandfather" of Midgets,
was still at sea and I was ordered to go with Fisanovich on his
first operational patrol.

We left our base in the evening of August 18 and steered a
course toward enemy shores. For two days running we looked
for the enemy. Now and again we spotted aircraft and small
launches like our MOs through our periscope. These launches
were no prey for a submarine, just as sparrows are no target
for artillery. No transport or other sizable ship was to be

Merskoi Okhotnik MO-038

seen, and Petsamo-Vuono Fjord with its Liinahamari Harbor drew us like a magnet.

"Do you think we might take a peep?" Fisanovich tactfully asked on the very first day, hiding his impatience.

"It's not worth it, Captain. It would be better to wait and look around," I replied. "Perhaps there'll be nothing to sink in the harbor."

It is my practice to avoid interfering in the handling of a submarine and to give the Captain as few orders as possible. But sometimes I can hardly keep myself from intervening. You watch the Captain doing something not quite well, something that you would have done simply and better. The order comes to your lips, but you hold yourself in check, saying to yourself that that is one way of doing it. You let him finish, otherwise it only throws him into confusion, and offends him to no purpose. Miscalculations can be examined later, at the analysis of the operation.

In Fisanovich's case I had practically nothing to do. He handled the submarine very efficiently and his reactions were excellent. He was absolutely tireless. I spent most of the time sitting on a folding stool in the control room, dozing off from time to time.

We approached the tempting fjord time and again. Fisanovich carefully hinted, "It's a fine little bay. A picture if there ever was one. There must be something in it. I feel it in my bones."

"Yes," I agreed, "there might be a net or, perhaps, anti-submarine mines."

I appreciated his eagerness. But there was no reason for plunging headlong into the bay. If there was anything in it, it would not escape us, for we were patrolling the entrance. Caution never hurt anybody. I knew these bays. . . .

At last, as we again approached Petsamo-Vuono, we saw a launch or a schooner leaving the fjord. The small vessel passed over us and disappeared. I felt that this was a good sign. It meant that either there had been no net across the entrance or that it had been drawn.

Fisanovich raised the periscope and put his eye to it.

"Comrade Divisional Commander," he said, "take a look."

The black smoke was wreathing deep in the bay. There was no doubt about its origin: it could only come from a ship getting under steam.

"What do you make of it?" I asked Fisanovich.

"Isn't it time we went into the bay?"

"Yes, I think it is," I replied.

Action stations was sounded. Through the periscope Navigator Butov took the bearings of landmarks at the tip of the capes and measured the height of the mountains: before entering the narrow gulf we had to know our position exactly. Tension mounted in the hushed silence as the submarine inched her way into the enemy fjord.

In our periscope we saw the slate-black, ridged mountains. The fjord grew narrower, giving us a better view of the shore. The clock, the gyrocompass repeater and the lag counter ticked audibly in the control room. I felt my heart slightly contract and a sort of numbness creep over me. We were really groping our way and, to use high-flown language, were in the maw of the enemy. He could at any time sink his fangs in us and we would not even know how he had struck at us.

We raised the periscope. About a cable-length away from us a launch was speeding into the fjord. We could not tell if it was a naval or civilian vessel, but judging by its behavior it had not sighted us. That was most important. And it was a good thing that it passed over us when our periscope was snug in its standard.

We took another look around. The launch had swerved to starboard. We now distinctly saw a small-caliber gun on it. It was heading towards the shore, away from us. Black smoke was wreathing to starboard. Our Navigator calculated that in another four minutes we would be in Liinahamari Harbor. In four minutes we would know definitely if we were wasting our time or if there were a suitable target for a torpedo strike.

"Time's up," Butov reported.

Through the periscope the captain and I saw houses, barracks, the quay, and no sign of a ship. That puzzled us, but it was too early for gloom because we had not yet discovered the source of the smoke. We cautiously moved forward, and the next time we raised our periscope we saw a troop transport lying alongside the quay. Black smoke was pouring out of its funnel.

"Tube Number One, stand by to fire," Fisanovich cried out. "Helm to starboard! Helm dead ahead! Tube fire!"

"Torpedo fired!" the torpedo station in the for'ard compartment reported.

The periscope gave us a good view of the transport—its sides just barely fitted into our field of vision. Men were working at the jib on the deck. Our torpedo was tracing a trail directly at its middle—Fisanovich had aimed at the funnel. It took only a few fleeting seconds for the picture to make a lasting imprint on my memory. In the next moment we dived to safety and began to turn toward the exit from Liinahamari. While we were swinging around, the submarine suddenly shuddered from an explosion. The torpedo had found its target thirty seconds after leaving its tube.

We laid a course toward the exit from Petsamo-Vuono and rose to periscope depth. The attack had been successful, but there might be unpleasantness yet in store for us. The Germans had wakened, and instead of being the hunter we might find ourselves hunted. In that case anything could happen.

The quay along which the transport had stood was enveloped in an impenetrable wall of smoke. A launch, the same one that we had seen on our way to the harbor, sped directly toward us. But this time, too, we escaped undetected. Hardly had we lowered our periscope than the launch tore past without seeing us. Shumikhin, our hydrophone operator, reported the drone of the propellers of another launch. Judging by the noise, the launches were in formation and heading for the open sea, gradually receding away from us. Depth charges began to explode, the reverberations rocking our submarine. There were three explosions in all. By then the launches had left the fjord. They could bomb the Barents Sea for all we cared.

We too left the fjord. Smiles appeared on the faces of the men. A load had been taken off their minds. The transport had been torpedoed; we had escaped detection. And now they could look for us as much as they liked.

"One feels at home in the sea," Karatayev said gaily. Everybody laughed with relief. Anything you said could now raise a laugh. There was no trace of the recent silence. All that had happened seemed simple, easy and even amusing.

"And those launches on a goose chase! Our little present made Fritz go off his nut completely," one of the men said, choking with laughter. The whole compartment laughed with him.

"Congratulations," I said to Fisanovich, shaking hands with him. "You and your men have done a good job. I'm sure that this is the first of a string of victories."

Life aboard the submarine settled into its usual routine.

"Supper!"

The word was passed along the compartments. The men from the bow compartment made their way to the galley.

"Pity I used up my vodka ration at dinner," somebody said in a tone of regret. "This is just the time to think kindly of the dead Nazis."

The men wolfed down their supper, cracking jokes and laughing hilariously.

Under cover of darkness we recharged our batteries, and in the morning resumed our patrol of the enemy coast. Until nightfall we cruised back and forth, constantly changing our course. We found nothing to attract our attention. Two enemy aircraft appeared and we dived. Soon afterward we rose to regulation periscope depth and looked around. Two launches were sailing at full speed along the coast.

"Look there, Captain," I said to Fisanovich. "The Nazis are up to something. Those launches have not been sent out for nothing."

The short dusk had already descended over the sea. In the

half-light it was hard to see anything through the periscope. But Fisanovich remained glued to the eyepiece.

"Comrade Divisional Commander," he said suddenly in an agitated tone. "Would you take a look. There's a spot on the surface."

I strained my sight. White as an iceberg, it was unquestionably a ship. Confirmation came from Shumikhin.

"Noise of propellers, 34, to port," he reported.

"Stand by to attack!" Fisanovich ordered.

A white vessel resembling a yacht could be distinctly made out moving against the background formed by the dark shore. Displacing about one thousand five hundred tons, she was a lovely ship, even evoking a feeling akin to pity.

The submarine was maneuvered into an attack course.

"Tube Number Two, stand by!"

That order issued in a loud voice made a caressing sound. It was soon followed by the order: "Number Two—fire!"

Some forty seconds later we heard an explosion. A minute or two after that there was another bang, loud and rumbling. It must have been the ship's boilers. Shumikhin reported that he could no longer hear the ship. Through the periscope we too did not find any trace of the white vessel.

The action had taken ten minutes. When we were leaving the attack area we saw several launches emerging from the fjord. But they failed to discover us.

Both our torpedoes had been used with good effect. It had been no picnic but it gave us confidence in ourselves.

We reached our base on August 23. The congratulations made Fisanovich feel as though he were walking on air, but it was obvious that the attention he got embarrassed him. His success had been estimated at its true worth. I was happy for his sake. He had been in command of his submarine for less than a month and had achieved more than veteran captains could boast of. There was more to it than Fisanovich's personal qualities as a commander. He had come to a submarine whose crew had escaped death by the skin of their teeth. The example of their former captain could only have demoralized them and they had had to be shown that they were more than a match for the enemy. Fisanovich had done a fine job of that, too.

In every respect the patrol was a noteworthy event in the lives of the crew. Four men—Helmsman Butov, Coxswain

Tikhonenko, Electrician Zaitsev and Wireless Operator Seregin—were admitted to the Party after it. They knew that sterner tests lay ahead of them and that by joining the Communist Party—incidentally, most of the crew were members—they had undertaken the moral obligation to be among the staunchest and the bravest.

As regards myself, I sailed in another Midget, M-171, early in September. Its skipper, Valentin Starikov, was a fine commander. On this patrol he searched for the enemy boldly, navigating his ship with extraordinary skill. True, there were some unpleasant moments. After patrolling the coastal area without result we made an attempt to steal into the port of Petsamo. There was a stretch of shallow water in the long and narrow fjord and our nose showed on the surface as we were feeling our way through it. No damage was done to the submarine but our conning tower was exposed to observation posts. Submarine chasers—there were no other vessels in the harbor—were alerted and we had quite a job eluding them. Some of the depth charges exploded much too close for our comfort. The first few explosions tossed the submarine a good four meters. But our casing and engines came through this barrage unscathed. The next explosions were somewhat farther away and sounded as though somebody were striking the casing with an iron bar. They were harmless altogether.

It was my first experience of depth charges, and I must admit I thought it would be much more terrifying.

Starikov maneuvered the submarine with admirable self-control and brought us safely out of the fjord.

We returned to our base without opening our score. But the patrol had shown me that in Starikov the submarine had a competent captain.

Without meaning to, I compared him with Fisanovich. Both were young and both were fine officers. Yet they were totally different, and not only by appearances—Starikov was a tall and handsome fellow who exuded self-assurance. They were different in character as well. Fisanovich was gentler and won people's confidence quicker. He had been in command of a submarine for only a short while, much shorter than Starikov, yet he was incomparably closer to his men. The crew really got to like him.

Different as they were from each other, the men serving in our submarines had one thing in common: they hated the enemy and were eager to come to grips with him. As time went by they learned the art of submarine warfare. So far we had not had losses. On the other hand, our score was nothing much to speak of, but there was no doubt that it would grow. We had come to know how a torpedo behaved when it was fired at a ship, and the sound with which it cut short a ship's life. We knew how to steal into an enemy-held fjord, the difficulties that this entailed, and how depth charges exploded near a submarine. This was not very much. But it was enough to enable us to say without exaggeration that we had passed the first test imposed upon us by the sudden outbreak of war.

RIGHT FLANK OF A MAMMOTH FRONT

Salute over a Bay

In the second half of September, after the failure of their July operations, the Germans launched another offensive. There was savage fighting in the region of the Western Litsa. Once again Soviet troops suffered heavy losses, and once again naval units fought shoulder to shoulder with troops of the 14th Army. Far from relaxing, the tough resistance that the Germans met with during the first days of the war in the North continued to mount, so much so that the Nazis themselves began to doubt the possibility of reaching their objective. At any rate, intelligence reached us that General Dietl, commander of a light infantry corps, reported to his supreme command that considerably more troops would have to be committed if he was to capture Murmansk. This mood could not fail to affect the enemy's morale. Naturally, it was all to our advantage.

Dietl requested greater sea cover for his army. At the time the enemy had about fifty ships in our theater. They included an auxiliary cruiser, eight destroyers and six large submarines. The Germans obviously felt this force to be inadequate. They realized that Soviet opposition was capable of much more than they expected. That preyed upon them.

We now knew for certain that the Germans were supplying their land forces from the sea, bringing supplies around Scandinavia. We also knew that they were shipping nickel ore out of the north of Norway and Finland. It was crystal clear therefore that one of the Soviet Northern Fleet's tasks was to wreck the enemy's communications. This job was assigned to our submarines. No other forces and means were available: our aircraft and torpedo boats were much too few in number to constitute any real threat to the enemy. The surface fleet had its hands full. In addition to its numerous assignments, it had the important duty of insuring the safety of Allied convoys, which were beginning to arrive in Archangel. In other words, it was covering our own external communications.

In the evening of September 19, after my return from patrol in M-171, I was sitting in my office at the shore depot and working my way through a heap of orders that had piled up in my absence. Few enemy aircraft braved the non-flying weather.

An artillery salvo suddenly boomed over the bay. I had half a mind to pay no attention to it, but looking out of the window I saw that instead of walking leisurely out of the mess as they usually did the men were running. I could not understand it. If it was an air-raid alarm why had it not been sounded?

I turned all the papers over to the clerk and hurried out into the street to find out what was happening. There I ran into Nikolai Stolbov, Captain of P-402.

"What's all this excitement about?" I asked him. "Who's firing?"

"It's K-2 trying to be original," he replied. "They've just come in from patrol and have fired a salute—to let us know that they sank a transport. The commander-in-chief's at the pier meeting them."

At the time I could not expect that that salute would initiate a tradition that would be cherished by the sailors and adopted throughout the Navy.

What had preceded this noteworthy salute?

K-2 had been with us, in the North, for a whole year. With her sister, K-1, she had come to us from the Baltic in 1940. Her commander was Captain 3rd Rank Vasily Utkin, in many ways a remarkable personality. His friends called him Vasily the Pomor. Indeed, he hailed from Archangel, coming from an old Pomor family. He went to sea when he was a boy, sailing in merchant ships and finishing a nautical school. Like many other navigators and ship's masters he was called to the colors when we started rapidly building up a submarine fleet.

At the time there was an acute shortage of officers. It was not to be wondered at, for it took much less time to build a

Katyusha K-Class (U.S.S.R.)

ship than to train an officer. The road to submarine captain, especially to captain of a large submarine, is by no means a short one. It requires three or four years of study in a naval school and another four or five years of service in various capacities in a submarine. Then there is the additional study necessary for promotion.

The problem was to shorten the generally accepted period of training for a submarine captain. Submarines were quickly coming off the slips and there was no time to wait. One solution was to call up sea wolves—navigators and ship's masters—from the Northern Merchant Marine. After two years' training under a special program they were assigned to submarines as first lieutenants and then, depending on their progress, they received independent commands. Discounting some inevitable misjudgments, this emergency measure fully justified itself. The merchant marine captains developed into superb submarine commanders who devoted themselves heart and soul to the navy and their new profession. One of them was Vasily Utkin.

Just before the war broke out he was found to be suffering from consumption. The doctors demanded his transfer to shore duty, but Vasily the Pomor categorically declared, "I shan't leave my submarine. Can you name a better cure than sea air? The sea and fresh cod will make me fit as a fiddle."

He loved raw cod, eating it like a Pomor, biting into a large piece and cutting it with a sharp knife before his very lips.

Utkin had his way: he remained in command of his submarine. Nobody could wish a better Captain for K-2. The Northern Theater was as an open book to him. He knew all the finer points of his Katyusha, and his men had a deep respect for him.

We pinned high hopes on the large Katyushas, which were the creation of the chief submarine designer, who was well known in the navy. Utkin had set his heart on showing what this magnificent ship could do when it was handled competently.

However, the first patrol did not bring the Katyusha any success. Utkin tirelessly looked for enemy ships and fired his torpedoes at them, but he failed to make a hit. All the greater then was the impatience with which the K-2 crew awaited their second patrol. The submarine put out to sea on September 7 with Kerim Gadjiev on board.

Five days later, Utkin sighted a ship near the entrance of Sulte Fjord. The ship was steaming at full speed, hugging the shore. But she was five miles away from the submarine and it was useless trying to hit her with a torpedo.

"So near and yet so far," Utkin growled with disappointment, turning the periscope over to Gadjiev.

"Take her to the surface, Captain," Gadjiev cried out, sparks dancing in his eyes. "You can get close enough to her to give her a light."

This, Utkin at once appreciated, was the best decision he could take. The Katyusha's surface speed was high enough to enable her to overtake the transport, and her two 100 mm guns were unquestionably sufficient to batter down any opposition. The risk of the submarine being damaged to the extent of being prevented from diving was negligible. Besides, Utkin had the advantage of being the first to attack and take the enemy unawares. This had been the Germans' trump against British shipping in the First World War and early in the Second World War.

Utkin acted quickly on Gadjiev's suggestion.

"Stand by to surface," he ordered. "Gun crew to control room."

Lieutenant Zarmair Arvanov, gunnery officer, ran into the control room followed by the gunners.

The submarine broke surface rapidly. The gunners quickly climbed out of the hatch and rushed to the guns, removing the plugs and setting the sights. Arvanov, his eyes running down the plot, sang out in a sing-song voice:

"Port 30. Mine shells. Range 40. Load guns. Stand by for salvo. Fire!"

The submarine was steering a course intersecting that of the transport. The first salvo was fired from a distance of some forty cable-lengths. It raised fountains of water in front of the transport. As the water slowly cascaded down two more shells whistled through the air. After the fourth salvo there were no more fountains. Instead the transport was enveloped in smoke. Arvanov had found his target.

The shells landed squarely on the transport. The burning vessel turned shoreward, evidently heading for a shoal. But the shells continued hitting her, and her stern soon began settling in the water.

"Aircraft to starboard, 120," the look-out cried out.

"Break off attack," Arvanov ordered. The deck was cleared. Just before the submarine dived Utkin saw the sea closing over the transport.

The aircraft dropped two bombs. But by then the submarine was well out of harm's way. Fifteen minutes later the men heard a drawn-out rumble. That could only have been the transport's boilers exploding. After a five minutes' wait the submarine rose to periscope depth, and Gadjiev and Utkin convinced themselves that there was no trace of the enemy transport.

The hero of the day was, of course, Arvanov. Unlike some other gunnery officers, who knew all the ins and outs of torpedo tubes but gave little attention to artillery, the god of war of surface vessels, he had masterfully directed the firing. Thanks to him the gun crews worked efficiently. This only went to prove that every naval officer must be equally proficient with all the armaments at his disposal. Even if the armament is not exactly in his line, he must under no circumstances treat it as of secondary importance. Anything can happen in war, and any neglect of part of one's duty may end in disaster.

When K-2 was approaching Yekaterininskaya Harbor, Arvanov asked Gadjiev for permission to fire a salute in honor of the victory.

The Divisional Commander thought it over for a moment and then said with a smile, "Go ahead."

Everybody liked the idea, and it was approved by the Fleet

Commander. From then on all submarines returning from patrol let the entire main base know how many victories they had scored. Each salvo meant one destroyed vessel.

K-2's September patrol was of special significance to us. During three months of war this was the first case of a submarine attacking an enemy ship with its artillery. Neither the Black Sea nor the Baltic Fleet had any experience of this. Naturally, we had drilled the men in the use of artillery against surface and air targets—that was the purpose of the guns. But nobody could tell exactly how effective artillery fire would be. Gadjiev was the first among us to show that a submarine could use its artillery with telling effect. Submarine captains could only thank him for it.

Team Work

D-3 was called "our old lady" by her crew with a shade of affectionate respect. Indeed, she was the oldest submarine in the Northern Fleet.

The "old lady" was noted for her crew. Many of them were Communists. The submarine's adornment and cementing core consisted of re-enlisted men. One of them, Warrant Officer Anashenkov, was in charge of torpedoes. He was also the submarine's Party organizer. He had sailed in the Baltic in Decembrists and had come to the North in one of them in 1933. Measuring up to him were Coxswain Neshcheret and Group Petty Officers Bibikov and Tugolukov. Each had had at least three years' actual sailing in submarines.

Fine seamen themselves, they passed their experience on to novices and were the bearers of the navy's best traditions. In the navy a great deal of attention has always been devoted to training new men.

The war found D-3 steeled and tested by storms. It was reassuring to sail with her crew. That explained my good humor when I went with them on their second war patrol. With us was Regimental Commissar Alexei Baikov, Brigade Political Department Chief.

Fleet Headquarters gave us clearance at 16.00 hours on September 22. There was a crowd on the pier to see us off. We would be gone for nearly a month.

We were on the bridge taking a last look at Yekaterininskaya Harbor as the submarine slowly pulled out.

Yefim Gusarov, D-3's Commissar, was, in the meantime, inspecting the compartments below. People who saw him for the first time thought him rather strange. Gloomy, frowning, with his brows angrily drawn together, he looked as though he were always discontented over something. At first sight one was inclined to keep away from him and think that somebody must have made a mistake in giving him the job of political instructor. In reality he was the kindest of men and, though he was apt to be gruff, it was obvious to everybody that he loved his men. His appearance did not scare away the sailors: in the three years that he had been serving in the *Decembrist* they had come to know him well.

Readiness No. 2 was ordered when we left the gulf. The men gathered for their political briefing. Gusarov told them of the situation at the fronts and in the North, and of their assignment on this patrol. Everything was, in general, known and clear about the latter two points. But the first made our hearts ache. Somewhere inside us we had grown used to the fact that the situation was serious at the fronts and that Soviet troops were still fighting defensive battles. Our consolation was that the enemy was suffering heavy losses and that sooner or later his offensive must peter out. But the circumstance that the Germans had reached the approaches of Moscow weighed heavily upon us. Although nobody said it aloud for fear that it may be construed as defeatism, we could not help thinking of the possibility of the capital being left to the enemy as in 1812.

Gusarov, of course, knew the situation at the fronts better than any of us and, though he was not much of a speaker, the men's faces brightened as they listened to his sober assessments and heard the strong note of conviction in his voice.

"It's difficult around Moscow. But put yourselves in the shoes of its defenders." Gusarov paused to enable the men mentally to transport themselves to the faraway approaches of the capital. "Would the fear of death make you flinch and leave your positions without orders? I don't think so. Moscow is being defended by men of steel. They are made of the same stuff as you, and have the same thoughts and opinions. They have learned to fight, and there are large reserves behind them. The enemy has ample equipment. Our lads will not lack it either. The Communist Party will see to it. We've been given first-class submarines, and they'll get all

they require. The Nazis will never see Moscow. Is that
clear?"

Storm winds were blowing in real earnest. The submarine
rolled heavily. It grew dark quickly and there was hardly any
visibility. Extra look-outs were posted on the bridge and I
went to inspect the compartments. The men were in good
spirits and kept watch alertly. The crew were obviously used
to our northern or, to be more exact, rough weather. The
Barents and Norwegian seas are seldom calm. There storms
are almost a natural condition. The frequent cyclones carry
the icy arctic air, whipping up a heavy sea that rolls even a
large ship, let alone a submarine.

Most of the time we sailed on the surface. At night, even in
our patrol area, we kept a look-out without diving, because in
the darkness the periscope is almost useless. Besides, we had
to use our electric power sparingly in case we had to give the
slip to the enemy. It was not easy to work on a rolling deck or
in the cramped space with its heavy, salt- and oil-saturated
air. Not every man can endure the unnerving onslaught of
seasickness. None of the men could afford to succumb to it,
particularly the men of the watch. Any relaxation of attention
could be fatal to the ship.

There are two cures for seasickness: work that makes you
forget the rolling, and habit. If both these cures fail, the only
alternative is to get a transfer from a submarine. A submarine
does not carry extra men. If anybody is seasick two others
have to keep watch not in three but in two shifts. It means
extra expenditure of strength, which may be needed in full
measure at any moment. It also means reducing the submarine's
fighting capacity.

The storm somewhat abated on the second day of our
patrol. The submarine's standing ailment made itself felt: the
diesel sluice valves began leaking again. She was an "old
woman" after all. Age is something not only man but also a
ship's organism cannot reverse. The trouble was more or less
remedied within half an hour, and almost immediately after
that we had to dive. Dawn had broken and we could not
remain on the surface within sight of German observation
posts.

Under water the sluice valves leaked again but it was
bearable. We steered for a small bay.

There were no ships in it, and except for a tiny village in

the distance there were no habitations on the shore. Through the periscope this landscape made one think of a black-and-white photograph: the dark water, the gray sky, and the black cliffs with small white, extremely clean cottages perched on them.

Who lived in these cottages and what was taking place beneath the sharp-pointed roofs? Perhaps honest Norwegian fisher folk, who hated the Nazis as much as we did lived there. Or perhaps the honest folk had been driven inland and the cottages had been given to inveterate quislings? Who knows?

We went on with our search. Time dragged by slowly. The seamen, who were off duty, were dozing or reading. As a matter of fact, more were reading than dozing. They called books moral weapons. I thought that a very apt description.

On patrol the life of a seaman is simple: four hours on duty and eight hours off. Tidying up and maintenance of machinery and guns. Four meals a day. Sleep. And over and above schedule—alarms and repairs. There is quite a bit of free time, and that is when the "moral weapon" is needed.

When left to his own thoughts for lengthy periods a man may fall victim to the blues. Long days of waiting to encounter the enemy, the feeling of mortal danger or bitter news from home are dead weights on the heart and shatter the nervous system. A man has a bad time of it on patrol if he has no book to read.

In D-3 as, incidentally, in all submarines, I've hardly met any non-readers. We got our books from the large brigade library. On this patrol Gusarov had been over-zealous, getting books from the library and Naval House as well, taking into account, so to speak, individual requests. The men were interested in a wide range of literature, reading political, military and technical books. The greatest demand was for fiction, of course, with Alexander Pushkin, Mikhail Lermontov, Nikolai Gogol and Lev Tolstoi heading the list. Other authors popular with the men were Vladimir Mayakovsky, Nikolai Ostrovsky, Mikhail Sholokhov, Alexander Fadeyev, Leonid Sobolev and Alexei Novikov-Priboi.

A good book awakens lofty feelings, fans hatred for the enemy, inspires fervent patriotism and sharpens the desire to do something heroic. That weapon is as powerful as a torpedo.

Unfortunately, our torpedoes were lying tranquilly in their tubes. We made an attempt to enter the large and deep Tana

Fjord. But we had to turn back because our "old lady" began to sink. We almost completely emptied our ballast tanks. That did not help. The submarine kept sinking as though some giant octopus were dragging her down. We turned and left the perfidious fjord at half-speed. Fresh water carried by mountain rivers after incessant rain had evidently accumulated in it. In fresh water a submarine grows heavy.

The diesel sluice valves continued leaking, letting nearly a ton of water into the hold in the course of an hour. The turbo pump had to be started from time to time. Filipp Konstantinov felt nervous, "We shall have to turn back because of these sluice valves, Comrade Divisional Commander," he said.

"I don't think I'll agree to that," I replied. "We'd be made a laughing stock at the base if we came running back like this."

"But this is not the sort of thing to be trifled with," Konstantinov argued. "We'll leave a track that will betray us to the enemy."

He was quite right. Water from the hold carries an admixture of oil and leaves treacherous rainbow patches on the surface. The noise of the pump was no asset either. Yet Konstantinov was wrong in the main thing, namely, that we should give up in face of our very first difficulties.

"I think you ought to consult again with your engineering officer and petty officers," I said. "They're always full of ideas."

In the morning of September 26 the weather was in our favor. There was a moderate swell, visibility was variable and snow squalls blew from time to time. At least, the patches of oil left by us on the water were not very easy to discern.

At 10.00 hours we sighted two motorboats at the entrance of Tana Fjord. Obviously they were there for a reason. Sure enough, a small transport, displacing about two thousand tons, appeared an hour later. The men were ordered to battle stations. They rushed to take their places, leaving open books in their bunks.

We were ready for battle. Two torpedoes were fired from a short distance. A minute later we heard one of them exploding. When we scanned the area through our periscope we found no sign of the transport.

The excitement of this first kill did not die away for a long time. The leaky sluice valves no longer seemed a hindrance to the fulfilment of our mission. Everybody was now certain that the engine-room artificers would think of something.

We had made a good beginning. On the next day, at approximately the same time, we came across a small tanker near Koi Fjord. It appeared suddenly from behind a cape, steering an eastward course. We fired two torpedoes from our aft tubes. One of them hit the target. This time we watched the vessel sink. It plunged into the water stern first, the bow sticking high in the air. It was all over in five minutes.

It must be terrible to be on a torpedoed vessel. If you come to the surface your chances of being picked up are extremely small. In these northern seas you can't swim for longer than 20 minutes. The cold overcomes your heart and it stops beating. But there was no pity in us for those who went under with the tanker. Why had they come to us to burn, pillage and kill? Whenever I pictured what was happening in enemy-held territory, my heart bled and a feeling akin to shame overcame me, for we had done so little toward victory. It made us all the more determined to hunt down the enemy.

The sluice valves continued leaking, and it was quite clear that they could not be repaired at sea. But the engine-room artificers did not disappoint us. Petty Officer Tugolukov suggested channeling the water trickling through the sluice valves directly into a trim tank without letting it go into the hold. That would solve the problem of the patches of oil. Engineer Officer Chelyubeyev was quick to appreciate the idea and the men got down to work under his supervision. Three of them—Krasnovsky, Chernyshev and Kotov—used a hose to connect the sluice valves with the steam distributor (which was used only when the submarine was at the base). The hose carried the water to the trim tank via the control room. It looked simple, but it entailed a lot of hard work, which in the end was crowned with success.

Now we could patrol the enemy shore as long as we liked, even in calm weather, without the fear of being detected. There would be no patches of oil to betray us.

In a battle situation men work faster and with greater resourcefulness. I have known of many cases where men took only a few hours on repairs that ordinarily required many days of work in a dock.

The submarine's wall newspaper was put out. It was devoted to the electricians and spoke of their work in the same respectful terms as of the work of the torpedomen and Petty Officer Neshcheret, in charge of torpedoes, who was directly responsible for the first two hits. As a matter of fact, the

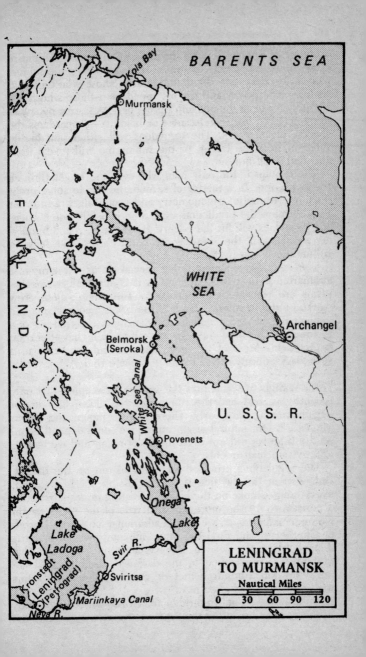

BARENTS SEA

Kola Bay

Murmansk

FINLAND

WHITE
SEA

Archangel

Belmorsk
(Seroka)

White Sea Canal

U. S. S. R.

Povenets

Onega
Lake

Lake
Ladoga

Svir R.

Kronstadt
Leningrad
(Petrograd)

Sviritsa

Mariinkaya Canal

Neva R.

LENINGRAD
TO MURMANSK

Nautical Miles

0   30   60   90   120

accuracy of a torpedo salvo depends upon almost the entire crew—those who ready the tubes, those who keep the submarine at the necessary depth and course, those who ensure it with electric power and the set speed, and those who listen to the noise of an enemy ship's propellers. An error by any of them—due to fear, carelessness or inability—jeopardizes the success of an attack. The torpedoes will either jam in the tubes or miss the target, or the submarine will reveal itself and find itself hunted.

The captain is the only man who sees the target through the periscope. In a matter of seconds he has to solve problems in arithmetic, trigonometry and vector algebra in order to determine the prediction angle, the invisible point where the torpedoes will hit the enemy. He is the eyes and brain of an attack, and the crew is its heart, arms and legs. A submarine is run by team work.

The engine-room crew enjoy special status. As long as a submarine is on patrol, as long as it is alive, all its mechanisms are constantly in operation. The engine-room crew worked uninterruptedly. Each of them was a courageous and vigilant fighter and a skilled workman with the training of a technician. The chief engineer himself had a higher education in his field. Most of the petty officers and seamen had a secondary education and training in some trade.

... At night we sailed on the surface. It seemed that only recently we had had the sun round the clock, but now it began growing dark early. There was no moon, and it was pitch dark. Our natural vision was all we could depend upon. At the time we did not even dream of radar, and we had no night-vision instruments.

The regulations provided for one look-out on the bridge. But even in the daytime it was impossible for him to spot everything—smoke on the horizon, floating mines, aircraft or a periscope. All the more was that true of the night watch. Going by experience, we posted additional look-outs. Decoder Chernetsov and First-Aid Man Shibanov were particularly dependable in this branch. But we could not be certain that nothing was overlooked in the darkness. Visibility did not range beyond a hundred meters. Besides, ships now sailed with their lights blacked out.

Gusarov stayed on the bridge almost the whole night long. In this respect he outdid the captain—Konstantinov could not stand the strain of an all-night watch and had to snatch a bit of sleep from time to time. But in Gusarov's case, nobody knew when he slept. In the daytime he could be seen in the compartments, commenting on the Soviet Information Bureau communiques received by the wireless operators, presiding over a short meeting of agitators, having a talk with the editorial board of the wall newspaper, or simply talking to the men in his taciturn but extremely sincere manner.

On this patrol part of his work was done by Regimental Commissar Baikov.

At about 14.00 hours on September 30 we were aroused by an alarm sounded by Lieutenant-Captain Sokolov, who was officer-of-the-watch in the control room.

"Two transports on a head-on course," he cried out.

Indeed, some 20 cable-lengths away I saw two ships moving toward each other. They were escorted by aircraft.

"All right, Captain, take over," I said.

Konstantinov took his place at the periscope. The submarine closed up for the attack. Ten minutes later the order "Fire!" was given and the submarine shuddered as three torpedoes left her. To prevent the submarine from rising to the surface, Chelyubeyev filled the rapid submersion ballast tank, but that failed to hold the submarine at a periscope level. We could not watch the torpedoes, and we did not hear explosions. But ten minutes later when we rose to periscope depth we saw only one transport, the one that had been on a westward course. It was now making straight for the shore. The transport that had been moving in an easterly direction— Konstantinov had selected it for his target—was not on the surface. Aircraft were circling over the spot where we had seen it.

An hour passed. Battle stations were sounded before the excitement of the first attack had died down. It looked as if we were having a streak of luck: a convoy of two transports and three patrol vessels was moving along the shore. It was the first convoy encountered by us. Thick-skinned as the Nazis were, it was beginning to dawn upon them that the Norwegian coastal waters were unsafe for lone ships. It was, of course, much harder to attack a convoy. On the other hand, there were many worthy candidates for the sea floor in it, we decided optimistically. Everything betokened that success was at hand.

Undetected, we dived under the convoy in order to be able to strike at it from the shore—that gave us a tactical advantage—and began wheeling to port to begin the attack. While we were steering the attack course a grinding sound put us on the alert. The submarine shuddered. We were mortified to find that we had grazed the seabed at a depth of ten meters and that now we were stranded on a sandbank.

By the time we got off the sandbank the convoy had disappeared. It was a dreadful disappointment. But nobody was to blame. Navigator Berezin was as steady as a rock. Konstantinov, who had been a navigator officer himself, had closely followed his calculations and determined the position of the submarine several times. I too had checked the position. But nobody could have known that instead of being 26 meters deep, as the chart showed, the sea at this spot was only eight meters deep. Had we turned somewhat to starboard we would have missed the sandbank. But in that case the convoy would have been beyond our angle of attack.

We had been too premature in congratulating ourselves.

Bad luck too comes in streaks. On the next day we tried to attack a large steamer, but the patrol vessel escorting it nearly rammed into us. We dived in the nick of time. The noise of the ship's propeller could be heard plainly without hydrophones. For some reason it left us alone.

For the next two days we hunted in vain, and the troubles that beset us were greater than anything we had encountered so far: the cable of the main periscope snapped, leaving us blind. True, we still had the zenith periscope but it was practically useless in a rough sea.

"We'll have to turn back, Comrade Divisional Commander," Konstantinov said gloomily.

This was no ordinary dilemma. It was the sort of damage that rarely occurred, and when it did occur the repairs had to be made in a dock. However, I felt that we had to give it a try ourselves.

"We can always turn back," I said. "But before we do that we must try and find some suitable steel cable."

"Where? You know yourself that we're not supposed to have a spare cable," Konstantinov replied.

"What about your mooring line?"

The indispensable Tugolukov applied himself to the job aided by Chief Electrician Bibikov, Petty Officer 2nd Class Roshchin and seamen Lebedev, Chernyshev and Yakovenko.

They worked all night. They dismantled the periscope winch, turned a new roller, inserted a bracket, stretched a new cable in place of the one that had snapped and straightened the tilting periscope standards. It was a remarkable feat.

The steel cable used for mooring a submarine is somewhat thinner than the conventional periscope cable and it was difficult to say how reliable it was. We decided to keep the periscope in its up position as long as the submarine was under water, and to lower it only when we surfaced. That was safer. In any case, we could carry on with our patrol.

. . . We were at sea for five days, keeping our eyes peeled for signs of the enemy. What with a storm of almost hurricane force raging on the surface that was a devilish task. It was all we could do to keep the submarine at periscope depth. We struggled to prevent the waves from forcing us to the surface, particularly when we moved at a slow speed. That was something we could not allow, because once the submarine was surfaced we would have a hard time of it diving. Besides, on the surface we would be running the risk of waves damaging our conning tower or the external casing.

At periscope level, therefore, we did not dare move slower than at half-speed. Our efficient pair—Chelyubeyev and Neshcheret—kept the submarine at the required depth, the former operating the trimming tanks and the latter manipulating the hydroplanes. This operation had to be performed quite frequently because after scanning the horizon we dived instead of downing the periscope.

If we had reliable sonars we would not have had to scan the surface so frequently. At the time, however, even in new submarines, to say nothing of "old ladies," hydroacoustics were far from being perfect.

The storm began to abate on October 11. However, it continued to snow, reducing the already almost zero visibility. One of these snowfalls hindered us from inspecting the results of a day attack on a transport of about five thousand tons. We had fired three torpedoes at it. A minute and a half after the salvo everybody on board clearly heard two explosions. The hydrophone operator reported that the propellers could not be heard. But when we surfaced we found ourselves enveloped in a jacket of snow. The snowfall soon passed and the sea around us was empty. This took place near Kongs Fjord.

Two days later we returned to Tana Fjord. It was deserted and we turned back. At the entrance the submarine suddenly reduced speed. We could not understand it. The electric motors were working at the required number of revs. All the other mechanisms were in order. It could only be some external trouble.

It turned out, as the periscope showed, that we were dragging a net with a large spar buoy flying a yellow flag. It raised a huge white bow wave, which the shore observation posts could easily spot. We changed speed in an effort to shake the net off. It did not help, and, besides, it was dangerous to maneuver like that. The net was clinging to the stern of the submarine and could at any second become entangled in the screws. That would be fatal. Even an ordinary hemp rope, if it winds around the propellers, will stop them dead. If that happened we would be a helpless target for enemy patrol boats and batteries.

We did not know if the net had been put up specially to expose submarines or if it was simply a fisherman's net. Whatever it was we had to get rid of it. To do that we had to surface, which in broad daylight and in a Norwegian fjord would have been, to say the least, a thoughtless act.

There was only one thing to do, and it was to dive deeper and try to sink the treacherous buoy. The depth meter showed seventy meters. Our engines were working at low speed, but the submarine hardly moved at all. We changed to medium speed. The submarine started moving very slowly. Our eyes were glued to the tachometer. We were worried sick that the propellers might be ensnared. The best solution would be to lie on the seabed and surface when it would grow dark. But it was too deep here for that—we would run the danger of being crushed by the water pressure.

After about an hour of suspense, we felt the submarine jerk forward as though she had been suddenly unfettered. We felt relieved, for it meant that the net had detached itself. But it did not mean an end to our anxiety. A piece of netting, which could endanger the propellers, had undoubtedly remained. Only the onset of darkness put an end to our troubles. We surfaced and sent two men to inspect the propeller guards. Wet to the skin and with teeth chattering, they reported that a long length of thin rope had wound itself around the guards. The net and buoy had detached themselves.

We cut off about fifty meters of rope. The rest we unwound and took into the submarine as a keepsake.

It was a beautiful night. The moon tipped the crests of the waves with silver. Every now and then Aurora Borealis filled the sky with a display of fireworks. It was something that could be seen only in the northern latitudes. But we had not much time for admiring nature. The diesels revved up and we steered a course toward the area where we usually recharged our batteries, which our cruise at medium speed with the net in tow had exhausted pretty thoroughly.

On the next day our "old lady's" sonar went out of commission. The vibrators sprang a leak. Although the acoustic system in the Decembrists was rather poor it would, in our age, be amateurish to fight without it. The breakdown of the periscope had blinded us, but now we were deaf. To say nothing of the difficulties of locating a target, we now could not always know if we ourselves had been detected by the enemy. Deep in the sea, where the periscope is useless, the hydrophones are our only means of knowing what is happening on the surface.

However, we did not have to sail "deaf" long. On October 15 we were signalled back to our base.

We proceeded to our base on the surface, zigzagging all the way to avoid becoming the victim of an enemy torpedo.

We returned home on October 17 after twenty days at sea. We caused a sensation by firing a salute of four rounds. As soon as we had made fast to the pier I hurried to Division Headquarters. There the officers who greeted me smiled mysteriously as though there was some conspiracy afoot. I did not attach any significance to it. But in my "cabin" at the depot I could not find my tunic. In its place hung a new tunic with the four stripes of a Captain 2nd Rank. It took me some time to realize that the tunic was mine but that the stripes on it were new.

In the navy or army, no matter how alien ambition may be, promotion is always exciting and pleasant. Our Brigade Commander Nikolai Vinogradov was also given a new rank, that of a Rear Admiral.

The Fleet Commander-in-Chief gave a good appraisal of our patrol. It was analyzed in detail at a conference with submarine captains and Commissars. All the pros and cons were thrashed out. I felt rather proud that the "old lady" had contributed her mite to the store of our collective experience.

But all this looked insignificant against the background of the grim and formidable events that were taking place on the decisive fronts, primarily near Moscow. Our attention was wholly focused on the capital. In one way or another all talk veered toward it. The natural outcome of this was a letter from the Y.C.L. members of D-3 to the Y.C.L.ers defending Moscow.

Reinforcements

"We have reinforcements," Kerim Gadjiev told me with a smile. I had already been briefed on the latest news in the brigade. I knew that 1st Division had received three new Katyushas—21, 22 and 23. They had sailed from Leningrad to Archangel via the White Sea Canal last summer and after final touches in dock they had come to us.

"Congratulations, Kerim," I said, shaking hands with my old friend. "You now have a large division. With the new submarines to keep you busy at sea I'll probably not see you until New Year."

This forecast proved to be close to the truth. We saw very little of Kerim. On one occasion, he returned from patrol at dinner time, changed over to another submarine and had his supper at sea.

1st Division now had five large submarines, and the sixth, the K-3, was expected soon. Those were not all of the

brigade's reinforcements. In addition to the Katyushas we received two Esses, at first S-102 and then S-101. These medium submarines were larger and newer than the Pikes. Together with D-3 they formed the core of a division, which now became known as the 2nd. This new division, which would grow, of course, was commanded by Senior Lieutenant Mikhail Khomyakov, who had brought the Esses from the Baltic.

The newly arrived Katyushas and Esses prepared for combat patrols. For them the war was only beginning, while our division of Pikes was already in the thick of it. While I was at sea in D-3, P-422 returned home with a kill to its credit.

On the evening of my return, its commander Lieutenant-Captain Malyshev gave me a detailed report on his twenty-five day patrol. He had encountered five enemy transports and had attacked each of them. Two of the transports had changed course and escaped. Three torpedoes missed their target because of errors in calculations. That had cast a gloom over the crew, and Malyshev himself felt nervous. It took all he had to meet his men's eyes and read their silent reproach. He felt they thought the misses were his fault and that as far as they were concerned there was nothing they could be blamed for. Indeed, on that patrol the crew showed that they were really competent.

At last, on the morning of September 12, Malyshev spotted a lone tanker of about six thousand tons. The submarine was some forty-five cable-lengths away. Malyshev made up his mind to make sure of this target at all costs. He shortened the

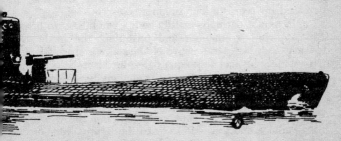

S-Class (U.S.S.R.)

distance to about five cable-lengths and fired a torpedo at that point-blank range. Seven men took turns at the periscope to watch the tanker sink. It made a tremendous impression.

There was much to learn from Malyshev's patrol. Five misses proved beyond argument the conclusion that had suggested itself long ago, namely, that it was ineffective to fire single torpedoes. Computation errors were inevitable in calculations. We did not have instruments that could accurately determine the course and speed of a target and the distance to it. Much depended upon visual observation, and certain allowances had to be made. Moreover, a target which detected a periscope or the track of a torpedo did its utmost to avoid being hit. In short, the answer to the problem was to fire salvoes of two, three and even four torpedoes at once or at intervals in order to cover possible errors. If instead of firing single torpedoes Malyshev had fired salvoes of two or three torpedoes, at least three of the six transports would have been sent to the bottom of the sea. This was a case where no torpedoes should have been spared. The lessons of P-422's patrol were analyzed by all submarine captains. It was explained to them that under usual, standard conditions they should fire salvoes. The only exceptions were Midgets, which carried only two torpedo tubes.

Victory salutes became common in Yekaterininskaya Harbor. The guns of the Pikes too began to speak. Stolbov and Moiseyev each fired another salute. Incidentally some time passed before Moiseyev let me have the details of his near escape from pursuit after he had sunk a coastal patrol ship.

P-421 fired a salute of three rounds. The commander, Captain 3rd Rank Nikolai Lunin was obviously out to make up for returning empty-handed from his first two patrols. True enough, on his fourth patrol, the last that year, he increased his score to four sinkings.

Lunin fought daringly, craftily and, I would say, with wide scope. Abrupt in manner and unsmiling, he made snap decisions and, like a true native of Odessa, was sharp-tongued.

In tactics, he had few equals despite his relatively short naval career. Like Utkin, he had been a master of a merchant ship and had sailed not in the North, but in the Black Sea. A true ship's master, he maintained iron discipline in his submarine. I had every confidence in Lunin: he was receptive to advice and was able to learn the lessons from success and failure.

*   *   *

Our division reached full strength after the November holidays. P-403 and P-404, which had been temporarily with the White Sea Flotilla, returned. As we had expected, their operations in the White Sea were not marked by any noteworthy results. But with these submarines on our roster we would have things easier. We would not have to rack our brains over whom to send on patrol to take the place of submarines in repair after a cruise or which had been damaged in drydock during air-raids. In short, we would now show our mettle.

The Story of a Torpedo

It was December 5, Constitution Day. A holiday is a holiday everywhere, even under water. Our cook went out of his way to turn the ration of groats and canned beef into a dinner worthy of the occasion.

We sat around the narrow table in the tiny wardroom. Our ration of vodka, 100 grams each, had been poured out. Senior Political Instructor Gusarov rose to his feet and proposed a toast to Moscow, where a tense lull had set in, and to the Motherland. We applauded standing. When the applause died down, Engineering Officer Chelyubeyev added, "And here's to our 'old lady,' may her battle score grow."

Yes, I was sailing in D-3 again. After the last patrol the submarine had received a new captain. It was no reflection on Konstantinov. He had skippered his submarine competently and efficiently and had been recommended for a decoration. But it became evident that the nervous tension of patrols was too much for him. Not everybody's nervous system has the same reserve of strength. It was found expedient to use Konstantinov in another capacity.

D-3's new skipper was Captain 3rd Rank Mikhail Bibeyev, one of the galaxy of former merchant masters, to which Utkin and Lunin belonged. But as distinct from them, he had graduated from a naval academy. Before enrolling in the academy he had commanded a submarine and his seniority in that capacity was not a short one. However, he still had to gain experience of navigation in the Barents and Norwegian seas.

For that reason the Brigade Commander had sent me on my

third patrol in the "old lady." This time I took with me our divisional torpedo officer, Lieutenant-Captain Alexander Kautsky. He had voluteereed to take the place of the First Lieutenant Sokolov who had fallen ill.

Alexander Kautsky was no novice in Decembrists. He had sailed in them as a rating in the Baltic, and as a re-enlisted coxswain he had come with them to the North. Then he had enrolled in a training school, and after graduation had returned to our Frigid Sea, as the ancient Pomors called it. He had served in submarines as Torpedo and Gunnery Officer and then became divisional torpedo officer. But he had his eye on becoming a submarine captain, and he did not miss the opportunity to sail as first lieutenant in a submarine, even if it belonged to a different division. He felt it would give him additional patrol experience.

The sea gave us a cheerless welcome. It was cold and dark. At this time of the year it either snowed or there was a mist. It stormed almost continuously.

On November 22, our first day at sea, our gyrocompass broke down. That was serious. The compass's wire pivot had snapped and we could not repair it. To sail without a gyrocompass was like running along the edge of a roof blindfolded. There could be no hope of a happy outcome.

We did not have an extra compass on board. True, there was a magnetic compass on the bridge with an optical transmission to the control room. But surrounded by such a huge mass of steel as a submarine, it could not be relied upon in general, let alone in the high latitudes.

In short, we had a problem on our hands. It was like a bolt from the blue. We would have been in our rights if we returned to our base. But that was exactly what we did not want to do. It would have been a pity to end the patrol without having really started out on it.

I liked the way Bibeyev reacted to the accident. He did not speculate on whether it was possible or impossible to continue the patrol. Instead he turned to Berezin.

"Navigator," he said, "have you eliminated the deviation properly?"

"Yes," Berezin replied not without pride. "The remaining deviation is negligible and has been determined accurately."

"What about reserve lamps? Will you be able to sail by the magnetic compass?"

"We've only got one spare lamp," Berezin said, starting out

on a comprehensive report, "but the lamp in the compass is almost new. Naturally, the deviation will change, but we shall check the corrections and be on our toes. The optical transmission is reliable. I've checked it. My opinion is that we can carry on."

Berezin was a little embarrassed by the responsibility he had undertaken and by his own boldness: after all what he said would count heavily in the captain's decision.

Bibeyev gave me a quizzical look.

"Inform the Fleet Commander-in-Chief and the Brigade Commander," I said, "that our gyrocompass is out of commission and we have decided to carry on by magnetic compass."

"Aye, aye," Bibeyev said with satisfaction.

We soon received a reply from the Fleet Commander-in-Chief. He gave us permission to carry on with the patrol but warned us to keep a vigilant eye on the magnetic compass, to be careful and not enter enemy fjords, and to return at once if we had any complications. That suited us.

On the third day, when we were approaching the Norwegian coast, we had another breakdown. This time it was the for'ard planes. It was a nasty business, but it could be tolerated. The aft plane was the main one and it was operating dependably.

When the batteries were recharged, the magnetic compass would run amuck. One had to give it one's undivided attention. We thought it would not let us down and moved closer to the coast, believing that we had about five kilometers' leeway. We were enveloped in fog and visibility was down to nil. But as soon as we turned toward the coastline the fog dispersed and we saw that we only had about two kilometers to spare. We had taken an awful risk getting stranded on a sandbank. In any case this was an extra reminder to be wary.

Our first encounter with the enemy took place on November 28. It was a wet and gloomy day, if the daylight hours of a polar winter can be called a day. Unexpectedly we saw a transport of about five thousand tons steaming out of a fjord. It was escorted by two mine sweepers. Their sweeps were probably lowered because they were moving slowly.

"All right, Captain, take over," I said, turning the periscope over to Bibeyev.

From a distance of six cable-lengths, when the clock showed exactly 14.00 hours, Bibeyev fired three torpedoes.

But at that very moment the submarine plunged down to seventy meters. It was Chelyubeyev. On the principle of "better more than little," he had let extra water into the trimming tank. Of course, it would have been worse if our conning tower showed above water. But this long dive deprived us of our possibility of observing the transport. There was a sharp explosion, and then silence. Which meant that only one of the torpedoes had found the target. Had it been enough to sink the transport?

When we rose to periscope depth there was nothing to be seen in the heavy fog. It was a pity. Perhaps we had only crippled the transport. True, our hydrophone operator reported that he could not hear its propellers. We had to be satisfied with that.

After the attack we dived to about 40 meters and set a course for our battery-recharging area. I went to the for'ard compartment where, directed by Torpedo Officer Donetsky, the torpedomen were reloading the tubes. The torpedo warheads glistened with a brick-red grease. Coxswain 2nd Class Zaborikhin and Leading Seaman Kirilyuk were tracing on it the words: "For the Motherland," "For Kiev," "For Minsk."

It had become customary to make such inscriptions. The men in the submarine hailed from many towns and republics. The abandonment of each town was like a stab in the heart for one or more of them—for it meant that relatives or friends had been left in it. Our war was totally unlike the war that was being fought on land. We did not see blazing, smoke-blackened towns and villages, the ashes of houses or sobbing children and women. But the acrid smell of fires penetrated down to us, under water, and made our eyes smart. The winds driving across Russia brought us the smell of gray ash, which plucked at our hearts and called for revenge.

On the torpedoes the seamen wrote the names of the towns that had been temporarily surrendered to the enemy and for which they wanted to take vengeance.

Until December 5 it was an uneventful patrol. The morning held out the promise of fine weather. There was a heavy swell. On such a sea it was not easy to spot our periscope, but it did not hinder us in any way. Visibility was variable. Snow fell now and then.

"Do you think we ought to move nearer to the fjord?" Bibeyev said. "Or even enter it? Remember that wireless intelligence said a convoy is expected to pass through our area today. It didn't give the time, though."

"Wireless intelligence is fairly accurate," I agreed. "The

convoy won't stay put in harbor in good weather like this. In other words, it will pass somewhere here in the course of the day. You are quite right to suggest waiting at the entrance to the fjord. If visibility permits, we'll be able to creep into the fjord, only we shall have to look about us more frequently."

We steered for the fjord.

If nothing untoward happens, the time table is rigidly observed. At 12.00 hours, Kautsky, who took over the watch, commanded, "All hands to dinner!"

In the wardroom we took our places around the festively laden table.

The wine was drunk. The herring, of which we were never short on patrol, was eaten. It had been deliciously prepared. Spoons were tinkling against the plates. Somebody praised the borsch. Suddenly Kautsky, who had ordered us to our holiday dinner, called out in a totally different tone of voice, "Battle stations!"

We jumped from our seats. I distinctly remember the excitment in Chelyubeyev and Berezin. Kautsky had made us the best possible holiday present. It gave us another opportunity of increasing our battle score. Everybody was eager to make the torpedo attack to go off smoothly.

When Bibeyev ran into the control room, Kautsky had already set a course toward the enemy. Ahead of us, rounding the cape, were two transports escorted by a Sleipner-class destroyer, which pugnaciously kept somewhat in front of them. The snow did not hinder Bibeyev. At first we maneuvered without a hitch. But suddenly, a shore patrol ship, which we had failed to see earlier, loomed in the periscope. Like the destroyer it sat deeper in the water than the transports and obstructed our view. We had to dive under it. Bibeyev and everybody else who was responsible for this maneuver coped with it splendidly. Now there was nothing to hinder us, and when we reached the attack position Bibeyev fired four torpedoes at the biggest of the transports. It displaced about ten thousand tons.

After firing the salvo we turned shoreward, because if the escort were going to look for us they would most likely turn their attention seaward.

We heard an explosion when some fifty seconds had elapsed, and then another, eight seconds later. Two minutes after that, when we came up to periscope depth, we saw the patrol ship speeding in the opposite direction from us a considerable distance away. The destroyer was near the transport we had aimed at. Before we could see any more, a sudden snow squall blotted our view.

We continued to maneuver near the attack area, at the entrance to the fjord. We felt perfectly safe, for the enemy was hunting for us somewhere else. Besides, we still hoped to see the results of our work. The snowstorm began to abate only forty minutes later, and when it did a strange object caught my eye. It resembled a box or a suitcase. Unquestionably, it was the transport, whose outline was distorted by the fast-falling snow.

Gradually it cleared sufficiently to enable us to recognize the transport. It was alone and sinking very slowly. Its bow was quite deep in the water, with the stern raised high in the air.

The situation was calm, and we allowed everybody in the control room to take turns at the periscope. The transport was in its death throes and it finally sank with helmsman Chernoknizhny watching it.

It took fifty-four minutes to sink. What had been in it for Dietl's infantry? Ammunition, clothes, food? Whatever it was, the loss to the Germans was quite a telling one. A transport of that size was equivalent to about ten trains.

At a depth of 40 meters we steered a course away from the attack area. In a cheerful voice Kautsky commanded, "Break off the attack. Readiness No. 2. Second watch on duty. All hands off duty to dinner."

Within five minutes, in an exuberant mood, we were resuming our interrupted dinner. It was a double holiday for us.

After dinner the torpedo tubes were reloaded. Warrant Officer Bibikov, editor of the submarine's wall newspaper, came up to me.

"Comrade Captain 2nd Rank," he said, "you owe us an article."

I did not argue and in half an hour gave him the fruit of my labor. The article was headed "The Story of a Torpedo." Here it is in full.

"1. I was born on 17/X/19. . . at a munitions plant.

"2. On 28/XI/19. . . I was assigned to a destroyer of the Northern Fleet.

"3. On 14/X/1941, after sailing for a long time I was transferred ashore to recuperate my enfeebled health.

"4. On 10/XI/1941, to my delight, the Torpedo Commission sent me to a submarine base.

"5. On 16/XI/1941 I reported for duty in the submarine *Old Lady* and waited impatiently for her to put out to sea.

"6. 5/XII/1941. It is Constitution Day today. We have been at sea for several days. After dinner I was given a combat assignment—to hit an enemy transport and send it to the bottom of the sea. I am proud that this assignment was given to me, doubly so that it is a holiday. You may be sure that I shall carry it out.

"7. 14.30 hours. Note the time. I attacked the enemy—for the Motherland, for Moscow.

"Note: The editors are pleased to report that the torpedo brilliantly fulfilled its task. The sixth Nazi transport hit by our submarine is on the seabed. The torpedo sends us greetings and wishes its sisters similar success."

I got all the data on the torpedo from the official service list, which I have kept in my files.

At about 14.00 hours on the next day near the coast we discovered a large transport escorted by two mine sweepers. We attacked without wasting time: a salvo of three torpedoes was fired eight minutes after we had sighted the ship. For fifty seconds we waited to hear the explosions. One torpedo scored a direct hit. A mine sweeper hurried in to help the transport. We wanted to attack it as well. But it withdrew and disappeared by the time we swung around to aim our torpedoes.

In contrast to the preceding transport, it sank stern first in twenty-six minutes. The spectacle was witnessed by five men besides Bibeyev and me.

That gave D-3 its seventh kill.

That night Chief Wireless Operator Tarasov received the latest Soviet Information Bureau communique on the start of a Soviet offensive near Moscow. It was a brief preliminary communication, but we were intoxicated with joy. It made our own victory symbolical: yesterday's transport had been sunk almost simultaneously with the launching of the offensive.

Three copies were made of the Soviet Information Bureau communique. One copy, on instructions from Gusarov, was hung in the control room, and the other two were passed from hand to hand. All subsequent communiques were treated in the same way.

None of us slept a wink that night. All our thoughts were

about the fighting near Moscow and we talked about it without end. That was the great turning point. It was the end to retreat. The myth of the Nazi army's invincibility would be finally exploded. One could understand that with their optimism on the upsurge many of the men overestimated the significance of what was happening and said that our troops would now march straight to Berlin. In our cold and confined steel box we dreamed of an early end to the war. None of us supposed that ahead of us were three and a half years of bloody fighting, that the road to victory lay across a gigantic battle on the Volga and through tank battles on the plains near Kursk.

Attack and victory were the only vent for the enthusiasm gripping the men. But though we hunted high and low we failed to contact the enemy. Moreover, our echo sounder went out of order. Without a gyrocompass and an echo sounder it was much too risky to enter a fjord. The inaccurate charts, the poor daylight, the inky blackness of the night and the endless snowstorms added to our difficulties.

On December 13 we were ordered home and were back at our base two days later. We were very warmly welcomed. The entire Fleet Military Council with the Commander-in-Chief turned out to meet us at the pier. Our "old lady" deserved it. Her bag of victories was now the largest in the brigade.

The "old lady" was really old, both in design and age. There was something about her appearance which bore a resemblance to the pre-Revolution Snow Leopards. She had an extra-tough hull. I usually advised the officer on night watch to ram the enemy if he was encountered suddenly and there was nothing else to be done. The "old lady" dived slowly, and when enemy aircraft appeared overhead we did not have to rush to the hatch. We could take our time, observe the aircraft from the bridge and instruct the helmsman in accordance with the situation. In addition, on each patrol the worn mechanism let the crew down: something either broke or went out of commission.

For all that the "old lady" was a formidable fighting machine. Her large bag of victories was due to her exceptionally efficient crew.

I was delighted to learn that for the latest patrol the entire crew had been recommended for decorations and that the submarine herself had been put forward for the Order of the

Red Banner. A month later, D-3 became the first submarine in the Brigade to carry an Order on her ensign.

Shoulder to Shoulder

It was now 1942. What had the past year given us? What had six months of war taught us and what results had they yielded?

The situation on the land front within the Arctic Circle had been stabilized. The German autumn offensive had collapsed. Soviet counterblows compelled the Germans to relinquish some of the ground they had won. But the enemy still had numerical air, artillery and mortar superiority. Our superiority lay in our boundless love for our country, our staunch morale, clarity of purpose and burning hatred for the invaders.

But that was not enough to drive the Nazis out. However, with all their numerical and technical superiority they were not strong enough to crush us. It became a positional war.

The part played by our brigade contributed toward preventing the Germans from assembling sufficient forces to move forward. Every tanker sunk by torpedoes kept German flyers grounded for lack of fuel. Every loaded transport sent to the bottom forced the German troops to dance in the frost without warm clothes, reduced their daily ration of food and made them economize on ammunition.

Early in the war we sank few ships. We now knew why. It was not only due to lack of experience. The enemy Lapland group had all it required, according to the calculations of the Nazi command, to capture Murmansk in a single lightning strike. The failure of the blitzkrieg was felt acutely here, in the North. For its second, autumn offensive and then for a positional war Dietl's Corps required additional resources and sizable reinforcements. The enemy's communication lines sprang to life. That gave us the work we had been waiting for. We fought shoulder to shoulder with the army, sapping the strength of the force opposing it.

We employed mainly positional tactics. The areas for lone submarines were demarcated along the entire route used by enemy transports and convoys from West Fjord and Tromsö in the west to Varanger Fjord in the east.

Varanger and Tana fjords, which were the nearest to the Soviet frontier, were stopped up by Midgets. These small submarines, whose fighting capacity was doubted by some people before the war, had proved their worth, making sceptics take their words back. In the hands of crack crews and competent officers these boats proved that they could do more than was expected of them. They had been designed for off-shore patrol duty. But from the very outset of the war they became active along the enemy coast, cleverly penetrating the harbors.

After Fisanovich had torpedoed a transport in Liinahamari, Yegorov in M-174 and Starikov in M-171 also broke into the same port where they wreaked havoc. Incidentally, Starikov's Midget was caught in an anti-submarine net at the harbor's exit. Starikov's self-control and resourcefulness saved the submarine from what looked to be unavertible disaster. Taking advantage of the tide and the choppy sea he virtually crawled over the net.

In September Fisanovich sank another transport in Varanger Fjord, increasing M-172's battle score to three kills. Other Midgets were likewise successful.

Praise was not all that was heaped upon these submarines. There were serious complaints as well. Firstly, they were poorly armed. They could not achieve much with their two tubes and two torpedoes. In most cases single torpedoes were ineffective. Secondly, the submarine only had one propeller shaft. That increased her swing angle, reducing her maneuverability.

These small and economic submarines proved well suited to the Northern Theater, where the enemy's operational bases were hard by ours. But their design had to be improved. They required heavier armaments and a double-shaft power plant. That would not greatly increase the cost of building them, but, on the other hand, would considerably enhance their fighting capacity.

The Pikes were medium-sized submarines with a range extending to Nordkapp, where the Barents Sea borders on the Norwegian Sea. Everything about them was satisfactory except their speed. There had been cases when because of the Pikes' inability to swing quickly into a firing position the crew had to stand helplessly by while enemy transports slipped out of their range.

However, that did not happen often, for we had prepared ourselves to fight with the means at our disposal. We developed reliable tactics fairly quickly—we hunted for the enemy in direct proximity to his coast, particularly in the region of ports and harbors, and salvoes greatly increased the probability of direct hits.

The enemy himself proved how correct our tactics were. Lieutenant-Captain Semyon Kovalenko, skipper of P-403, which had joined us after he had returned from the White Sea, decided to amend the tactics we had adopted, reasoning that the Germans could not have failed to see that when they sailed two or three miles from the shore they were constantly attacked by submarines. He felt they would try to avoid these attacks by going farther out to sea.

In his patrol area Kovalenko lurked in wait about ten or twelve miles off shore.

But in an effort to think for the enemy, he had out-maneuvered himself. The Germans remained true to their favorite course. P-403 failed to spot anything not only visually, which was quite natural on account of the polar night and the frequent snowstorms, but also with the aid of her hydrophones. Kovalenko's calculation did not justify itself. However, on his next patrol in the second half of December, he hunted for enemy ships where they were hunted by other submarines and returned home with a kill.

It is worth mentioning that after Kovalenko had entered Porsangen Fjord he recharged his batteries there without going to the area specially assigned for the purpose. That enabled him to carry on his hunt and, besides, a violent storm was raging in the open sea. Additional look-outs were posted on the bridge, and one of the guns was manned. In this position the submarine encountered a convoy consisting of a transport of about ten thousand tons, four patrol ships and several submarine chasers.

The enemy was on a favorable course angle, and the torpedoes were ready for firing. All that had to be done was slightly to alter the course to make allowance for the darkness and issue the orders "Stand by!" and "Fire," for which only a few seconds were required. At the same moment that the torpedoes were fired, a patrol ship, which had not been noticed before, drew up alongside the transport, with the result that both ships were hit. This was the first double hit in the fleet. The explosion was accompanied by such a dazzling flash that the light went through the bridge hatch and illumined an engine-room artificer standing near the ladder in the control room. Some sort of dirt covered everybody on the bridge. That was not to be wondered at, for the hits were scored less than three cable-lengths away.

After this, without diving, the submarine hid in a tiny bay and was not discovered by the escort vessels.

In short, everything turned out well. But had the submarine been discovered and forced to dive she would have been in a desperate predicament with her uncharged batteries. Attention was drawn to this point when the patrol was analyzed. No objection was raised to sailing on the surface at night, even under the enemy's nose, but the batteries had to be fully charged. Submarines had to have a power reserve to enable them, when necessary, to dive and stay under water for several hours.

On the whole, P-403's patrol proved the efficacy of our hunt tactics. Further proof of this came from P-404, which was on patrol at approximately the same time. She hit an enemy transport with two torpedoes from a distance of ten cable-lengths.

The Pikes were also suitable for creeping up to the enemy shore and, unobserved, land a reconnaissance group or, on the contrary, take such a group aboard after a special assignment. Sometimes, submariners witnessed mute tragedies, when a scout group would be overdue and they would have to leave without it.

As I have already mentioned, in addition to Pikes we had two Esses. But it was still too early to pass judgment on them. So far only S-102 had been on patrol. Her first two patrols had been unsuccessful. But on her third patrol she landed a scout group and then took it back on board, and attacked two convoys. In the first attack she sank one ship, and in the second Lieutenant-Captain Gorodnichy repeated Kovalenko's double hit. Firing from a submerged position, he sank two transports with a single salvo. In short, we expected much from these submarines and their crews, for the Esses were more modern ships than the Pikes, much faster, with a large range, and their artillery was as powerful as that of the Decembrists.

With their torpedoes, mines and artillery our heavy submarines operated in the Norwegian Sea beyond Nordkapp. The road to the Germans' western bases was blazed by Avgustinovich in K-1. The others followed in his wake.

The Katyushas laid mine fields in the path of convoys, an operation that required navigational accuracy and complete secrecy. Everything would go to pot if any of these conditions was violated. Our submarines, however, did their work efficiently and Captains reported fires in the mine fields—water, as we all know, does not burn.

K-3 sailed in the Lopp Sea, a region of skerries along the Norwegian coast. This was Lieutenant-Captain Malofeyev's first patrol and Gadjiev, who had just returned from sea, went with him as Instructor Commander taking Divisional Navigator Vasilyev with him.

The submarine laid mines in the enemy's sea lanes near Hammerfest. After that she safely negotiated enemy mine fields and entered the skerries, where on December 3 she contacted a convoy consisting of a large transport, a patrol ship and two submarine chasers.

Two of the four torpedoes fired by K-3 hit the transport and it began to sink. But the submarine was detected when she fired the salvo, and the escort vessels attacked her with depth charges. K-3 dived. A depth charge exploded near her. She lost her buoyancy and hit the seabed with her bow. The depth-charge attack continued. The submarine tried, without success, to maneuver, and then settled on the sea floor. The depth charges were dropped accurately—one of the fuel tanks sprang a leak and the telltale oil rose to the surface.

This put K-3 in a desperate plight. The enemy knew where she was and was determined to finish her off. Kerim took the only possible decision: to surface and engage the enemy with artillery. He had had experience of this. True, that experience had been gained in K-2 against a transport. This time he had to contend with warships. But the caliber of their guns could not be larger than that of K-3's artillery. At any rate, the 100 mm guns gave K-3 a good chance.

The submarine surfaced and the gunners led by Lieutenant Vinogradov rushed to their stations. The patrol ship and submarine chasers approached on the port side, and opened fire at once. A lucky hit from a large-caliber machine-gun put the for'ard gun out of action. But the aft gun, commanded by Petty Officer 2nd Class Konopelko, was quickly readied for action.

It fired three rounds before the enemy gunners could find the range, and the patrol ship went under in flames and smoke. She was hit in her bow where the ammunition was stored. The submarine shifted her fire on a chaser which had rushed to the sinking patrol ship. The chaser disappeared in the water, joining her partner. The second chaser swung around and took cover behind the nearest cape.

The battle had taken only seven minutes. Thirty-nine shells were fired by our gunners.

Artillery was also successfully used by K-22, which was commanded by Victor Kotelnikov, a veteran of the Northern Fleet. On one of her patrols, with Brigade Commander Vinogradov on board, the submarine's artillery sank first a steamer and then three small ships. K-23 likewise sank a ship—a mine sweeper—with her guns. Her captain was Leonid Potapov, an experienced sailor.

In short, the Katyushas were making good use of their artillery.

In 1942 the Northern Fleet's submarines became the main force operating against enemy sea communications. This was recognized not only by our Command but by the enemy too. His ships no longer dared to sail alone, as they used to at the outset of the war. They were escorted by warships and aircraft. Furthermore, the enemy communications were protected by anti-submarine mine fields. All this sustained tension in the Nazi navy. The Germans reinforced their fleet based on the Norwegian coast with destroyers and small ships. Submarines, cruisers and the battleship *Tirpitz* were transferred to the North.

But we were not the cause for the appearance of submarines and large warships. They were levelled against the Allied convoys that were now regularly sailing to Murmansk. Another assignment, that of covering our own sea communications, was now added to those we already had.

THE SEA—ALLY OF
RESOURCEFULNESS

To Those Who Are at Sea

Our life was sharply divided between the sea and the base.

The sea was our front. It began at the exit of Kola Bay and stretched for hundreds of miles to the east, west and north. Like hunters tracking game in a forest, we furrowed the ocean in search of the enemy. Through our periscope we saw the clean and cozy little town of Berlivog, on the Norwegian coast, with its sloping, tiled roofs and tall white churches—a fragment of peace time, which seemed to have been overlooked by the war.

Sometimes the hunt was abortive. But more often than not we found and sank the enemy. The deep rumble of an exploding torpedo that would come as a climax to long minutes of maneuvering would compensate, tactically, materially and morally, for several patrols. On the other hand, more and more frequently, the hunter became the hunted. A submarine would be attacked and pursued for a long time, sometimes for hours on end.

But whatever the result of a patrol (except a fatal one, of course), a submarine inevitably heads for the only geographical point to which it is tied by an invisible but unbreakable thread—namely, its base at Polyarnoye.

Bases play an extraordinarily big role in a submarine war. They are more than a source of fuel, ammunition and food, and more than a place where men can recover their exhausted strength. They give a "rest" and "cure" to the submarine herself, whose "health" is put to a gruelling test on each patrol. Precisely that is the most laborious form of maintenance, being linked up with advance, prewar preparation, with a proper account of the economic potentialities of the base area.

When war broke out the shipyards in Murmansk began to cater for the navy. We, of course, had our own naval repair facilities, one of which was the Krasny Gorn floating dock that had been turned over to our brigade. It arrived in the North from Kronstadt in the summer of 1935, bringing with it many of its veteran workers. These people had dedicated themselves to the navy.

The Krasny Gorn staff were closely bound up with submariners. They were headed by Andrei Shchur, who had been engineering officer in P-401. The chief engineer, Konstantin Stepanov, had served in the same capacity in D-1.

Shchur and Stepanov, who knew submarines inside out, managed the floating dock efficiently. Krasny Gorn was busy day and night, despite the air raids. The men of the submarines in repair lent a hand.

Training continued in the intervals between patrols. The main form of training, which was compulsory for all crews, especially those with young Captains, consisted of practice attacks. These exercises were held in Kildin Reach near the exit from Kola Bay. This was a relatively calm stretch of water though the submarines exercising in it frequently had to dive to escape enemy aircraft.

The shore base supplied us with everything we needed for training, battle and life. It was commanded by Captain 3rd Rank Grigory Mordenko and Battalion Commissar Vasily Shuvalov. Both had seen service in submarines and knew the requirements of ships and crews.

It was a large base with a numerous personnel. As regards the spirit and mood of the men, the following gives an eloquent picture. When naval detachments began to be formed for the land front in summer, four hundred men of the base personnel volunteered. Two hundred and seventy-three were selected, because all could not, naturally, be sent to the front. Somebody had to remain behind for the difficult job of preparing submarines for patrol.

At any time of the day or night, in any weather, submarines may require fuel, torpedoes, food, distilled water, lubricants or oxygen. All these supplies were handled by seamen of the shore base. Diesel engines were always on hand to recharge submarine batteries. And if anybody in a submarine fell ill and could not go to sea, the shore base, which had seamen of all submarine trades, provided the replacement.

The men of the shore base selflessly performed their routine duties, which at first glance seemed to have no room for heroic deeds. I cannot remember a case where a submarine was delayed through their fault. Submariners justifiably regarded them as a party to their victories.

On shore each submarine and division had its own crew's quarters and cabins. All of us were under emergency orders.

Few people live permanently in Polyarnoye. Now it was inhabited almost exclusively by the military. We spent our short leisure hours at Naval House, which had regular film shows. Or there would be a performance by a naval song and dance company directed by Boris Bogolepov, or a play by the Northern Fleet Theater. As a matter of fact, there was always something going on that gave our lives some variety.

Last summer, for example, we had British seamen staying with us. They were from the submarines *Tigris* and *Trident*. We received them hospitably. On the very first day a group of British and Soviet seamen gathered near the shore base buildings. Animated discussions, chiefly with the aid of gestures, were started. The British seamen were offered Russian cigarettes, and in their turn, they offered our men their cigarettes. Photographs of relatives were handed around. But the mutual interest was soon exhausted due to the language barrier. The Englishmen spoke no Russian, and our men knew very little English. These meetings petered out of themselves. True, contact between officers continued. From time to time they invited each other to dinner.

We could not help comparing the organization in the British and Soviet submarines. One striking thing was that the Soviet submarines were cleaner and tidier. Moreover, our discipline was better. Our submariners had a smart look about them, wearing their uniforms according to regulations, and they saluted each other, something that could not be said of the British seamen.

When *Tigris* and *Trident* scored hits they returned flying Nazi flags upside down, and sounding their siren to show how many ships they had sunk. Our seamen would throng the pier to congratulate them. The British seamen reciprocated this courtesy.

Later *Tigris* and *Trident* were replaced by *Sea Wolf* and

Sea Lion, which were likewise successful. British submarines used Polyarnoye as a base until 1943.

Dinners featuring roasted suckling pig were a pleasant relief in our routine. These wartime luxuries were reserved for victors. It all started with a joke, when Avgustinovich, keeping a straight face, said to Mordenko, "I don't see any jubilation at the base. We sink ships in the sweat of our brow and come in firing salutes. But you seem not to notice it. You could at least serve a suckling pig for each victory. It would make us feel better."

Mordenko took this seriously. There and then it was agreed that each crew returning home with a victory would be treated to roast suckling pigs according to the number of hits. The shore-base personnel kept their word. The new custom became popular, and soon Mordenko had to keep a fairly large pigsty. Often he could be heard complaining, "Just think of it, we've had to roast two suckling pigs for one Midget. The crew's so small they'll never eat them. Besides, where am I supposed to get pigs from?"

However, his fears were groundless. Although hardly anything was left on the tables after gala dinners, the pigs multiplied with sufficient rapidity.

The Fleet Commander, the Member of the Military Council, the Brigade Command, the Divisional Command and all submarine captains, who happened to be at the base, would be invited to these dinners. In the restful and congenial atmosphere we would hear sea stories and details of battles. In contrast to official analyses, these stories were more detailed and were told with greater zest. Nothing interested us more than these reminiscences of hunts and torpedo attacks, artillery battles and escapes from enemy pursuit. After all, this was our life.

I vividly remember Victor Kotelnikov's story about a patrol in January. Everything began with an attack on a transport anchored near the shore in a small bay.

"We fired a salvo from our for'ard tubes from a distance of about ten cable-lengths," Victor said, beginning his story. "Nobody heard the explosion and I thought I had missed. We raised the periscope and there was the transport riding its anchor unscathed. I cursed myself for missing and decided to swing around for an aft salvo. After firing two torpedoes I took another look through the periscope. You could have knocked me over with a feather, for the transport seemed to have a charmed life. There was nothing we could do to it. There was only about twelve meters of water under our keel. The bay was too small to allow us to maneuver safely. The only thing to do was to surface and sink the transport with gun fire.

"As soon as we surfaced, Sapunov and his gunners scrambled to the deck and rushed to their guns. Imagine our surprise when we saw that the transport was sinking slowly. We had hit it after all. A patrol ship, which seemed to have materialized out of thin air, was speeding to the rescue. It was too late to dive, and Sapunov opened up with both guns.

"The patrol ship caught fire after our second salvo. We turned our attention to the transport once more. It was, poor thing, unable to sink and we decided to give it another push down. However, when our guns started blazing away at it, we saw the sea around spouting—it was the shore battery. We started maneuvering, firing away all the time. After the fourth salvo the transport quickly disappeared under the water, and suddenly, we could not believe our eyes, we saw it standing as though nothing had happened. I began wondering if I was having hallucinations. I rubbed my eyes, and then realized that it was another, smaller transport. It had been anchored behind the one we had sunk and we had not seen it. We shifted our fire to it.

"Hardly had it sunk than the patrol ship brought the fire on it under control. Sapunov put a few more shells into it, but at that moment we saw another patrol ship rounding the cape. However, when it saw that its sister ship was in a tight spot it turned and fled. In the meantime the patrol ship burst into flames again, listed and sank quickly.

"During the battle it seemed to me that a shell had hit us in the stern. When it was all over, I ordered the quick diving tank to be blown and we sailed out of the bay by diesel power."

"What about that submarine attack you had to ward off, Victor?"

"Nothing much to it," Kotelnikov shrugged. "When we were well out of the bay, Kirichenko, who was on watch, cried out at the top of his voice, 'Torpedo, port, 45!'

"That warning came in the nick of time. We just managed to get out of the torpedo's way. But the next moment Kirichenko saw the trails of three other torpedoes, this time aft of us. We got up full speed, with both diesels working for all they were worth, and veered to starboard. For a fleeting moment it was touch and go. Had it not been for Kirichenko, we would not have been sitting at this dinner.

"Then the German submarine raised her periscope and showed her conning tower. Our look-outs spotted her at once. Our 45 mm gun opened fire, and the submarine quickly dived out of sight. It was difficult to say if she was hit. That's the whole story. When we got to our battery-recharging area we found that our stern was undamaged. The German shelling had been inaccurate."

"Comrade Kotelnikov, have you any idea of what was in the transports that you sank?" Golovko asked.

"Not the faintest, Comrade Commander-in-Chief."

"They were taking sheepskin coats for the Lapland group. Thirty thousand sheepskin coats. The Germans themselves complained in their newspapers that the Russians were not fighting according to the rules, that they were acting inhumanly. The light infantry would now freeze from the cold."

"Let them dance in the frost," Victor laughed. "They came unasked."

These gala dinners often produced constructive suggestions. The atmosphere at them warmed our hearts and filled us with pride for being with such wonderful and staunch friends.

The Fleet We Served In

Friendship and the feeling that we were bound together by common work and interests had come to us long ago, as had our affection for the Northern Fleet. These are not empty words. Anyone who had served in it for several years, had grown used to it and come to appreciate the charm of the northern landscape did not feel he was a chance comer. Such a person was not oppressed by the many months of cold and the polar night. You grew accustomed to it and treated it as something quite ordinary. But the thing that one could not get used to, a thing that never failed to move and gladden one, was the consciousness of playing a part in the navy's growth and development. Like any young organism, the Northern Fleet grew and matured rapidly. We watched and helped it to mature.

I frequently look back to the distant and yet near year of 1933. I was stationed in Kronstadt. It was the month of May.

The ancient lime trees in the Petrovsky Park were just beginning to put on their new finery. The Gulf of Finland had discarded its blanket of ice. But we were filled with the poignant sadness of having to part with places we had come to love, with the Baltic where we had felt at home.... We were members of a Special-Purpose Expedition, known as SPE-1, and we had to say good-bye to all this for a long time, perhaps forever. Ahead of us was the frowning, unexplored North. This was not a usual mission and we were troubled by thoughts of what service in a new place would be like and whether we could accustom ourselves to our new environment quickly.

All of us knew that a real, fighting fleet was needed in the North. There the country had its sea gates in the ice-free port of Murmansk with its free access to the ocean. The North was the country's right flank, a flank that had no protection whatsoever. Foreigners were fishing in our waters and even landing on our shores. They had to be given a rap on the knuckles.

The North had to be developed in the interests of the state. It needed a fleet. This was appreciated long before 1933. But we did not have the ships to send to the polar seas. Then there were diplomatic obstacles. The Western powers refused to allow our warships out of the Baltic into the North Sea. It was then that the simple and wise idea was conceived of building the White Sea-Baltic Canal. That was well within the possibilities of the Soviet Union, which had by then become stronger. The canal was, in the main, completed within twenty months.

SPE-1 set out on May 18, 1933. It was composed of the submarines D-1 and D-2, the destroyers *Kuibyshev* and *Uritsky*, and the patrol ships *Uragan* and *Smerch*. The expedition was commanded by Ivan Isakov (Chief-of-Staff of Baltic Fleet, now Admiral of the Fleet of the Soviet Union).

In the evening we completed the passage from Kronstadt to Leningrad. And in the night of the 19th, when the bridges were raised, we weighed anchors and sailed upstream along the Neva. On that night in May, many of us, perhaps for the first time, really appreciated the beauty of Leningrad, which we had not noticed before.

I was in D-1 as Torpedo Officer. Most of the officers in the submarine were young. All of us had graduated from training school approximately at one and the same time. The course for gunnery officers was a year longer than for navigation officers.

Our navigator, Victor Kotelnikov, for example, joined the Navy on a Y.C.L.* assignment and was sent to a naval training school. From there he went to the Frunze School, which he finished in 1931. After that he sailed as Navigator in a Snow Leopard and then received a transfer to D-1. He was straightforward and honest, and entirely devoted to his work. Despite his youth he made a splendid Navigator. It was pleasant to serve in the same ship with him and to have him as a friend. It was in those years that we became close friends.

*Young Communist League

The senior generation of submariners was represented in the submarine by Captain Boris Sekunov and Commissar Nikolai Ralko. Everybody in the brigade had a deep respect for our captain. There was little he did not know about seamanship. He had joined the navy before the Revolution and had fought in the Baltic during the Civil War. For many years he commanded a Snow Leopard, and when the first Decembrist was commissioned he became its Captain.

Restrained and imperturbable, he was always courteous and attentive to his men. He never seethed or lost his temper when somebody made a mistake, but his remarks, spoken in a calm voice, made one feel more embarrassed than a furious dressing-down accompanied by choice epithets. He never lost his equanimity, even during torpedo exercises.

During fleet exercises in the summer of 1932 our subma-

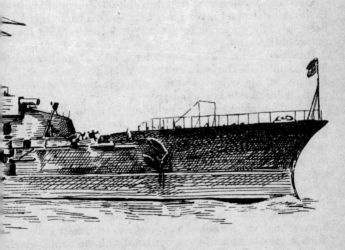

Marat

rine attacked the battleship *Marat*, which sailed under the ensign of the People's Commissar for Defense. Sekunov fired one torpedo and "hit" the battleship in its most vulnerable spot. All of us were jubilant over the Letter of Thanks awarded to Boris by the People's Commissar. Our ambition was to be like him, for to us, young officers, he was a model submarine commander.

The First Lieutenant Mikhail Popov was stern-faced, short-spoken and exacting. We respected him for his seamanship and, frankly, were a little afraid of him. Already then he was regarded as the most likely candidate for the command of a submarine, and nobody was surprised when he became Captain of D-3 that same autumn.

Our expedition sailed along the Neva, crossed Lake Ladoga and entered the turbulent Svir River. There the landscape was familiar to me, for prior to joining the navy I had sailed along the Mariinskaya Waterway from Rybinsk to Leningrad many times. I could not help boasting about it to my comrades. There was, after all, something special about the Svir. Navigation in it was such a complicated matter that if a tugboat had a barge in tow, both the tugboat and the barge needed a pilot. They would take the vessels over their sectors and then yield their place to other pilots.

We made our first long stop near the settlement of Sviritsa in the river channel making fast to a wooden barge that had been specially prepared for the purpose. That evening I was officer-of-the-watch.

It proved to be a long stop indeed, for the canal was not fully completed. The locks on the Svir rapids were not ready. But we did not waste any time, filling it in with exercises, drills, political education and sports.

Finally our submarine was pulled into the specially adapted lock. A chain, 100 meters long, was lowered into the water from its stern to prevent it from yawing at the turns and on the rapids. The pilot came on board—he was a bearded old man, who had sailed on the river for about forty years. With him was his assistant, or pilot's apprentice, to use a local term. The apprentice was much younger, of course, but his beard was as long as that of the pilot.

Four tugboats approached, made fast to us with steel hawsers and we continued our journey. In Onega Lake the ships left the locks, and there our bond with the Baltic, which had become symbolic, was cut short. Lev Galler, Fleet

Commander-in-Chief, arrived to say farewell to us, speed us on our journey along the canal and wish us luck.

At Povenets we entered the White Sea Canal. We had to wait until the evening of July 20 for the canal to be ready to receive us.

After we had passed several locks, we looked back and found ourselves catching our breath in surprise and admiration. From our elevation Lake Onega looked as if it were nestling at the foot of a tall mountain. The tops of trees were sticking out of the water in the quiet reaches, adding to the novelty of the landscape.

On July 21, after passing through the last, nineteenth lock, the ships of SPE-1 entered Soroka (now Belomorsk). That brought us into the White Sea.

Preparations were started for the passage to Murmansk.

It proved to be an extraordinarily uneventful passage. In the Barents Sea the weather was calm. Frolicking grampuses followed us all the way to Kola Bay. Excitedly we chatted about Murmansk, which would be our new home.

Nobody doubted that there would be difficulties, but most of us were planning on a long term of service in the North. We speculated where the submarine base would be, on shore or in a mother ship, whether officers and re-enlisted men would be given separate quarters, and when we'd be able to bring our families. We were eager to settle down.

We entered the port of Murmansk on August 5, 1933. On that day it was announced that the Northern Naval Flotilla had been set up by a Government decree. Zakhar Zakupnev was appointed Flotilla Commander, and Pyotr Bairachny, Chief of the Political Department.

The whole town turned out to welcome us.

The flagship *Komsomolets*, formerly a training ship, was already in Murmansk. The *Umba*, a small transport provided by the Northern Merchant Marine, served as a depot ship for the submarines.

Training was soon started with emphasis on a study of the area, which was new to us.

The Northern Naval Flotilla, which was subsequently reorganized into the Northern Fleet, thus began its existence.

A month later SPE-2 arrived in Murmansk. It consisted of the destroyer *Karl Liebknecht*, the patrol ship *Groza* and the submarine D-3, whose Captain was an experienced submariner named Konstantin Griboyedov.

Our three Decembrists and the *Umba* were formed into a Submarine Division. For a short while the division was commanded by Maxim Skriganov. In the autumn that veteran submariner was transferred to the Pacific Fleet, and his place was taken by Griboyedov.

Mikhail Avgustinovich, a graduate of the Black Sea Naval Coast Defense School, was our divisional artillery officer. Submarines fascinated him and he applied himself assiduously to navigation, frequently going out to sea. With time Avgustinovich became captain of a submarine, Divisional Commander, Brigade Chief-of-Staff and, as the reader knows, was, at his own request, appointed captain of K-1.

Murmansk was a temporary base. The year that we arrived in the North, building was started at Polyarnoye to turn it into the fleet's main base. The work, which went on day and night proceeded with unprecedented rapidity.

We strove to keep to the same rapid pace in our study of the Arctic Ocean. The conditions for training were markedly different from what we had been used to. On the one hand, the climate was much more rigorous than in the Baltic. But, on the other, the sea was ice free and we could train all year around. In Kronstadt, we had trained from May to October, when the Gulf of Finland was free of ice. Here we could sail at any time, and we gradually grew accustomed to the tempestuous sea, the gales, the thick fogs and the long polar night.

A new commander, Konstantin Dushenov, was appointed early in 1935. Under him the work of building up the Northern Flotilla was accelerated, and in the autumn, just before the anniversary of the Revolution, we moved to Polyarnoye.

The ships, Headquarters, the Political Department and seamen's families were all moved in one day. On the shore of Yekaterininskaya Bay, where once, amid the mountains and cliffs, there was the tiny fishing village of Alexandrovsk-on-Murman, we saw a handsome town with large modern buildings.

Frequently, particularly during our first year at Polyarnoye, everybody would turn out for voluntary work on Saturdays and Sundays. I remembered we filled a large ravine with earth and stones, and in its place there appeared the northernmost sports stadium in the Soviet Union. The Commander-in-Chief, Konstantin Dushenov, worked as hard as everybody else.

It would be impossible to overestimate Dushenov's contribution to the building up of the new fleet. He would be seen wherever there was building in progress—in the port, at the piers and at the sites being cleared for airfields and shore batteries. Wherever a hitch occurred he would be on the spot with advice. But sometimes his powers and abilities as an organizer were insufficient. There was a shortage of critical materials, and not all his plans for the fleet and shore defenses were supported "at the top." When that happened, he would go to Moscow even if it meant incurring unpleasantness for himself. In pressing the point that the northern defenses were of the utmost importance he was sure that he was doing the right thing and that the questions brought up by him would be tackled properly, in a Party spirit.

He was not mistaken. His advice, recommendations and calculations helped to speed up the development not only of the fleet but also of the shore and frontier defenses.

He directed the fitting out of moorages, naval repair shops, bases and storehouses. The Krasny Gorn floating workshop, mentioned above, arrived from the Baltic when he was Commander-in-Chief.

While being a strict disciplinarian, Dushenov encouraged democracy in relations with people. He was accessible to the men and had their interests at heart. At that time he had just turned forty. But already then he had the qualities of an outstanding naval commander, and a distinguished political leader. It was the natural outcome of his life.

During the Revolution, as a twenty-two-year-old seaman, he was secretary of the Party committee on the *Aurora*. On the day the Winter Palace was taken by storm, he insured liaison between seamen and the Smolny Institute, and then commanded the guard at the Winter Palace after it was captured. Dushenov and his sailors honorably discharged the important Party assignment of preserving the priceless treasures of the Hermitage for the people.

During the Civil War he took part in the defense of Petrograd against the whiteguards, and then fought on ships of the Volga Flotilla. After the war, in which he had demonstrated his staunchness and his devotion to the Revolution, he was appointed Commander and Commissar first of Sevastopol and then of Baku.

Then he held key posts in the Baltic Fleet, and later headed the Academy, where he had studied himself, and did

Aurora

much to improve its organization. After that he was Chief-of-Staff of the Black Sea Fleet.

With this experience behind him, he went to the North. Under him, the flotilla became a fleet early in 1938. He received the rank of Flag Officer 1st Rank. This did not detract from his restlessness or simplicity. He could be seen visiting the home of a warrant officer, on the bridge of a warship on a long cruise, at an amateur performance, or speaking to sailors or the inhabitants of Murmansk.

In the autumn of 1936, two submarines—D-1 and D-2—set out on a cruise flying the ensign of the Commander-in-Chief. This cruise was part of the specially planned exercises. We sailed to the Kara Sea via Matochkin Shar Strait, and visited Russkaya Harbor on Novaya Zemlya. Dushenov spent more than two weeks at sea with us.

His popularity in the fleet and in Murmansk Region was enormous, and he was elected a Deputy to the First Supreme Soviet of the U.S.S.R. But soon afterward the irreparable happened. Falsely denounced, he was arrested and sentenced to death.

That was one of the heaviest blows sustained by our navy. In the three years that remained before war broke out, Dushenov would undoubtedly have done much more to increase its fighting capacity.

Despite setbacks, the fleet continued growing and becoming stronger. It was reinforced with new, Soviet-designed destroyers, patrol ships, mine sweepers, submarine chasers and torpedo boats. The Submarine Division became a brigade, whose main strength consisted of Pikes and Midgets. Katyushas began to appear in it on the eve of the war.

All this was closely intertwined with our lives. Veteran and experienced officers were moved up in rank. After a spell as gunnery officer in D-1, I was sent to officers' training courses in Leningrad. Upon my return I was assigned to the same submarine as First Lieutenant to Vyacheslav Karpunin. Then I became captain of a Pike, after which I returned to D-1 as captain. In the autumn of 1938 I was appointed Commander of a Pike Division.

The careers of many other officers, who went to the North in 1933, were much the same.

Bombs Rain Down

In P-422's control room there is a placard with the words: "Submariners, you are going into battle with your country's blessings. The blood of brothers, fathers and mothers tortured to death by the Nazis calls for revenge. Sink the Nazis. Death and nothing but death to them!"

Every man on board passed that placard several times a day, and all knew the simple words of this appeal by heart. It found a response in the heart of each of us. The war had affected everybody in the cruellest possible way.

There was electrician Stepan Chernousov, for example. I had known him for a long time as a thoughtful sailor with an excellent knowledge of his trade. He hailed from Smolensk Region, and his village was occupied by the invaders. He had no news from his relatives. It was a bitter pill. I could appreciate what he felt. I had myself, for the hundredth time, re-read a letter from my wife that I had received in December.

Though not in occupied territory, she was in besieged Leningrad, where the people were enduring famine, frost and daily shelling. A frail woman, Zoya could not boast of health. I was worried that she would not live through this terrible winter.

"Grandmother died yesterday," Zoya wrote, "but she was very old and the strain had been too much for her. Mother works in the port day and night. I, too, am working as far as my strength allows: I helped to dig trenches, and then kept watch on the roofs for incendiary bombs. I also did duty at the gates. But now I don't feel well. I'm afraid it's my lungs again. But don't worry, it'll pass.

"Look after your men, darling, and have no mercy for the Nazi scum. Pay them in their own coin for the people they have killed, for our country.

"You say you want me to go to your mother in Yaroslavl Region. But, believe me, I can't leave Mother here alone...."

Many of the men received letters like these. They pull the most sensitive and treasured strings of the heart, and intensify love and hatred. They awaken a wrath that beats against the chest and tries to burst out, but its only outlet is through clenched teeth. We had to muster all our will power to remain calm and cautiously seek out the enemy in the sea and sink him.

With these thoughts filling our minds we set out on patrol.

Before this patrol, P-421 had undergone repairs in Murmansk. As always, the plant director Tsapanadze, the chief engineer Usach and the foreman Levkin had given the submarine every attention. The friendship between the submariners and the plant personnel was of old standing. When war broke out it became even stronger than before.

While the repairs were under way, the crew joined one of the work teams to help the plant recommission the submarine ahead of schedule. Despite the air raids, the work went on for 14-16 hours a day. We felt at home at the plant, and when news was received that a submarine that had been repaired there had sunk an enemy ship, the workers rejoiced as though they had made the kill themselves.

We left our base in the night of January 9. It was cold and Kola Bay was bathed in mist. Warmed by the Gulf Stream, the water smoked in a myriad of spouts of vapor, which collected into a thick fog bank. To a bystander it was a picturesque scene, but it was no fun sailing in such weather. You had to keep your eyes peeled if you did not want an accident.

When we passed Rybachy not a trace of the cold or the vapor remained. Instead, a stiff wind rose and was followed by short snowfalls.

"We certainly had a rough time of it yesterday," Andrei Zharov said as he took over the watch 36 hours after we had left the base. Silently we agreed with him. There had been a savage storm. We did not even dive when we sighted an enemy plane: it was impossible for it to spot us amid the huge waves. The submarine was tossed like a cork. She was almost completely covered by colossal sheets of water. Tons of water cascaded through the hatch into the control post, and the pumps had to be kept going all the time. On the bridge, the men on watch had to lash themselves securely to the railings.

But this sort of thing was not new to submariners. We were used to it. All the troubles that they experience in a storm are quickly forgotten, and for that reason nobody spoke much about yesterday's storm. I turned to Zharov. "You are like a hunter. Now the submarine has only your two eyes. Keep them wide open so that the beast does not slip away. The success of the hunt now depends upon you."

Naturally, Senior Lieutenant Zharov did not have to be reminded of his duties—he knew his business, but, as they say, you can't spoil porridge with an extra bit of butter.

My allusions to a hunter were not accidental. As I have already mentioned, there are many elements of a hunt in our work. But it was not only that. Andrei was a passionate hunter in the direct sense of the word. He spent every leave hunting in the environs of Leningrad or somewhere along Lake Ladoga or the Svir. About two days before the war broke out, when our anti-aircraft batteries were already firing at German scouting planes, a huge flock of homing pigeons suddenly appeared near Polyarnoye. Andrei got a fowling piece from somewhere and excitedly chased after them. But he did not bag anything.

I liked this energetic and cheerful officer. He had a way with people and was friendly with his men. Officers of his type, who know when to crack a joke, are obeyed quickly and implicitly. The artillery crew commanded by him was noted for its efficiency. There had never been a case of the submarine's guns failing.

Navigator Officer Mikhail Pitersky was another commander of the same type, well-trained and efficient.

We patrolled an off-shore area, looking into the fjords. But luck was against us. An occasional submarine chaser or an aircraft would force us to dive.

"Horizon clear," reported the officer-of-the-watch from the periscope. "Horizon clear," reported the hydrophone operator.

Three days passed. How many more would pass before the alarm would be sounded and the long-awaited order given to stand by for a torpedo attack. Regretfully, on this score we could only speculate. If we had air reconnaissance our immediate prospects would have been clearer. We would have been told where a convoy was being formed, when and where it was setting out from, and in which sector we could expect to encounter it.

True, we were sometimes given a helping hand by wireless intelligence, which listened in to enemy conversation and drew conclusions about his movements along his lines of communication. We had not yet developed a means of receiving wireless signals under water. The men had many good ideas in that line, but these ideas had not yet been translated into technical means and were nothing more than fantasy. In short, we did not have the possibility of regularly receiving wireless communications because we could not surface in daylight in sight of enemy submarine chasers and shore observation posts. We sometimes received tempting intelligence a day late, when it had lost all significance.

On patrol tension does not relax for a single moment. Although the routine of a patrol had become second nature to us, somewhere deep down in each of us there was the sense of danger which kept us constantly alert. The men read, talked, or played chess, yet any foreign sound or the least break in the usual rhythm of the mechanisms instantly caught their attention. There was no escape from this. Even when one slept one's nervous system was turned in for the signal of alarm. One might draw a parallel with the mother of an infant. Noise does not disturb her sleep, but the slightest squeak from the baby immediately brings her to her feet.

A submariner must have steady nerves. To avoid overstraining our nervous system we adopted an unerring recipe that had been worked out by many generations of sailors. We rigidly followed a set time table. Under no circumstances were officers allowed to lose their equanimity, to show irritation. Every effort was made to inculcate a team spirit in the men.

Commissar Dubik did much in this field. He saw to it that the submarine's news bulletin was issued regularly. The men were kept abreast of the situation on the land fronts. The daily Soviet Information Bureau communiques still further wetted their eagerness to come to grips with the enemy. The crew were still bitter about their last patrol, when they sank only one ship in five encounters. They were itching to make up for lost time.

But that was exactly what we were falling short of. The weather was fair but there was no enemy to be seen. One night we sailed into Tana Fjord, but there was nothing doing there either. Besides, after we had covered only a few miles ice began to form on our deck. The conning tower shone with ice. The wireless antenna and the gun barrels grew thick with it. We had no alternative but to turn back. As soon as we left the fjord the Gulf Stream relieved us of our icy armor.

January 17 was a memorable day for me. At about midnight, when I was dozing, I was awakened by Malyshev.

"Congratulations," he said.

"What's the occasion, Captain?" I asked.

"A radiogram from the Commander-in-Chief. You have been made a Hero of the Soviet Union."

I was wide awake now. Was this a joke? Yet no submarine captain would dare pull the leg of his Divisional Commander on patrol. A mistake? But Malyshev was showing me the message written in the hand of the decoder. It contained congratulations from the Fleet Commander-in-Chief, the Member of the Military Council and the Chief of the Political Department. Officers and men who had heard the news crowded around me.

It made me feel a little dizzy. I had been decorated with the highest military award. I could not account for it. It was the men with whom I sailed who had sunk German ships. What was my advice, knowledge and experience worth without them? I owed this great honor to them. My heart filled with gratitude to my comrades-in-arms, who shared this joy.

After dinner on the next day we attacked a small coaster of about six or seven hundred tons at the exit from a fjord near Hamvik. We hit it with two torpedoes. But, in our turn, we were attacked by a submarine chaser. The depth charges dropped by it fell wide off the mark and we eluded it in the open sea.

In the region of Omgang we were nearly caught by fishing nets. The sea was full of them—the Norwegians went on fishing in spite of the war. In these bleak places fishing is the only means of livelihood for the coastal population. But for us, as I have already said, their nets could spell disaster. To get your propellers entangled in a net in enemy waters was almost tantamount to destruction.

To avoid the nets we had to maneuver with our engines pulling in different directions to enable us to turn quickly, with the minimum angle of swing.

When we were clear of the nets we moved farther away from the shore to reload our torpedo tubes and recharge our batteries. It wasn't a very impressive victory, but it gave us the uplift we needed. It was the submarine's first hit in the New Year.

The next two days passed in monotony. The land was gripped in frost. The fjords were enveloped in vapor and an impenetrable fog hung over the water. There was nothing for us to do—we would have been unable to see anything anyway. Besides the Germans would hardly have risked sailing in the fjords when visibility was down almost to zero. We sailed along the coast where from time to time the sea was unusually calm.

Near Nordkyn we dived and entered Sand Fjord—by then the fog had lifted and we could count on prey. But before we had proceeded several miles, a submarine chaser attacked us. Somehow we had betrayed our presence. There was a series of explosions. The men on duty stood stock-still at the mechanisms. Those who were off duty leaped to their feet. The last two depth charges—the sixth and the seventh—exploded somewhere quite near. Bits of cork showered down from the ceiling. We felt the submarine tossing.

"The electric steering gear is out of commission," Coxswain Zavyalov reported.

"Change over to manual control," the captain ordered, reacting immediately.

Engineering Officer Lyamin and Stoker Petty Officer Tabachkov dexterously manipulated the handles of the valves, letting in additional ballast. The submarine dived deeper.

The chaser evidently lost all signs of us or it had used up its depth charges. At any rate, the bombing stopped. We lost no time getting out of the inhospitable fjord.

At last, on January 23, when we were sailing near Nordkyn, the officer-of-the-watch, Pitersky, reported, "A large transport escorted by two patrol ships."

We began the attack. From a distance of about twelve

cable-lengths we fired a salvo of four torpedoes. Within a minute and a half we clearly heard two loud bangs.

"Surface the submarine, Captain, and let's see our handiwork," I said to Malyshev.

But almost as soon as Malyshev raised the periscope and took a glance at the large, listing, eight-thousand-ton ship enveloped in steam, two deafening explosions shook our submarine. The lights went out, and cork, paint and the glass of the smashed bulbs showered down on us. Some invincible force seemed to be tearing the submarine to pieces. The hydroplanes jammed. And we felt as though we were in a fast lift that was descending—the submarine lost its buoyancy and hit the sea floor at a depth of eighty-five meters. It seemed as though we had received a direct hit somewhere in the region of the control room. In addition, we got the alarming report that there was water in the engine room.

During these few, awful, long-drawn-out moments, I won't hide it, I thought that the end had come. Everybody else must have felt the same. None of us had been bombed with such accuracy. But will power and fortitude took the upper hand. Nobody panicked. To say that nobody abandoned his post would be superfluous. In a submarine you could not run anywhere, you could not avoid sharing the fate of your comrades. Here panic and the hypnosis of horror can manifest themselves in loss of self-control, in disorderly, incorrect action or in complete passivity, in inability to carry out orders.

But, I repeat, nothing of the sort happened. With the engine room sealed tight there was no danger of water flooding the rest of the submarine and depriving her of the buoyancy of surfacing. The damage was quickly located and repaired, and the submarine stopped shipping water.

When we hit the seabed the situation did not seem to be hopeless any longer. The danger was not as great as we had thought. All we now had to do was to stay on the seabed and wait. Besides, it was the only sensible thing to do, for to rise we would have had to pump the water out of the trimming tanks and the enemy would only have thanked us for the noise of the turbo pump. It was best to lie low.

I ordered all instruments and mechanisms, including the gyrocompass, to be switched off.

Depth charges continued exploding within earshot. It struck me that diesel oil might be escaping and giving us away to the enemy. I could not discount this possibility in view of the explosions. If this continued we would have to find some other way out. I quickly thought over possible variants of further action.

Pitersky, who was standing at the chart table, was counting the explosions off with matches.

After he had taken the fifteenth match out of the box the sound of the explosions began to recede. Was it accidental?

"Navigator, is there a current here?" I asked Pitersky.

"According to the sailing directions the current here has a speed of one and a half or two knots," he reported.

The situation was growing clearer. I had been right in thinking that diesel oil was leaking out of one of the fuel tanks. But before it could reach the surface the current carried it away. The enemy failed to take this into consideration and was dropping his depth charges over the oil spots. It was certainly a lucky break for us and we began to breathe easier.

Three hours dragged by. Pitersky had used up all the matches in his matchbox. The explosions had become quite faint and it grew quiet. Our hydrophone operator could not hear the noise of propellers. The Germans had evidently decided that they had sunk us and had gone off. We could now surface.

There was no sign of the enemy. When we surfaced we got the whole picture of the damage. The first series of depth charges had punctured the upper tank, which contained fourteen tons of diesel oil. There was a sizable dent in the tough casing. Had the casing not been as tough as it was the seabed would have been our last resting place.

The men's reaction to what had been experienced was manifested in a rise of spirits. Merriment provided the outlet for hours of concealed tension, relieving the excessive strain on the nerves. Life looked doubly large after our harrowing experience. We had prevailed over the enemy and that multiplied our optimism.

Once more we were sailing in coastal waters past fjords. A light southeasterly was lacing the land with frost. At sea the temperature was above zero. There was not a cloud in the sky. At night the moon shone brightly and Aurora Borealis blazed in all its splendor. This made our nocturnal prowling a hazardous game. We had to keep to the dark side of the horizon to avoid being caught unaware by the enemy.

That is almost what happened on the night of January 27. True, we spotted the silhouettes of enemy ships first and swung to attack them without diving. But Aurora Borealis and the moon path into which we sailed helped the enemy. A Nazi destroyer opened fire and sped in our direction before we could get into battle position.

Three explosions shook our submarine as we dived, blasting the lamps in half of the compartments. Paint peeled down from the ceiling, the light failed, but all this was much less stupefying and frightening than the first time. The next three depth charges exploded much farther away and caused no damage to the submarine. Half an hour later the destroyer gave up the chase. We wasted no time in surfacing and reporting the position, time and course of the convoy which had shaken us off. It was sailing eastward and we reckoned that the submarines patrolling in that area could be put on its track. That is exactly what happened. Starikov's M-171 had a gala day.

That night we recharged our batteries and repaired our port diesel, which began giving us trouble after the shake-up received by our Pike. The morning watch was taken over by Georgy Kovalenko, the First Lieutenant. A fine officer, he fully merited an independent command. At 11.00 hours he sighted two transports escorted by several destroyers and patrol ships—visibility was poor and it was impossible to give their exact number.

When the captain and I ran into the control room, Kovalenko was already getting the submarine into position to attack the leading transport, which displaced about six thousand tons. We had an excellent view of the vessel and fired two torpedoes at it. It proved to be a scrimpy salvo, for the third torpedo did not leave its tube, which jammed at the moment it was being prepared for firing.

A bang, which we heard about a minute and a half after the salvo, told us that we had scored a hit. But when we took a peep at the convoy to see the results, we found a destroyer coming at us at full speed. It was so close that it blotted out the view in the periscope.

To avoid being rammed, we dived without seeing what happened to the transport. Depth charges rained down on us. Three of them gave us an uneasy moment. The other six exploded somewhere far away. It took us about twenty minutes to get rid of our pursuer.

Pitersky came on watch at 20.00 hours. At the very end of the watch we heard his voice from the bridge, "Torpedo attack! Course 195!"

The submarine headed in the direction of a convoy, whose silhouettes could be seen vaguely in the darkness. But when we drew closer we could see that it was not a convoy at all, but two warships—a destroyer and a patrol ship. Once again the situation was not in our favor—we were on the bright side of the horizon. The ships opened fairly accurate fire; the first few shells splashed into the water much too near for our comfort.

An emergency dive saved us from being rammed. The destroyer's propellers roared past directly overhead. Then there was an ominous rumble as three depth charges exploded somewhere very near. We were plunged in darkness. Broken glass crunched underfoot. The coxswain reported that the electric controls of the helm had broken down. There was other trouble, which we had not had before: our wireless failed, and in the diesel compartment the cooling pipe had burst and some of the rivets in the input had been torn out and now a thin jet of water was rushing in through the hole.

Naturally, we did not ascertain all this damage at once. The submarine was dropping like a stone. Below us we had a depth of about three hundred meters, which was quite enough to crush us. We did all we could to stop this fatal plunge. The Captain issued orders energetically in a calm voice. Lyamin, the engineering officer, and his men once more demonstrated their uncanny skill. In the inky blackness they managed to hold the submarine at a depth of ninety meters. This was the first step toward salvation.

We had developed a kind of immunity to depth charges. Although the damage was much more serious than on any previous occasion, the men performed their duties with greater confidence. The light came on. Methodically the men repaired the damage. The gyrocompass was the only thing that had us baffled. It had been too delicate to stand up to the rigid test of a bombing. For us it was a most unpleasant blow.

We were like a blindfolded man who was forced to spin on one spot and then told to find the right direction. The enemy was at our heels. To get away from him we changed course and speed. This threatened us with complete loss of orientation, especially as we could not use our magnetic compass while we were submerged. We were in danger of running aground in close proximity to an enemy-held coast.

A solution was found unexpectedly. Somebody suggested that we use our boat compass, which we kept in the bow compartment. In a submarine, with metal on all sides, this compass is a shameless liar. It can lead you into an error of as much as 30 degrees. Still, it was better than nothing. We could at least have an approximate bearing with regard to the sea and the shore.

We began our unprecedented underwater voyage by a boat compass. It did not fail us. We ran in circles under water for about three hours before we finally rid ourselves of pursuit. From time to time, to avoid sinking to the seabed and remaining there forever, we had to blow our main tank. The bubbles gave us away, of course, but of the two evils we had to choose the lesser one.

Although we were pursued for a long time, the enemy dropped only eighteen depth charges, and only three of them caused us any damage.

We surfaced at about 04.00 hours and proceeded to our battery-recharging area. In the end we got the gyrocompass back in operation, but the next two days were uneventful. On January 30 we were ordered back to our base.

At night, on our way home, Malyshev suddenly ordered an emergency dive, thinking that we had been spotted by a dive-bomber. But at periscope depth we found that it was not an aircraft but an ordinary star twinkling peacefully through a gap in the clouds. We had a good laugh all around.

On the steel-gray water of Polyarnoye Bay our submarine gave the impression that it was a glittering white iceberg. When we arrived a smoky-red ball, the first sun that year, was peeping over the horizon, making the snow-blanketed shore sparkle with a rosy light and giving the water blue-green hues. The "iceberg" fired three salvoes, as though saluting the sun. This scene was photographed, and somebody even made a drawing of it.

The Commander-in-Chief and the Member of the Military Council were at the head of the men welcoming us at the pier. There were handshakes and warm, heartfelt greetings. A lump rose in my throat. I thanked everybody for their congratulations and said to the Commander-in-Chief, "I am well aware that I owe this coveted decoration primarily to the men and officers of the submarines in which I have sailed."

In the evening I paid a visit to D-3. On January 17 this veteran of the Northern Fleet had been decorated with the Order of the Red Banner. It gave me great pleasure to congratulate the submarine's fine crew with whom I had been on several patrols.

What Cannot Be Helped. . . .

We had kept our score only with victories. Of course, each of us realized that losses were inevitable, for such was the inexorable law of war. But nobody wanted to think of it, and nobody spoke of the hazards of operational patrols. Deep in our hearts we sometimes wondered about our invulnerability, and even somehow grew accustomed to it. That made what could not be helped—our first loss—all the greater.

The bitter score of losses in the brigade was opened by M-175. She was due to return from patrol when I was at sea in P-422. But when it was overdue, when the maximum period that submarines of that type could remain at sea was up and no reply was received to base call signals, we had to face the grim truth that the submarine would never return.

How had the Midget perished? Had she been hit by a depth charge after she had attacked a convoy? Or had she run into an anti-submarine mine? Or had a torpedo fired by an enemy submarine sowed death in its compartments? Anything could have happened. We had nothing to go by and perhaps never would.

One thing we were sure of was that the fine crew and their commander, Lieutenant-Captain Melkadze, died as soldiers.

I met Mamont Melkadze for the first time in the spring of 1937, when he was Torpedo Officer in a Pike that was making the passage from the Baltic to the North. Two years later he was given command of M-175, which had then just been commissioned. Honest, courageous and sober-minded, he gave promise of becoming an outstanding commander. This was substantiated by his handling of his submarine on operational patrols.

On her last patrol M-175 carried Engineer-Lieutenant-Captain Victor Shilyayev, the divisional engineer. He had joined us in the North only recently, having been engineering officer in a Midget in the Baltic. Shortly before that fatal patrol he told me of a narrow escape that he had had in July 1941.

The submarine in which he served was attacked by an enemy U-boat near our shores before she could dive. A torpedo hit the stern, the explosion hurling the captain and everybody on the bridge into the sea. The submarine sank in shallow water. When she was hit Shilyayev was in the second compartment. Finding that the aft compartments were flooded and that the men in them were dead, he organized the rescue of the survivors in the first three compartments. Under his direction, eight men donned their life-saving gear, climbed out of the fore hatch and, holding on to each other, swam toward the shore. They were soon picked up by a boat from a shore observation post.

He escaped with his life in the Baltic thanks to his self-control and professional training, only to perish in the Arctic Ocean.

Some time later we suffered our second loss. True, only one life was lost. On February 19, a radiogram signed by the First Lieutenant was received from P-403 which was on patrol. It read: "Submarine rammed by enemy destroyer while diving. Conning tower smashed. We have suffered other damage. The captain has been killed."

On the day after that radiogram was received, the mutilated submarine entered the base and we learned details of the recent battle and the death of Semyon Kovalenko.

On the night of the 19th, P-403 carried on with her patrol, recharging her batteries at the same time about two miles off the enemy coast. There was a moderate sea with occasional squalls.

Through the snow the look-out and Shilinsky, the officer-of-the-watch, suddenly sighted an enemy destroyer and patrol ship on the starboard side, in the dark part of the horizon, not more than two cable-lengths away.

During these crucial seconds the fate of the submarine was in Shilinsky's hands. Shilinsky meanwhile was put to the sternest test that any officer-of-the-watch could face. Properly speaking, if there was an unexpected encounter with the enemy it was his duty to take the place of the captain until the latter could reach the bridge.

To give Shilinsky his due, that was exactly what he did. He

ordered the helm to be put hard to port, stopped the recharging of the batteries, and called the captain to the bridge.

These orders were issued in good time. But one could not say that the decisions in these orders were of the happiest. Shilinsky was afraid he could not dive to escape being rammed and for that reason began maneuvering on the surface. A simple tactical calculation would have shown that the submarine could and should have dived. There was plenty of time, at least six or seven minutes.

Navigator Belayev was in the control room. When he heard the order "Hard to port!" from the bridge, and Shilinsky calling for the captain, he thought the submarine was in danger of being grounded. He rushed to the bridge, and the first thing he saw was a destroyer rapidly approaching astern.

"Aft tubes, stand by to fire!" he ordered without a moment's hesitation.

Kovalenko and Polyansky, the Commissar, appeared on the bridge. This, I believe, was the last opportunity they had of diving without sustaining any substantial loss. Things were evidently moving too fast, and the captain had no time to get his bearings.

Before the submarine completed the swing begun by Shilinsky, the destroyer tore past about fifteen meters astern of her. The maneuver had upset the German commander's intention of ramming the submarine. Tracer bullets cut through the darkness as the destroyer opened up with quick-firing guns and machine-guns. Small-calliber shells and bullets showered down on the bridge.

The navigator cried out with pain. Coxswain Kuzkin groaned, "I'm wounded."

"I've been hit, too, Coxswain, and pretty badly," Kovalenko muttered, falling near the helm in the forward, covered part of the bridge, or the limousine, as we called it.

It was dark on the bridge. Belayev, who was lightly wounded, thought that the captain had gone down to the control room. He took over. First Lieutenant Shipin knew nothing of what had happened. He was in the control room, which was his station during a battle alarm.

In the meantime, the destroyer was swinging around for another attempt to ram the submarine. Kuzkin, who was wounded, had released the helm, and until another helmsman could take over at the second helm in the control room the submarine veered to port side. The destroyer had a greater swing angle than the submarine, and for some time both vessels described concentric arcs. That saved the Pike. Belayev quickly appraised the situation and shouted, "Clear the bridge. Emergency dive!"

He looked around the bridge once more and asked in a loud voice, "Is there anybody in the limousine?"

He did not get a reply and slammed the hatch shut.

Just before the submarine disappeared in the water a 20 mm shell made a hole in its casing.

"Where's the captain?" somebody in the control room asked.

But these words were drowned by a deafening bang—the torpedo had, after all, hit the bridge and the aft gun guard with its stem. Then three depth charges exploded one after another. . . .

The Pike lost her captain. Semyon Kovalenko was an able commander with extraordinary erudition and technical know-how. He had studied at the physics and mathematics department of an institute, and was a skilled tactician. He knew as much about the theory of ships as any diploma'd engineer, and was constantly searching for the most effective ways of utilizing submarines in battle. Had he lived he would undoubtedly have mounted to prominence in the navy.

A chain of circumstances played an essential role in this tragedy. But it would be wrong to attribute everything to circumstances. Shilinsky, as I have mentioned, had not performed his duties in the best tradition, but part of the blame devolved on Kovalenko. The captain's fault was that when tension had reached its peak there had not been precise order on the bridge.

But the episode showed the excellent training that the crew had been given by Kovalenko. It manifested itself in Belayev's resourcefulness and initiative, which saved the submarine, the irreproachable work of Engineering Officer Saltykov, who ensured the emergency dive, and the efficiency and skill of seamen Zverev and Isayev, who quickly plugged the hole in the casing. Further, it showed in Shipin's actions as well. After the submarine had dived, the first lieutenant steered her toward the enemy coast and lay low on the seabed. The enemy probably thought he had sunk the submarine, for he soon left the area. Shipin surfaced before dawn, reported the battle and brought the submarine to the base.

With the submarine captains we carefully analyzed the entire incident. Every point was debated and nothing meriting praise was glossed over. It was agreed that there had to be no relaxation in the training of officers-of-the-watch, that the organization of our Submarine Branch had to be constantly improved.

Konstantin Shuisky, who, as the reader will remember, was first lieutenant under Malofeyev, was appointed captain of P-403. We could not have hoped for a better successor.

At that time we suffered a "peaceful loss" in the brigade. Captain 3rd Rank Zhukov was relieved of his command of K-21. He was a veteran sailor and an experienced submariner, but his addiction to the bottle nullified much of all that. After one of his binges on shore he had to be relieved of his command. Of course, everybody was sorry about it but nobody thought the decision unjust or unwarrantedly severe.

When Nikolai Lunin was named as his successor, I whole-heartedly subscribed to it, feeling that he had the experience to be in command of a submarine. This was borne out by the seven victories scored by P-421 under his command.

Lunin's first assignment was not quite in the usual run of things.

P-402 reported that she had unexpectedly run out of fuel and was stranded near the enemy coast.

Before finding herself in that disastrous situation, P-402 had sunk a large transport and a mine sweeper and damaged another vessel with a torpedo. She was bombed and during one of these attacks her external fuel tanks sprang leaks. When finally the enemy was shaken off, the captain ordered these tanks blown with air and scavenged with water so that no treacherous oil slicks could betray her position. He thought that the fuel in the inner tanks would last him until the end of his patrol.

But he miscalculated. The tanks were empty. The submarine radioed her plight and waited for assistance, every minute risking discovery. There was nothing worse than to have to wait helplessly. Mother wit came to the rescue. The torpedoes were drained of their benzine, which was mixed with lubricating oil. This mixture did the trick. The diesels began to work and the submarine moved away from the dangerous coast. But there was not enough of this improvised fuel to take her home.

K-21 was under repairs when she was ordered to go to

Stolbov's assistance. There was three or four days' work left to be done, but this was impossibly long. Seamen under Engineering Officer Vladimir Braman undertook to get the submarine ready in a few hours. They successfully coped with this task and soon, with Lunin in command and Kerim Gadjiev on board K-21, set out on her rescue mission.

The Katyusha had to give the Pike enough fuel to enable her to return to the base. This was unprecedented in our practice. No method of transferring fuel from one submarine to another had been evolved. In peace-time we simply had not been able to foresee such a contingency. Besides, we did not have the necessary technical facilities. Gadjiev and Lunin had to improvise.

The heavy swell made it not only incredibly difficult but also dangerous for the submarines to tie up alongside each other. But it was the only thing to do, for the hose was not long enough to allow them to keep at a distance. This was when the two captains' training and seamanship stood them in good stead.

The submarines came alongside each other and were secured with manila rope. Sailors with axes stood by at the bitts to cut the ends of the rope should the necessity arise. The guns were manned.

A fuel hose was passed through the fore hatch and into the tank throat in the Pike. The hose was suffiently slack to allow for the rolling.

Within a relatively short span of time, which seemed unendurably long to the submariners, P-421 received fifteen tons of fuel, which was quite enough to see her home. A hundred and twenty kilos of lubricant was taken on board in bags specially used for distilled water.

The submarines did not dent each other, and neither the ropes nor the hose snapped. In short, this operation, extremely complicated from the seaman's point of view, was completed successfully despite the continuing swell.

It was a victory over the sea, and as much honor went with it as with a victory over the enemy.

Both submarines returned to Polyarnoye safely. In that operation Lunin demonstrated his superb seamanship.

I had a serious talk with Stolbov. There was no excuse for an experienced Engineering Officer like Bolshakov to have made that miscalculation over the fuel. The captain had to bear the responsibility for gross blunders by his subordinates.

We had no right to create difficulties ourselves in order to overcome them heroically later. If that became a practice the Nazis would never be defeated.

A Solar Calendar

An abstract drawing on a sheet of Whatman with wavy lines between the different colors hung on the wall of my "cabin." It was the work of Divisional Navigator Boris Kovalev.

He had created this small masterpiece with colored pencils and with the help of a marine astronomical almanac, and called it a solar calendar. In the Arctic Circle it is the kind of calendar that no commander can do without. It was essential for battle planning. It told you at once if on a certain day you would have the sun on the horizon, how long daylight would last, what would be the duration of evening and morning dusk, how long and how dark the night would be, and whether there would be a moon. It gave you an exhaustive picture. The only thing it could not forecast was when Aurora Borealis would start its fireworks.

The war, the calendar told me, broke out on the day of the summer solstice. We began our patrols during the polar day. Our score of victories mounted unabated into the continuous northern darkness. January, too, brought a good crop.

During that month, according to our data, the torpedoes and artillery of our four Katyushas sank a total of six transports and other vessels, and laid a fairly large number of mines along the enemy's supply routes. An episode eloquently characterizing our seamen occurred during one of these operations.

K-23 was laying mines in an enemy fjord. This required the utmost secrecy. The starboard mines were laid without incident. But when the turn of the port mines came the mine-laying device, which was far from being perfect, jammed. The prospect looked dismal. To repair the damage in the ordinary way, the submarine had to surface and open the mine-ballast tank. But with that tank opened the submarine could not dive. It did not require much imagination to foresee how all this could end in a busy area of an enemy fjord in moonlight. Captain 3rd Rank Potapov felt he could not risk the submarine.

The other alternative was to send a man into the tank to batten it down while the damage was being repaired. That would enable the submarine to dive if necessary. But it meant certain death for the seaman in the tank. Only a volunteer could be asked to take such a risk.

Many of the men volunteered, but Petty Officer Nosov insisted on doing the job. A re-enlisted man, he had trained many first-class seamen.

"Don't worry about me, Captain," he said in an embarrassed voice. "If you have to dive, don't hesitate to do so. Nobody'll do the job faster than me."

Potapov let Nosov have his way.

While the petty officer was busy in the tank, the Captain and the look-out saw a German ship passing nearby. Luckily, it was snowing and the enemy did not notice the submarine.

Everything ended happily. Nosov mended the damage quickly, and the mines were laid exactly in the assigned area. Some days later K-23 sighted a lone transport in the distance. She surfaced, overtook the ship and virtually riddled it with 100 mm shells. After the twenty-first hit, the ship sank near the coastal settlement of Sverholt.

In January all the Divisions reported victories although it was difficult to hunt for the enemy in the dark of the night.

There is more tension during a night hunt than during a torpedo attack. An attack follows a clear-cut pattern: the target is in sight, the computations are made, and all that is needed is to speed up the firing of the torpedoes and elude the escort vessels in time. But when a submarine is hunting it is completely surrounded by the unknown. The captain has to be constantly weighing pros and cons, to steer a course which would keep the submarine from being spotted by shore posts, and, at the same time, look out for convoys. The strain on the men's nerves never slackens. . . .

All the submarines of our division, except P-402, were on patrol in January, and all of them reported kills. P-404, commanded by Captain 3rd Rank Vladimir Ivanov, made the first kill. Moiseyev sank two ships. Lunin sent three ships to the bottom on his last patrol in P-421; true, two of them were sunk in February.

The ordinary, wintry weather continued into February, but to make up for it we had some real daylight, with a tiny, bleak sun. When there's daylight one feels the joy of living, and fights with greater vigor.

That month S-101 went on her first war patrol. Commanded by Captain 3rd Rank Vekke, she had Divisional Commander

Khomyakov on board. It was a successful patrol. The submarine torpedoed a transport of about five thousand tons and landed a reconnaissance group on the Norwegian shore.

Our Midgets, led by their "Grandfather" Morozov, fought bravely. The loss of friends in M-175 had not discouraged them. Each realized, of course, that the same thing might happen to him. But at the mention of lost friends their faces grew stern, and one knew that they were determined to seek revenge.

Fisanovich and Starikov returned victorious from almost every patrol. In March Starikov attacked a German U-boat that had carelessly surfaced in Varanger Fjord. It was a battle between submarines, and it was significant that our submarine prevailed over a vastly experienced enemy.

Among the Midgets only M-173 was regarded as unlucky. She had a good, fighting crew, and her commander, Lieutenant-Captain Kunets, was regarded as a competent officer. But he lacked resourcefulness, resoluteness and tactical sharpness. In the course of eight months of action the submarine more than once put out to sea and encountered the enemy but every time Kunets had extremely bad luck. Either he delayed adopting a decision, or was slow with his computations, or issued muddled orders. Whatever happened the fact was that the attack did not come off. In the end we got to the bottom of this run of bad luck. It was a case where nature had not endowed a man with the qualities of a submariner. The only thing that could be done in the circumstances was to transfer Kunets to an Es as First Lieutenant and appoint somebody else in his place.

His successor, Lieutenant-Captain Valerian Terekhin, had everything Kunets did not have. This was demonstrated during the very first patrol, on which the submarine had the Divisional Commander on board. On March 16, Terekhin sank a transport which was escorted by two mine sweepers.

He followed this up with the kills on each of the next three patrols. But I am getting ahead of my story by mentioning what happened in April.

This was March. And although it was still frosty, with storms and blizzards, the solar calendar gave promise of a longer day. We were nearing the spring equinox. And looking at the solar calendar I joyously told myself that we had learned to sink the enemy both by day and night, in summer and in winter.

HURDLING ALL BARRIERS

A Sail on the Periscope

In March I had my hands full putting Fyodor Vidayev through the mill for his independent command of a submarine.

When Lunin was assigned to a larger submarine, I recommended Vidayev as his successor. My recommendation was accepted. Indeed, Fyodor had sailed in P-421 as First Lieutenant and it was time he had his own command. He was an old-timer in the brigade. Back in 1938 he was navigator in D-3 under Kotelnikov, and had been with him on the expedition to Jan Mayen Island with the mission of rescuing Papanin and his men from a drifting ice floe. Fyodor proved to be a competent navigator. His knowledge of the polar seas stood him in good stead—he had sailed in them with fishermen prior to his service in the navy.

Four years had passed since then. Vidayev had become a submariner in the full sense of the word. He had had splendid training under Kotelnikov and Lunin. A thoughtful man with an analytical mind, this training had given him a lot. He was easy to get on with, level-headed in face of danger, and there was, I think, only one thing he was afraid of; and it was to draw attention to himself.

When he was appointed captain, his place as First Lieutenant was taken by Kautsky, who had for a long time wanted active duty. Day after day we made practice runs in the region of Kildin Reach. We used one of the bays near our training ground as a base so as not to waste time on passages to Polyarnoye.

I was not surprised that things went smoothly, for Vidayev

had been an efficient first lieutenant. He had had to maneuver a submarine in every conceivable situation, for Lunin, like any good captain, had seen to it that his first lieutenant could take over at any time. However, Fyodor still had to settle into his duties as captain, and here the psychological aspect played a quite considerable role. It was one thing acting for the captain and another when you know you're responsible for a submarine.

I was satisfied with Vidayev's progress, and finally, on March 20, I went with him on his first independent patrol.

We were greeted by a murderous sea. The submarine rolled crazily, taking a list of 40 degrees. We had a long way to go, having been assigned to one of the most distant patrol areas.

Lieutenant-Captain Afonin, commander of L-22, which was being completed at Archangel, was officer-of-the-watch. He had commanded a submarine in the Baltic during the war against the White Finns, and he had come with us on this patrol to acquire combat experience under northern conditions.

Leaving him and Vidayev on the bridge, I climbed down the hatch. In the third compartment Commissar Afanasyev was discussing something animatedly with the Party organizer, the Y.C.L. organizer and the editor of the wall newspaper.

I looked into all the compartments. The watch were attentively going about their duties. The men off duty were having their evening tea. Only two or three of the younger men refused their tea: they were on the seasick roster. The nucleus of the crew, however, consisted of veterans of the Finnish War. The weather did not affect their capacity for work or their appetites, although a heavy sea had an effect on them as well. That was only natural and they were used to it.

Early in the morning we were ordered to Area N to provide an Allied convoy with cover against large enemy surface ships. This assignment did not come as a surprise, for more and more convoys were now sailing to Murmansk. Shortly before we went on this patrol, we had a party to which British seamen were invited. They told us that their mission in the Barents Sea was the toughest they had had. That was true. Even practised sailors like the British find themselves hard-driven.

The convoy in question was PQ-13. As in previous cases submarines were diverted from their patrol areas to give them added protection. The Germans had considerable naval forces, including a modern battleship, in Norwegian ports and these could inflict heavy losses on the clumsy, show convoys and their escort. We therefore extended our area of operations not only to the German supply lines but also to our own sea lanes.

We were part of the screen for two days during which we did not encounter the enemy. The convoy passed us, and we were ordered back to our patrol area.

The days were growing longer, and this forced us to spend more time under water. There were no other signs of spring. The weather was stormy, it was as cold as before, and snow fell frequently.

Although we had not yet come to grips with the enemy, Vidayev did not betray the impatience I am sure he must have felt. I was eager to see him in action, in a torpedo attack, which was the crucial test for the moral right to be the captain of a submarine.

The test began at 14.32 hours on March 28 near Porsanger Fjord. Vidayev, who was at the periscope, looked away from it for a moment and said with a broad smile, "I think we've found our convoy." Then in a louder voice with an undertone of severity, "Stand by for a torpedo attack!"

A transport and two patrol ships were following a zigzag course along the coast heading for the fjord. The enemy was far away from us, but our position made it possible for us to attack him.

The minutes dragged by as we began to close in. We looked at the transport in turn through the periscope. From time to time the hydrophone operator reported the enemy's position, and Vidayev corrected the course accordingly. Vidayev was handling the situation calmly and it was not necessary for me to interfere. One could see he had confidence in himself and in his men.

I felt it was time he ordered the aft tubes to stand by. Instead, the captain raised the periscope and groaned with disappointment. Silently, he stepped aside to let me have a look. The convoy had sharply changed its course, and was now rounding the cape at the mouth of the fjord. Although we were now virtually a stone's throw away from the enemy, the change in the course angles made it impossible for us to fire. In this situation it would surprise nobody if the attack was called off. There was only one possibility of still hitting the enemy, but not every captain would see it.

However, before I could say anything Vidayev ordered, "Helm to port, course 165! Coxswain, take her down to twenty meters." Turning to me he said, "I'm going to dive under the convoy for an aft salvo."

That was exactly what I had in mind. My opinion of him soared. He was displaying enviable tenacity.

The noise of the German propellers passed overhead. We rose to periscope depth and got into a position to attack.

"Aft tubes, stand by!"

Just then, as ill luck would have it, the convoy again changed course, dropping out of our angle of attack. It was those blasted anti-submarine zigzags. They were impossible to foresee. Vidayev, however, with a commander's insight, which helps to divine the development of events, saw through the enemy's intention.

"They've changed their course again," he said. "We'll have to go into the mouth of the fjord and wait for them there."

The submarine headed for that invisible point where the captain planned to strike at the enemy. Through the periscope we watched the convoy now drawing near us now moving away as though it had decided to get away. Fyodor kept the submarine steady on course. The attack was taking nearly an hour, and the captain was covered with sweat. He took off his cap and unbuttoned his padded jacket. Cut off from his surroundings he would have looked like a young chap engaged in heavy manual labor.

The convoy finally completed its last turn and everything fell into place. It seemed to have deliberately readied itself for an attack. We steered an attack course.

"Aft tubes, stand by!"

There was a muffled explosion under water—it was a depth charge. I glanced at my watch. It was 15.28 hours. Why had the Germans released a depth charge? As a preventive measure? We were positive that we had not been spotted. At 15.31 hours there was a series of seven explosions. We stuck to our attack course.

"Aft tubes, fire!" Fyodor ordered at 15.38 hours.

We felt four jolts one after another. The torpedoes had left their tubes. It was a good thing that we had a bubble-free firing system which did not give us away.

Within fifty seconds we clearly heard two explosions. A look into the periscope showed us that the transport was sinking. We began a post-salvo maneuver. At 15.45 hours we heard the first of the depth charges aimed at us exploding. Vidayev dived deeper. The Germans kept up their attack until 17.37 hours, dropping forty-four depth charges, but all of them exploded astern of us. A sudden snowfall had, evidently, spoiled the enemy's accuracy. We got off lightly— only our gyrocompass failed us for a short time.

Once more there were long, uneventful days and nights. The monotony was broken on April 4, while we were recharging our batteries. A radiogram from Fleet Headquarters informed us that P-421 had been decorated with the Order of the Red Banner.

All day on April 8 we hovered under water in the vicinity of Porsanger Fjord, where Vidayev had made such a successful debut. There was nothing doing there and we sailed north to be able to recharge our batteries when it grew dark.

We were on course 20. In the ward room the steward was laying the table for evening tea. The men off duty were resting—reading or getting ready to sleep. Suddenly, at 20.58 hours, a terrific explosion shook the submarine. We felt it tilting. Bunks and regeneration cartridges clattered to the floor. Water gurgled somewhere. Some of the men in the sixth compartment were hurled into the fifth. And at once the trim in the stern began to change.

When Vidayev and I rushed into the control room, Kautsky and Engineering Officer Slavinsky had already ordered the submarine to surface. Before clearly realizing what had happened, they had, in fact, immediately taken steps to keep the submarine afloat. Indeed, had they hesitated or begun to find out details, the water pouring into the aft compartment would probably have deprived us of all possibility of surfacing.

An order to secure the door and begin patching up the hole in the casing was passed to the aft compartment from the control room. The six men in the compartment instantly sealed themselves off from the rest of the submarine. By the iron-clad law of the submarine service they remained in the inky darkness, single-handed against invisible gaps in the casing, against the icy water. They knew that it might cost them their lives, but at that price they would save the submarine. At the same time, their only chance to remain alive was to save the submarine.

There was nothing but snow on the horizon and we surfaced. That gave us the opportunity of taking stock of what had happened. We had unquestionably touched off a mine although nobody had heard the mine-rope gnashing against the casing. Even a first glance showed that we had suffered considerable damage. The bridge hatch had been wrenched out of shape. The upper lid had been torn off and the compartment had not been flooded only because the lower lid had withstood the pressure of the water. The parapet of the aft gun was bent. In the control room the wireless set was jolted out of its place and seriously damaged. The gyrocompass broke down.

The first thing we did was to pump the water out of the seventh compartment, where under Petty Officer Dryapikov the men were desperately fighting to keep the sea out. Seamen Kachura, Mitin, Zhavoronkov, Novikov and Fevralev found the holes, stuffing everything they could put their hands on into them. Where nothing helped, they pressed themselves against holes until assistance came.

This was not a case of exceptional bravery. It was the natural result of training. The crew of D-3 had faced the same emergency during their last patrol in March, when a depth charge seriously damaged the casing. The submarine returned home only because the crew had managed to prevent the water from flooding the compartments.

Dryapikov and his men battened down the door, turned on the pressurized air to counter the pressure of the sea, and stopped up the holes, displaying resourcefulness and enterprise. All the other men, too, did their bit, and that, properly speaking, saved the submarine.

But had we been saved for long? A cape, where we knew the enemy had an observation post and an artillery battery, could be seen through the fast-falling snow. We were in no condition to dive. And we did not know if we were navigable. It was only a matter of time before we would be a sitting duck for the enemy. And if the wireless defied our efforts to repair it we would be unable even to ask for assistance.

Luckily, the snowstorm continued unabated until the onset of the short April night. But our worst fears about our being able to move independently were confirmed by 23.00 hours. We had lost our propellers. However, our wireless operators Rybin and Svinyin repaired the transmitter by 23.20 hours and I sent the following message to the Fleet Commander-in-Chief. It read: "Hit a mine. Unable to move or dive. Position. . . ."

In the meantime, Navigator Marinkin reported that a slow current of about one and a half knots was steadily carrying us shoreward. The outlook certainly looked black. Yet, when a situation seems to be hopeless, a solution is found though ludicrously absurd at first glance, yet not without practical sense. We were sailors, damn it. Why, we asked ourselves, should we not act as such and use a sail. We could make one from the diesel hoods, and use the periscope for a mast.

"What about it?" I asked Vidayev and Kautsky not very confidently, outlining my somewhat offbeat plan.

"We had thought of it ourselves. We only need to put about ten miles between ourselves and the coast. Once we're safe we can think of something else."

"All right, carry on," I said.

It was difficult to tell what would come of it. Would the improvised sail work? Would it be sufficient to get the submarine moving against the current? Computations would not help. Solely the attempt itself could provide the answer, and there was no reason why we should not make the attempt.

The sail was ready by 01.00 hours. We fitted it on the periscope with the help of a makeshift beam. A periscope and a sail! A modern optical system, a 20th-century instrument fulfilling the role of a wooden mast for a sheet of rough canvas, which had served ships since time immemorial. The sail filled, and the submarine moved away from the coast, driven by a fair wind.

We moved slowly, but nonetheless the log began to count off miles. The magnetic compass showed we were on a course of 350 degrees. Everybody was delighted. After 04.00 hours we received a message from Headquarters. It informed us that K-22, patrolling a nearby area, was coming to our rescue. This raised our spirits.

After about an hour of this bizarre journey, we had to haul down our sail. The wind dropped, visibility improved and Nordkapp and Cape Helnes could be seen distinctly. Consequently, if we had not lowered our sail we would have been spotted by the enemy.

We looked at it with the greatest of respect. It had enabled us to cover nine miles. This was the distance that gave us the chance of avoiding immediate detection by the enemy.

Soon we received another message from the base. It confirmed the first. It stated: "K-22 ordered to go to your assistance. If unable to save the submarine, save the men and destroy the submarine."

We raised our sail again at 07.00 hours when it began to snow and a light wind blew. At 09.00 hours visibility returned and we lowered the sail. To keep out of sight as much as possible we filled the main ballast tank, so that the deck could hardly be seen above the water.

The men did not idle. The engine-room artificers and electricians recharged the accumulator batteries, and the stokers refilled the pressurized air tanks. The compartments were tidied up. Routine was kept up to distract the men from thoughts about the possible outcome of our venture.

There was no telling how it would end. If the sail let us down the current would carry us toward the enemy coast at a speed of a mile and a half an hour. Would Victor Kotelnikov reach us before we were detected and sunk by the Germans? It was difficult to say. In any case we had to be prepared for the worst. Both our guns were manned, for we were determined to fight to the end. We made preparations to blast our artillery magazine for we did not mean to surrender even after exhausting all our means of resistance. Kautsky had the task of blowing up the magazine, and Dyba, the Artillery Officer, was given the assignment of exploding one of the aft torpedoes.

All these preparations were made unobtrusively but the men got a hint of them, as they always do in such cases. Commissar Afanasyev reported that they were calmly discussing the possibility and the outcome of an encounter with the enemy. All of them were prepared to die rather than be taken prisoner.

As I learned later, Vidayev slipped Rybin, the chief wireless operator, a note with the memo: "Send this when you get the order from me." The message consisted only of seven words: "Am dying, but am not surrendering."

We were still drifting shoreward. The tidying up was completed. Vidayev ordered the men to clean and polish the mechanisms. . . .

In the meantime, K-22 was speeding to our rescue. She had left Polyarnoye six days after us, and had been bombed heavily twice. On April 3 she attacked a convoy consisting of one transport and three patrol ships. Kotelnikov fired two torpedoes at the transport and, after quickly changing the angle of attack, fired another at one of the patrol ships. These were sniper's shots: all of them found their mark.

The remaining patrol ships pursued the submarine, dropping twenty-two depth charges, but none of them caused any substantial damage. Kotelnikov shook off his pursuers, and on the next day revisited the area where he had attacked the convoy. There were life belts, pieces of wood, suitcases and a portrait of Hitler floating on the surface.

"Crap always floats," the seamen said.

Like us, K-22 had had no luck during the next few days.

On the night of April 9 she sailed to her battery-recharging area. In the early hours of the morning the diesels ceased their racket. A pre-dawn frost was in the air. Lieutenant-Captain Bakman, the First Lieutenant, glanced at his watch. It was almost time for the submarine to dive: the enemy shore was comparatively close. Exactly at 05.00 hours Bakman woke the Captain who was dozing and reported that the submarine was ready to dive.

Kotelnikov inspected the battery compartment and climbed to the bridge. The shore was still enveloped in dense twilight. Prickly snow was falling. Kotelnikov postponed the dive to 06.00 hours to give the batteries a chance to cool and be ventilated properly. Visibility was low enough to allow him that luxury.

This delay decided the destiny of P-421. At about 06.00 hours, K-22's wireless operator received the message: "To the captain. Submarine P-421 ran into a mine. Her engines are disabled. Proceed to her assistance. If she cannot be saved, take the crew off and sink the submarine. P-421's position is so and so. Fleet Commander-in-Chief."

At 08.45 hours K-22 arrived in the assigned area and began looking for us. The watch peered into the blue haze in the distance, worrying that they were late. K-22 searched for more than an hour. . . .

At 10.50 hours, Senior Lieutenant Marinkin, who was officer-of-the-watch in P-421, saw a dark spot in the northwestern part of the horizon, on starboard course 30. He took his bearings. The spot was moving.

He ordered the guns manned and inspected the spot through his binoculars. The minutes dragged slowly by. Finally, Marinkin lowered his binoculars and yelled joyously, "It's a Katyusha!"

The men cheered.

"It's Victor at last," Vidayev said, sighing with relief, and ordered the signal flags to be hoisted. Soon the Katyusha could be clearly discerned with the naked eye. Then we recognized the men on the bridge. Finally our rescuer stopped in the heavy swell some fifteen meters away from us.

I briefly recounted the situation to Kotelnikov through a megaphone. In his turn he communicated the orders of the Fleet Military Council, which we already knew, namely, that he would try to take P-421 in tow and, if that failed, he would take our crew on board and sink the submarine.

The towing lines were made fast at about 12.00 hours. The gun crews stood by, and K-22 started moving. Five minutes after we were taken in tow, the treacherous swell did its work: the lines snapped. K-22 came alongside and tried to tow that way. But nothing came of it either because of the swell. We tried fixing the hawsers again stern to bow, but they not only snapped once more but also tore out the Katyusha's bitts.

We decided to try the anchor chain. But before we could do much an aircraft appeared. It fired several flares in our direction and turned shoreward. It was 13.20 hours and visibility was excellent. A ship appeared in a fjord in the distance. The situation was becoming desperate for we now ran the risk of losing both submarines. On the authority given him Kotelnikov ordered us to abandon ship and take with us our secret documents.

We went alongside the Katyusha and aided by two of her seamen, the crew began jumping onto her deck.

We began abandoning our ship in the nick of time, for soon another aircraft appeared and then flew in the direction of the shore. We could expect to be attacked at any minute.

With Vidayev I inspected all the compartments to make sure that nobody was left in them. Then we climbed to the bridge and stopped at our wet, storm-frayed ensign. That minute of silent farewell was a bitter pill to swallow. We were brought out of our trance by Kotelnikov's megaphone-amplified voice, "Hurry or we'll lose both ships!"

It was a well-advised reminder. I glanced at Vidayev. He had pressed himself to the ensign and there were tears in his eyes.

"Come," I said.

First I and then Vidayev (whose duty and prerogative it was to be the last to abandon his ship) went over to K-22. I spied the corner of a naval ensign peeping out of his pocket. Catching my glance Vidayev said, as though justifying himself,

"It's the newer one. I took it as a keepsake. The old one is there, flying."

Silently I shook hands with him. He was a good lad. In this most poignant grief for any ship's captain he was keeping a tight hold on himself.

We climbed to the bridge. Besides the Captain and officer-of-the-watch there were Alexei Petrov, correspondent of *Krasny Flot*, the naval newspaper, Brigade Flag Signals Officer Volonkin, and Afonin, Captain of K-22. K-22 moved away from the disabled Pike and swung around at a distance of about one and a half cable-lengths.

A torpedo raced out of one of her stern tubes and ploughed swiftly through the water. We bared our heads. There was an explosion and a column of water wrapped in black smoke rose into the air. Some ten seconds later, when the column subsided, all trace of P-421 had disappeared. She had not survived to receive the Order ensign, which she had won.

"Aircraft to starboard, aft, 30," the look-out cried.

"Clear the deck. Emergency dive," Kotelnikov ordered.

. . . K-22 entered Polyarnoye at midday on April 10. After firing two salutes she hoisted P-421's signal flags and fired another salute in honor of her last victory.

The Brigade Commander came on board as soon as the gangplank was in position. He shook hands all around and said, "My congratulations on your victory and on saving your ship's company." Then he took me aside and added, "You must bear a stiff upper lip. Zoya has died in Leningrad."

Prepared as I was for this news, I could not control the tears filling my eyes. A tight knot in my throat prevented me from saying anything in reply.

We Serve the Soviet Union

June 12 was a clear, windless day with a light frost. A fine snow fell from time to time.

On the pier, near the submarines tied up alongside it, were more than two hundred ratings, petty officers and officers lined up in rigid formation. There had never been so many submariners lined up on the pier ever since the outbreak of the war.

In front of the formation was a table covered with a red baize, and on it small boxes with Orders and medals, Order certificates and letters of thanks. At the table, facing the formation, were the Fleet Commander-in-Chief, the Member of the Military Council, a representative from the Presidium of the Supreme Soviet of the U.S.S.R., and the Commander and Commissar of our brigade.

The decree was read:

"For exemplary fulfilment of assignments from the High Command in the war against the German invaders and for displaying courage and heroism, the title of Hero of the Soviet Union and the Order of Lenin and the Medal Gold Star are awarded to..."

My name headed the list. I marched to the table. Arseny Golovko presented the award to me, shaking my hand and congratulating me. I was congratulated by the other men at the table.

There was much that I wanted to say in reply. For example, that, if necessary, I would, without hesitation, sacrifice my life for my country, for the Communist Party, because without country and without the Party life would be meaningless to me. For it was my country and the Party that had turned me from a semi-literate river seaman into a naval officer, into the commander of a unit, and brought me to the forefront of the struggle against the enemy. My country's destiny was my destiny.

I wanted to say that we were not letting ourselves be deluded by our first victories in the naval war, that we could see our mistakes and our shortcomings, that submariners would fight with more skill and with greater ferocity, that the intensity of our struggle against the Nazi invaders would steadily mount. Marxism-Leninism could not be reconciled with Nazi philosophy. We had a deadly hatred for the enemy. Our personal grief merged with the grief of the entire country. And we would fight without showing mercy, until complete victory was won.

These thoughts crowded my mind, but I pronounced the short and meaningful regulation formula, "I serve the Soviet Union."

These words covered the entire purport of our lives, of our day-to-day service in the navy....

Nikolai Lunin, Valentin Starikov and Israel Fisanovich were called to the table. They were decorated with the title of Hero of the Soviet Union by a Decree of April 3.

The words "I serve the Soviet Union" resounded in the frosty air.

Victor Kotelnikov received the Order of Lenin. Only three days before that he had been at sea, rescuing the crew of P-421. Perhaps tomorrow he would be back hunting the enemy.

The Order of the Red Banner was presented to Kerim Gadjiev, who had eleven patrols to his credit.

Karpunin, Submarine Department Chief at Fleet Headquarters, Brigade Commander Vinogradov and Brigade Commissar Kozlov were likewise decorated with the Order of the Red Banner. This award was presented not for "general" armchair leadership. They had won it at sea, on patrols in which enemy ships had been sunk.

By order of the People's Commissar of the Navy, D-3, K-22, M-171, and M-174 were named Guards Submarines. M-172, P-402 and P-421 were decorated with the Order of the Red Banner.

P-421 had not survived to receive the Order. The Order ensign for her would now fly at the flagstaff of some other ship that had distinguished herself. Within a space of nine months she had scored seven victories under Lunin and one under Vidayev. It was an impressive score.

Naturally, we realized that the lost ship was only a cold steel casing with a maze of mechanisms, systems and instruments, that all her victories were the work of the men who sailed in her. Yet it was difficult to rid oneself of the habit of regarding a submarine as though it were a living being. The reason for this was perhaps that for a long time she had been the home of seamen, that her intricate mechanisms cleverly obeyed the will of her commander, that she had a cast of her own. Then again, perhaps, the reason was that this modern war machine mirrored the brains and labor of the men who had made it.

In any case, the submarine herself is decorated with an Order, which remains with her even if the entire crew is changed. But if a submarine is lost, her Order is not turned over to a new master. Each vessel must have her own battle traditions.

Even by being lost, P-421 had done us a service. We now knew that there was an anti-submarine mine field in the area where she received her fatal wound. Submarine captains were instructed to pass through this area at a greater depth to avoid the mines. That saved many ships.

Later, captains reported that in negotiating the hazardous area they had heard mine ropes grazing against the casing. But a correctly executed maneuver enabled them to get through the mine field safely. The mines were left suspended high in the water and even if they exploded they would not have caused much harm. Avgustinovich told us of one of these explosions. There was a loud bang and the submarine shuddered violently. However, there was little damage. When K-1 surfaced, mine fragments were found on her deck and bridge.

As regards the crew of P-421, most of them remained in the brigade, being posted to submarines or to Headquarters. The reader will meet some of them in the succeeding chapters. Others were assigned to various units. All of them did their duty to the very end.

In the autumn of 1960 I met Mikhail Bogdanov, who hailed from the village of Bozhkoyka, Rostov Region. He was one of the three P-421 veterans about whom we had had no news for years.

All of us remembered the anxious period at the end of the spring of 1942 when the Nazi threat hung thick over the North Caucasus and the area between the Volga and the Don. During that spring the Northern Fleet had rushed preparations to send a naval unit to help the troops fighting in the South. Submariners were included in that unit: warrant officers and ratings from the shore base and three men from P-421—Electrician 2nd Class Prikhodchenko, Electrician Yerofeyev and Motor Room Able Seaman Bogdanov.

The unit was seen off in July. Our men joined in the land fighting, which was new to them.

Nikolai Lunin was among those who saw the unit off. He came to wish good luck to the men who had served under him. He gave Bogdanov his dirk.

We had no news of these three P-421 veterans for many years.

In 1959 I got a letter from Bogdanov. We corresponded for more than a year and, finally, we met eighteen years after our roads had parted during the war.

The three seamen were separated from each other long before they could get to the firing lines. Their train was heavily bombed by aircraft on a hot noon at Baskunchak Station. Yerofeyev, who was near Bogdanov, was killed. He was buried there and then, in the salt-marsh steppe. Prikhodchenko was wounded and taken to a hospital.

The echelon was reformed and the naval unit moved on. In those days travel was slow in Russia. Hurried preparations had been made to send the unit from Murmansk in July, but now it was well in the middle of August. A battle was raging on the banks of the Volga. The sailors hoped they would be sent into the hottest sector of that battle. But the echelon arrived at Poti, where the men were assigned to different units.

Bogdanov found himself in the 416th Marine Guards Mortar Regiment. It consisted of motorized rocket mortars, nicknamed Katyushas, a name that fell caressingly on the ear of the submariner. The name became popular, and the people associated it more with these rocket mortars than with the large submarines, whose existence was not even suspected by very many people. The land Katyushas became famous in the literal sense of the word. Every schoolboy knew about them.

The regiment, commanded by Captain 2nd Rank Moskvin, former artillery officer on the battleship *Marat*, had already made a name for itself in the battles near Moscow. It made any man proud to serve in it, and Bogdanov did his best to uphold the honor of a Northern Fleet submariner.

In the Caucasian foothills the regiment made a noteworthy contribution to the victory of the Maritime Army. Bogdanov was in the ranks, when in front of the regiment, which was drawn up in formation, General Petrov, Commander of the Maritime Army, embraced Moskvin and said that, if it had been physically possible, he would have embraced every seaman.

In November 1943, when the Nazis were driven out of the Taman Peninsula, Bogdanov returned to the sea. He served as mechanic in a mine sweeper based on Kerch. But he sailed in the mine sweeper for only three months. She was blown up by a mine. In contrast to P-421, the small vessel sank instantly. The mechanic was badly wounded, and he was unconscious when he was fished out of the water.

He spent six months in a hospital. The end of the war found him in a ship repair company in Nikolayev.

"And here's the dirk that Lunin gave me. I had it with me throughout the war," Bogdanov said, finishing his story.

In front of me sat the father of four children, and the builder of houses for miners. But I saw him as the young and efficient Misha Bogdanov that I knew many years ago, as the sailor who carried out orders promptly and was prepared to lay down his life.

It was more or less the usual story of a man of his generation. Stories of this sort went to make up the military history of the victorious Soviet people.

Farewell, Friends

April was a month of farewells.

P-401 went on patrol on the day the submariners were presented with decorations. I distinctly remember the usual pre-patrol bustle. Navigator Paushkin hurriedly charted the preliminary course. Commissar Veresovoi climbed on board with pamphlets and books under his arm. The cook, Gornostayev, emerged from the base repair shop with utensils that had had to be mended.

Gornostayev, a sprightly Muscovite, was the best cook in the division. Cooks were held in high esteem by submariners. A cook had not only to be well-versed in the culinary art but also inventive, in order to make delectable meals every day in the course of several weeks from tinned food and concentrates. Unpalatable food simply stuck in the men's throats, for on patrol they have little exercise, and sometimes they do not have even enough fresh air. A cook had to have great stamina because the crew is broken up into three watches. The cook has no help. He has no right to be either seasick or ill. Lastly, like all other submariners, he has to know his way about a submarine blindfolded. In battle, he takes his place among the other sailors, having nothing to do with an electric stove but with valves and repair tools.

Gornostayev was just such a cook, neat and tidy.

Arkady Moiseyev came up to me and said, "Comrade Divisional Commander, the doctor has put Firsov in hospital. Who are we going to replace him with?"

Firsov was his first lieutenant. He had to have a replacement, of course, because no ship could do without a first lieutenant. I thought it over and found there was no one I could send except the divisional navigator. I stopped a sailor and said,

"Find Senior Lieutenant Kovalev and tell him to report to me."

Honestly, I was sorry to have to send Boris to sea—he had not yet had his rest after returning six days ago from a patrol in P-404 with Vladimir Ivanov. It had been a harrowing patrol. Enemy ships had pinned the submarine to the seabed with depth charges. However, Ivanov managed to elude the enemy by virtually crawling on his belly. On that patrol, the submarine sank two transports. There was a chance of sinking another, but due to rank negligence on the part of torpedo-man Sinyakov, the tubes jammed. On the whole, it had not been an easy patrol for Kovalev either. But there was nobody else I could send with Moiseyev.

Kovalev reported to me, looking smart and cheerful. He listened to my order and replied briefly, "Aye, aye!" and at once set about his duties as first lieutenant.

Finally, we got through all our anxieties and bustle. The submarine was, as always, ready to sail at the appointed time. She pulled out accompanied by the cheers of the men on the pier.

Kerim too made preparations to sail. He had just returned from a patrol with Lunin in which they sank a large transport. Since the outbreak of the war, Kerim had spent a total of four solid months on combat missions.

Now he was making preparations to go as Instructor Commander with Leonid Potapov in K-23. As always, Divisional Navigator Lieutenant-Captain Vasilyev, known better as Kuzmich, was going with him.

Near the pier I met Battalion Commissar Galkin. He carried a small suitcase and had a mixed, gay-and-troubled look on his face.

"Going far, Dmitri?" I asked.

"To K-23," Galkin said, stopping.

"As a representative of the Political Department?"

"No. For good. I've been appointed Commissar."

"What, all of a sudden?"

"No, I waited for the opportunity. It's what I wanted. I feel much happier in a submarine, closer to the men."

This was said sincerely. I had known Galkin for four years and had been at sea with him for quite a long time. He had told me a lot about himself.

He was born in Western Byelorussia. When war swept into

Byelorussia he had just turned twelve. Kaiser Wilhem's troops were advancing from the West, and the village where the Galkins lived found itself in the fighting zone. Refugees moved eastward together with the retreating Russian troops, saving themselves and their meager belongings. The Galkins were among these refugees.

Villages were in flames. Shells burst near by. The road was enveloped in dust. The frightened livestock brayed, bleated and neighed. At one of the turns of the road the Galkins' cow broke loose and ran across a field. "Good Lord," the mother groaned. "Dmitri, do something about it!" And the boy ran after the cow.

He had almost caught up with the animal when something incomprehensible happened. A winged monster, roaring awesomely, suddenly appeared overhead. It flew across the sky as though it were alive. The boy looked up, gazing at the strange machine as though he were bewitched. When it finally disappeared he could find no sign of the cow. The human torrent had carried his parents away with it, and the boy wept pitifully.

The lost lad was picked up by bearded soldiers. "You'll come to Russia with us, little fellow," they said, putting Dmitri in their train at a small station. "You'll get lost here."

Soon Dmitri Galkin was put in an orphans' home in the heart of Russia. Some time later he was earning his own way. When the Great October Revolution rolled across the country the lad got the opportunity to study, but he did not give up working. Life had taught him to be independent at an early age. He made every effort to find his parents, and his last hope was dashed in 1920, when Western Byelorussia was seized by squire-ruled Poland.

By that time Dmitri was in the Red Army, having linked his destiny up with it. The ideas which the army of the Land of Soviets upheld were his ideas. In those years people's class consciousness matured rapidly. The young man went on studying, and with time he became a trained political worker.

In 1936 he was transferred to the navy. At first he served in shore building units, and then as Political Department Instructor in the Submarine Brigade of the Northern Fleet. I was Divisional Commander when he was appointed Commissar in P-401. We became friends. This was facilitated by the fact that we were of the same age and had both had a difficult youth.

When Western Byelorussia was liberated, Dmitri renewed his inquiries about his family. He learned that his father had been dead for many years, but that his mother and brothers were living in the same village, which he had left as a twelve-year-old when it was shelled by the Germans. He decided to spend his next leave with his family in his native village.

On a summer evening in 1941 he approached his parents' house with a palpitating heart. The people he met on the way greeted the strange naval officer. Only the mother recognized her son in the gathering twilight. Her small Dmitri was now a different person. But the life he had left a quarter of a century before had not changed. Here people were only awakening to the new life. They could hardly believe that the son of an impoverished peasant had become a naval officer, as though he were a squire's son. Of course, they knew that this was usual in the Soviet Union. But it was one thing to know and another to see for themselves.

Galkin's leave was cut short in the cruellest fashion. War broke out. By an evil coincidence he left his native village again under fire. Shells whistled, bombs exploded. On chance trucks and even getting lifts in tanks, he got his family out of the war-ravaged area. He sent his wife and children to the East, and returned to Polyarnoye, where he reported for duty in K-1, in which he was Commissar. With that rank he was posted to the Fleet Political Department.

Now Dmitri was returning to a submarine, to the work he loved. The crew were only gaining by it. I heartily congratulated him on his new appointment and wished him every success. A familiar yet always exciting moment arrived. K-23 was pulling away from the pier. A smiling Gadjiev was standing on the bridge. Men who were shortly due to sail themselves crowded the pier.

Kerim waved his cap and shouted something in reply to the good wishes. But his words, drowned in the roar of the diesel engines, were carried away by the gusty wind.

But I could not manage even a smile. I was worried about Moiseyev. On April 25, after he had reported that he had used up all his torpedoes, he had been ordered to return home. Three days had passed, but there was no word from P-401.

The May Day holidays, marked modestly under wartime conditions, passed. It now looked as though our worst fears were becoming the bitter truth. We would wait, of course, but the spark of hope was growing ever dimmer. Moiseyev had been only eighteen hours' journey away from the base. A week had elapsed. K-23 scoured the area but returned empty-handed. Miracles don't happen. . . .

We had another blow on May 12. Gadjiev reported that they had torpedoed a transport and then engaged two patrol ships in an artillery duel, but serious damage prevented the submarine from diving. That was our last message from K-23.

By comparing intelligence reports with Gadjiev's last communication we got a more or less clear picture of what had happened to K-23.

The submarine was bombed after she had successfully torpedoed a transport. Evidently, she had been unable to escape the patrol ships and, to avert disaster, had surfaced and engaged the enemy in an artillery duel. As usual, the submarine's gunners rose to the occasion and destroyed the two patrol ships. However, the submarine was damaged and could not dive. She lost her principal weapon. German aircraft took over, and it was more than the wounded submarine could withstand. K-23 perished in an unequal battle.

The brigade lost its best and most experienced Divisional Commander. He was an unusually gifted man and a striking personality.

Kerim had hardly turned thirteen when civil war flared up in the Caucasus and spread to his native village in Daghestan. The boy joined a Red Army unit, soon became a machine gunner. He fought on the Terek and in Southern Daghestan. After the war, when he was demobilized because he was a junior, he found he could not remain in his native village. He went to Baku. The Caspian, which he had seen during the war, had captured his imagination, and he had made up his mind to become a sailor.

Reality outstripped his wildest dreams. The Y.C.L. sent him to a naval school in Leningrad. The prospect that opened before him was much more alluring than the master's bridge of some schooner in the Caspian. But the difficulties confronting him were incredible. He was semi-literate and had a poor knowledge of Russian. In spite of that he worked steadily toward the goal he had set himself. His burning desire reinforced by unyielding tenacity won out. He became a naval officer. After graduation he was assigned to submarines.

Kerim was known in all the Soviet fleets. He had served in the Baltic and in the Black Sea, and had commanded a submarine in the Pacific. After finishing the Naval Academy in 1939 he was sent to the North, where at Fleet Headquarters he was put in charge of submarine organization and training. Anybody who knew this conscientious and erudite staff officer could never imagine that he had been an illiterate boy from a mountain village who could hardly speak Russian.

Almost every day, soon after the flag was hoisted, he would be seen on some submarine. He was always about when a submarine's machinery had to be inspected or given a trial run after repairs, or when the crews were put through their paces. He was not one of those dispassionate observers whose sole concern was to note shortcomings and report them to his superiors. His nature was such that he could not help intervening if he saw that something could be improved, and when he did intervene he did it tactfully, without hurting other people's feelings. All the officers soon saw for themselves that his advice and suggestions were useful.

But most frequently Kerim could be seen on the bridge of a submarine setting out on patrol. He was a strict mentor, but submarine captains never found his presence a burden. Far from it, Kerim knew submarines inside out, and he quickly found his bearings in the Northern Theater.

In spite of everything, he did not particularly care for staff work. He was always eager to be with the men, in submarines, where he could apply his knowledge. He finally got what he wanted. In the autumn of 1940 he was appointed commander of 1st Submarine Division.

In this capacity he was able to show what he could do. Under him everything was subordinated to combat training. Kerim had his own firm, independent views on tactics. "In a war the best decisions of a commander are those that are adopted in time, even if they are not as happy as those that are adopted belatedly," he used to tell his subordinates. "Stick to your decision. Do not change it if you feel there are insufficient grounds for taking another decision. Drive away all doubts and suit your actions to your initial decision."

Kerim trained his officers along these lines, requiring that they act thoughtfully and quickly, that they be prepared to take a justified risk without flinching. Torpedo attacks under complicated conditions and artillery fire in face of difficulties were his favorite method of training. He made it a point that submariners should be equally proficient in the use of all ship's armaments, that no weapon should be regarded as primary or secondary. As though foreseeing war patrols, he laid stress on the training of gun crews, which had been somewhat neglected.

Among Divisional Commanders Kerim quickly became regarded as the best. It happened naturally, of itself—he never attempted to stand out among his comrades to emphasize his superiority in anything. But his extensive experience, his training at the academy and his talent for leadership put him into the role of our adviser. We turned to Kerim whenever we were in difficulties, and he took these difficulties as close to heart as we did.

When war broke out he redoubled his efforts to improve the skill of submarine captains. This training went on primarily during war patrols. Under his direction, captains learned to hunt the enemy, to carry out successful torpedo and artillery attacks with devastating effect. Kerim's attacks were always swift, sudden and masterfully executed. He never failed to inspire the men, to fire them with eagerness to engage the enemy, to fill them with confidence in victory and in their weapons. In their turn, the men were prepared to follow him anywhere.

He was born for the sea. His best years and his greatest accomplishments were linked up with the sea. And the sea became his grave.

By a decree of October 23, 1942, Kerim was posthumously decorated with the title of Hero of the Soviet Union.

Captain 2nd Rank Victor Kotelnikov became the new commander of 1st Division.

A Duel of Nerves

With the onset of spring the enemy light infantry in the North came out of their winter hibernation. Hitler appointed General List commander in Finland. The Lapland group was reinforced with additional aircraft, for the Germans were planning a new offensive on Murmansk. The town was bombed continuously, and, with the exception of the port and the ship-repair yards, it was reduced to heaps of rubble.

Aiming to disrupt the offensive, Headquarters of the Supreme Commander-in-Chief ordered 14th Army and the Northern Fleet to begin active operations at the close of April against the German troops on the maritime flank. Here the objective was to rout and destroy the enemy 2nd and 6th infantry divisions.

A frontal attack by infantry and the landing of the 12th Marine Brigade near Motovsky Bay were decided upon with the objective of breaching the enemy defenses. The brigade, with its light arms and field artillery, was successfully landed despite the extremely difficult conditions and the icy water. This was the result of short but intensive training. By May 1, the task force widened its bridgehead. There was heavy fighting, with both sides constantly attacking.

The 14th Army, which was advancing from the Western Litsa, was unable to break through the powerful German defenses. The task force went over to the defensive, suffering heavy casualties. By decision of the Karelian Front Command it was evacuated in the course of May 12 and 13 to the eastern bank of Malaya Bay in the Western Litsa.

The objective set by General Headquarters proved to be unattainable because of the enemy's numerical superiority. We were unable to dislodge the two infantry divisions. But the end purpose of the operation was achieved. The enemy could not now even dream of an offensive not only against Murmansk but even against Sredny Peninsula, from which our artillery harassed shipping in Petsamo Bay.

Our fleet played a big role in these battles. Surface vessels landed the task force and supported it with fire from the sea. Naval aircraft covered the landing from the air. That, of course, insured its success. Lastly, 12th Brigade was composed of our men.

As regards our submariners, they continued wrecking the enemy's communications. In their preparations for the offensive and then in repelling our attacks, the Nazis were compelled to make more extensive use of their sea lanes. Consequently, in April and May we knew not only the bitterness of loss but also the happiness of victory.

Utkin and Bibeyev each fired a salute when they returned to Polyarnoye—K-2 had torpedoed a transport and laid a mine field in enemy waters. Andrei Zharov was her artillery officer. He had been transferred from P-422, winning a promotion. Petty Officer Dryapikov, whose heroic action had helped to keep P-421 afloat after she had struck a mine, was appointed in charge of torpedoes.

D-3, commanded by Bibeyev, went on patrol carrying Brigade Chief-of-Staff Captain 2nd Rank Boris Skorokhvatov as Instructor Commander.

The outbreak of war found Skorokhvatov serving in the Pacific. When the Germans started their offensive against Moscow, he volunteered to form a marine brigade as part of forces defending the capital. He became its first commander. The marines gave a good account of themselves during the December offensive. But by that time Boris was no longer in command of the brigade. He was an experienced submariner and knew the ins and outs of staff work, and in November he was recalled to the navy and sent to us, in the North, as a successor to Avgustinovich, who had been given command of a large submarine.

For the Chief-of-Staff this was the first operational patrol. The "old lady" came into contact with the enemy three times, and on each occasion Bibeyev led her into an attack. The torpedoes found their mark, sinking one transport and disabling two others.

All of us were delighted with the successes of 4th Division.

Midgets stay at sea a week at most. While Pikes and Katyushas were on patrol, Midgets would complete two and sometimes three patrols. But even a short cruise in these submarines exhausts the men. The sea tosses the Midgets as though they were corks. The cramped space adds to the men's hardships. Besides, the crew is only big enough for a double-shift watch. In other words, to use the vernacular, the men had a twelve-hour working day. To this must be added the alarms, the attacks and the bombings when the entire crew are at battle stations. In short, there is very little time for leisure. Yet when they return to the base, the Midgets do not stay long if no repairs are required.

In April and May, three of our Midgets completed eleven patrols between them. These submarines—M-171, M-172 and M-176—torpedoed thirteen vessels.

Some of these patrols are worth mentioning.

Starikov, for example, came to grips with a patrol ship. It happened like this. M-171 torpedoed a transport, eluded pursuit, which lasted for three hours, and finally surfaced to recharge her batteries because there was almost no energy left to allow her to proceed under water. But when M-171 surfaced she found an enemy patrol ship only about fifty cable-lengths away. The enemy at once attacked, opening up with his guns.

What had Starikov to do? Dive? But under water he would be almost immobile and the patrol ship would easily find and sink him with depth charges. The captain decided to sail surfaced to Rybachy, where he would get cover from our shore batteries. It was by no means a short journey.

The submarine steered a course toward our shore. The diesels developed their top speed of twelve knots in record time. But the patrol ship was faster, of course, and gradually drew ever nearer, sending salvo after salvo at the submarine.

To avoid being hit, Starikov steered an irregular, zigzag course, keeping the enemy on his swing angles. The submarine was unable to use the 45 mm gun in her bow—had she attempted it she would have exposed her side to an enemy salvo.

The captain displayed remarkable self-control. Psychologically it would have been much easier to accept battle, even if it was unequal and there was little chance of victory, than to proceed helplessly under enemy fire.

This harrowing pursuit lasted for more than an hour. Luckily not a single one of the 100 mm shells hit the submarine. Near the zone of action of our shore batteries the patrol ship did not risk giving further chase and turned back.

Fisanovich too had been forced to seek the protection of our batteries. But the circumstances were much more dramatic.

M-172 came across an enemy convoy near Ekkerei Island. The transport selected by Fisanovich was heavily guarded. To make sure of hitting it, Fisanovich dived under the escort vessels and found himself in the middle of the enemy convoy. He fired from a distance of three cable-lengths, hitting his target.

But the submarine was discovered and chased. Depth charges exploded near her, putting out the lights and crippling the gyrocompass. But the worst part of it was that the diesel oil tank sprang a leak, and the submarine began leaving a treacherous trail on the surface. In addition, the power reserve in her batteries was small. This meant that she could not move at her normal speed.

Using his magnetic compass Fisanovich steered toward Rybachy. The explosions shook the submarine. The sailors worked on the damage using flashlights. The submarine was kept at her cruising depth with enormous difficulty. Hydrophone operator Anatoly Shumikhin nearly went deaf from the explosions, but he did not for a moment take off his earphones. His reports allowed Fisanovich to take his bearings in the situation and elude his attackers, for a direct hit would have been fatal. The regeneration system failed and it became increasingly more difficult to breathe. Luckily, Brigade Flag Surgeon Major Gusinsky was on board and he strewed the contents of the regeneration cartridges in the compartments. That brought some relief.

This nightmare journey continued for ten hours. The enemy dropped three hundred and forty-two depth charges. Yet the submarine reached the cover of our shore batteries, and the enemy ships were compelled to turn back.

This same period witnessed another noteworthy episode in which M-172 played the main role. It was interesting chiefly from the viewpoint of tactics and the ability of the sailors to take more from machinery than it was called upon to give.

The submarine was patrolling an area near Kibergnes. Visibility was down to a few tens of meters due to a snowstorm. In this weather it was only Shumikhin's keen hearing that helped to detect a target. Among the many-voiced sighs of the sea he caught a sound that unquestionably came from the propellers of a fast vessel.

At this point, I must note that in those days our sonars could give only the direction of a sound source in the water, without indicating the distance to it. Hydrolocators, which solved this problem, had not yet been supplied to our ships. For a torpedo attack it was necessary to know both the direction and the distance. That was why an attack without the aid of a periscope, with data only from the sound-tracker, was regarded as a fairly hopeless venture.

However, a skilled hydrophone operator could determine the course of a moving ship with greater accuracy than was allowed by his apparatus, and even give the approximate distance to it. Anatoly Shumikhin had the gift and the training. The captain knew how dependable he was and decided to attack the ship. The submarine set a course towards the invisible target.

Twenty-eight minutes passed. As before, nothing could be seen in the periscope which was plastered with wind-driven snow. Yet the computations showed that it was time to swing into an attack course. Fisanovich started the swing. Another six minutes passed—it was time to fire. But the enemy remained invisible. Worrying, his mind full of doubts whether to believe or not to believe in success, the captain changed his course. This allowed delaying the salvo. Fisanovich hoped that at the last minute the target would heave into sight and disperse his doubts.

The silhouette of a large ship displacing about ten thousand tons loomed out of the snow at the end of the third minute after the submarine began its swing. The ship was moving in exactly the course that had been computed on the basis of Shumikhin's reports. Fisanovich did not have to correct his own course. Three minutes later two torpedoes struck the enemy.

This was the first periscope sonar attack in the fleet. It was accomplished years before such attacks became usual for our submarines.

Anatoly Shumikhin was the hero of the day. A hard-working, disciplined sailor, he had wonderfully developed his natural ability, his musical ear. Without this natural gift one could not become a good sound-tracker no matter how one tried.

In the brigade we selected our hydrophone operators carefully, for they were indispensable assistants of the captain on a patrol, during an attack and during post-attack maneuvers. As a rule, our hydrophone operators coped with their duties superbly.

Hydrophone operator Adamyuk made a large contribution to the noteworthy battle under Captain 3rd Rank Joseph Bondarevich. News of that battle spread throughout the brigade like lightning.

Joseph Bondarevich of M-176 was our most successful submarine captain during the spring patrols. In his five patrols that spring he torpedoed six ships. Of these attacks the most spectacular was accomplished at the close of May.

Toward dusk on May 28, M-176 was recharging her batteries about twenty-five miles away from the Norwegian shore. The captain was on the bridge with Coxswain Gordii. An aircraft suddenly appeared from behind the clouds. It described a circle over the submarine and turned shoreward. The coxswain did not follow the aircraft with an idle gaze, as a novice would have done, but by force of habit continued scrutinizing the sea in his sector. This habit was rewarded. In the distance Gordii saw a black object, which he immediately reported to the captain, "Starboard 60, range 30! Comrade Captain, it's either a torpedo boat or the conning tower of a submarine!"

Bondarevich saw that it was an enemy U-boat and ordered M-176 into an emergency dive.

It was 18.22 hours.

The U-boat dived almost at the same time as M-176. Our submarine's torpedo tubes were ready for firing. But what was the use? Bondarevich could not permit himself to fire without being certain of his target, without seeing the enemy. He had only two torpedoes. The enemy was a medium-sized U-boat with at least ten torpedoes. Bondarevich, therefore, could not afford to expose himself to an attack. But there was little doubt that the enemy would attack and Bondarevich acted on this assumption. He took M-176 to a depth of forty meters and ordered Adamyuk to report the U-boat's location every minute.

Hardly had the submarine reached the set depth than Adamyuk cried out that the enemy had fired two torpedoes. They passed high overhead—M-176 was safely at a forty-meter level.

An unprecedented underwater duel began, and it all depended on whose nerves were stronger.

Bondarevich maneuvered his submarine at three knots, constantly changing course and depth and provoking the enemy to attack him. In the end the U-boat commander's nerve failed him and he fired another two torpedoes.

Then followed a period of caution on the part of the enemy. He likewise maneuvered, either attempting to get into position to fire a salvo or hoping that our submarine would fire her torpedoes. Time dragged on slowly. An hour went by. It became more and more difficult to breathe. But the men did not notice it. They had never been so close to death before. But instead of breeding fear it only braced the men. The crew waited tensely for orders, and nobody doubted that whatever orders would be given would be correct. They had always had implicit faith in Bondarevich, and more so now than ever before.

Petty Officer 2nd Class Adamyuk monotonously reported the enemy's position, and then suddenly called out, "The fifth torpedo! The sixth!"

"He's getting rattled," Bondarevich thought with satisfaction. He pictured the German captain to himself. Like him, he was getting regular reports from his hydrophone operator, and was hardly able to restrain his fury against the invulnerable enemy submarine, which was keeping silent for a suspiciously long time.

Bondarevich had on several occasions nearly succumbed to the temptation to fire at least one of his torpedoes, feeling that he could not miss. He argued that even if he missed he would frighten the enemy and provoke him into firing again.

"Seventh... eighth..." Adamyuk counted. At last he pronounced the long-awaited word:

"Tenth!"

This meant that the enemy had used up all his torpedoes.

Bondarevich wiped the sweat off his forehead with his sleeve. The duel had entered its fourth hour.

"The U-boat is surfacing!"

With a habitual glance at his watch Bondarevich noted that the time was 21.48 hours, and thought, *The German has probably decided that we have no torpedoes*. He ordered the submarine up to periscope depth. At 21.50 hours he saw the U-boat in the periscope. The course angle was favorable for an attack, the distance being not more than eight cablelengths. His torpedomen were already standing by and he at once ordered both tubes to fire.

Sixty-eight seconds later everybody in the submarine heard a sharp explosion. Adamyuk, naturally, heard more: the reverberation of air and some strange noises.

The U-boat disappeared from the surface. The noise from its propeller stopped. Only air continued to reverberate. But even that sound ceased fifteen minutes later.

The Soviet captain had won this underwater duel of nerves. We were proud of Bondarevich and his crew, appreciating fully how difficult it was for our submariners to defeat an experienced, dangerous and much stronger enemy. Today, when modern technical means have brought recognition to the idea of submarines fighting submarines, it is quite in order to recall that battle of more than twenty years ago. Battles like it laid the foundation for tactics of the future.

Graduation

One of the most pleasant feelings that a person can have, I think, is that of a teacher who is satisfied that his pupil can make his way independently in the sea of life. I have never been a teacher in the professional sense of the word, but I know that feeling. Many aspects of the work of a commander and a teacher are similar. I had devoted many years of my life to my work, and I have had to send pupils out not into the figurative sea of life but into real independent voyages in a real sea.

I experienced this pleasure when I congratulated Konstantin Shuisky on the receipt of an order from the Commander-in-Chief permitting him to go on independent operational patrols.

P-403, which had been rammed by the enemy, was recommissioned after a "course of treatment" in Murmansk, and then Shuisky himself had to be settled into his command, for a period of three years had elapsed since he had commanded a submarine. True, he had made up for some of the lost time as first lieutenant in a Katyusha. Moreover, he had gained much new experience, for patrols under combat conditions had only some external aspects of peace-time sailing. Each patrol was a school in itself.

Yet, a submarine captain required training that could not be got in any other capacity. Shuisky had to be put through that training.

I'll never forget the day P-403 slid down the slips into the water. We were setting a course toward Polyarnoye when the air-raid sirens began to wail. The AA guns in Murmansk and on the ships opened up. Enemy bombers shrieked in the air over us, and fighters went up to intercept them. An air battle raged. Several tens of aircraft circled in the blue, twilightless sky. One of the Junkers suddenly traced a smoky arc over the gulf and plunged into the water some distance away from us. A moment later another bomber, spouting tongues of flame, also began dropping like a stone. A single glance was enough to tell that it was falling directly on us.

"Full speed astern!" I shouted to the captain. The water churned up at the stern, washed over the deck, absorbing the submarine's forward momentum. We stopped and moved slowly back. The bomber hit the water directly in front of us, raising a column of water.

Then, suddenly, there was silence. The all clear was sounded. . . .

We sailed to Polyarnoye.

The period of training passed quickly. The submarine completed all her tests, and Shuisky carried out all his training assignments. On June 1, Brigade Assistant Liaison Officer Engineer-Lieutenant-Captain Frenkel and I took our kitbags aboard P-403.

We set sail on a quiet, bleak evening. A north-westerly, which had blown continuously for several days, had put up a swell on the sea. Huge, blue-green waves with mirror-smooth surfaces rose and fell. The submarine rolled heavily and rhythmically. This rolling was hard to endure if you were not used to it.

We dived after passing Rybachy, for enemy U-boats were known to be prowling in this area.

Senior Political Instructor Kulyasov, the new Commissar, went through all the compartments where he told the men what our assignments were on this patrol. He also told them of the situation in Sevastopol, which was now attracting the country's attention. The Black Sea fortress was fighting with its back to the wall. As military men, we realized that our troops there would not hold out much longer. We were having a much easier time of it here, in the North, despite the whims of the stern climate. The situation on the Northern Front was incomparably more stable than anywhere else, and our bases were well-organized.

The weather changed when we got to our area. A wind rose, stirring up a choppy sea. It was what we wanted. This was the kind of sea that did not worry a submarine much, and it was hard to spot either a periscope or the track of a torpedo in it.

We prowled in our area all day on June 3. Shuisky was in an excellent mood, laughing and joking. It was the job he had been waiting for.

He had quickly won his crew's respect. He did not regard them as simply the "ship's company," and had already come to know many of them quite well. In their turn, the men saw that though the captain was easy to get along with, he was strict where duty was concerned. He was not a fault-finder, but he never passed by any dereliction of duty. Without raising his voice he would pass a remark in such a tone of voice as to make the man concerned want to sink through the floor. If Shuisky showed the same quality in battle he would be assured of the men's devotion and affection.

It was past 18.00 hours when the hydrophone operator reported the noise of propellers. About forty cable-lengths away from us a large transport was steaming under escort of three mine sweepers and two submarine chasers. Glancing at Shuisky I saw not the good-natured man I knew but a grim fighter with a hardened face. Throughout the attack he was collected, capable and efficient. I hardly had to correct him.

We drew up to within twelve cable-lengths of the transport and fired four torpedoes at intervals of six seconds.

After the fourth torpedo I had to order the coxswain, "Take her down to forty meters!"

Although the escort vessels did not see us, one of the mine sweepers was on a course that put P-403 in danger of experiencing all the charms of being rammed once more. It was something none of us were very eager about.

We heard a loud bang fifty-eight seconds after we fired our salvo. Fourteen seconds later there was another explosion. Soon afterward eight depth charges went off somewhere far astern of us—it was the submarine chasers looking for us.

When we surveyed the horizon we found no trace of the transport. The mine sweepers could be seen in the distance, and the chasers were creeping about the area of attack.

"Congratulations, Captain," I said shaking hands with Shuisky. He beamed, becoming once more his merry and witty self. He was pleased with his men and submarine, and somewhat embarrassed about his own self.

It was a promising beginning. Our first day on patrol had been a complete success. We had not even had to go through the agony of being bombed.

The next three days were uneventful. We had to sail dived for ever longer periods, for the polar day was at its height. It was a terrible strain on our hydrophone operators. Their job of sitting with earphones and listening to the voices of the sea looked easy. But the nervous tension was colossal.

A medical commission headed by Professor Prikladovitsky had checked up on the health of submariners at our base. They weighed, sounded and measured the men before and after patrols. I was particularly struck by one of the conclusions drawn by them. On patrol, the captain and the hydrophone operators have to bear the greatest nervous strain. They even lose weight. On the other hand, the rest of the men do not lose any weight, in fact some even gain weight—due to the lack of exercise.

Hard as our hydrophone operators strained their hearing they did not hear any foreign noises. There was nothing to be seen through the periscope either.

We surfaced and posted extra look-outs. One of them was Senior Military Surgeon's Assistant Kamensky, who was extremely dependable. He put his heart into whatever he did, whether it was his direct duty as first-aid man or that of a look-out. Actually, he was our ship's doctor, Senior Military Surgeon's Assistant being his official title. If somebody were to omit calling him doctor, he would have been extremely surprised and even somewhat hurt.

As I have already said, surgeon's assistants were called doctors throughout the submarine service. This innocent exaggeration was a tribute to their modest but selfless work. On the other hand, at sea, far from the shore, the surgeon's assistant was the only medical man in a submarine and, essentially, performed the duties of a doctor. He had to keep an eye on the crew's health, provide medical aid to anybody who fell ill or was wounded, and supervise the quality of the food. In addition, he was responsible for the ventilation and the drinking water, and had to make sure that the air humidity was right and that the oxygen and hydrogen content in it was normal. At the base, he supervized the receipt of food for the entire period of a patrol, and then gave an account of it, in other words, he performed commissary duties. In addition, many surgeon's assistants were used at the hydroplane helm or as messengers during an attack.

The crew thought highly of Kamensky. He kept himself abreast of developments in the medical world, reading and re-reading textbooks and manuals. When the submarine was at the base he cheerfully did spells of duty at the hospital, seeing it as an opportunity of gaining practical experience.

Such was our doctor. He volunteered to act as an additional look-out. But neither he nor any of the other look-outs had any luck on that patrol. The days followed each other monotonously, the only change being in the weather which sometimes "pampered us" with snowfalls despite the fact that it was June.

At last, on June 11, the hydrophone operator helped us out: at 05.30 hours he heard the noise of propellers. Judging by the sound it was a transport. But the whirling snow hid it from us.

"Take your bearings from the sound," I advised Shuisky.

The submarine turned and blindly groped her way toward the target. When we were some thirty cable-lengths away, visibility improved and through the now scattering snow we saw the outlines of a transport of about five thousand tons. Shuisky went into an attack course, firing four torpedoes from a distance of ten cable-lengths. Soon, with an interval of seven seconds, there were two explosions. The pair of minesweepers escorting the transport did not give chase. But the snow, which began falling with redoubled fury, did not allow us to check on the results of the attack. Moreover, the hydrophone operator heard the noise of a vessel which, judging by its location, was entering a nearby bay. We never knew if it was the transport torpedoed by us or some other ship.

That evening we were ordered home.

In my report to the Brigade Commander I said that Shuisky had shown all the qualities of a competent submarine captain and that I was confident he could carry on independently.

Konstantin Shuisky justified my confidence in him. Among other decorations he won two Orders of the Red Banner and was one of the first naval officers to receive the Order of Alexander Nevsky. Under him P-403 was awarded the Order of the Red Banner in 1943.

At the close of 1942, Shuisky went on five independent patrols. During the first of them he did not meet the enemy, but when he was returning to the base, he was attacked by a U-boat. Three large air bubbles on the sea surface and then the tracks of three torpedoes racing toward the Pike were noticed by Shilinsky, who was officer-of-the-watch on the bridge. The lesson he had learned in the battle that had ended with Kovalenko's death now stood him in good stead. Without losing any time, he maneuvered the submarine strictly in accordance with the rules covering just such a contingency. That saved the submarine.

On the next patrol, Shuisky attacked the enemy twice, damaging one transport and sinking another. In the chase after these attacks the enemy dropped one hundred and eighteen depth charges. But the captain proved to be equal to the situation. The Pike escaped from her pursuers with little damage. The third patrol was unsuccessful. After scouring the sea futilely for three weeks, the submarine was again attacked by a U-boat. And once again she was saved by the vigilance and skill of the officer-of-the-watch. This time it was the First Lieutenant Shipin.

The fourth and fifth patrols gave the Pike victories which cost the enemy a mine sweeper and a large transport.

At the very end of the year the submarine underwent repairs. She had to have new hydrophone apparatus and batteries, her engines had to be overhauled, and her mauled casing straightened.

NORWEGIAN SEA

Nordkapp

Ingö I.

Hammerfest

Porsangen Fjord

Lopo Sea

Arnøy I.

Skerries

Alten Fjord

Tromsö

N O R W A Y

L A P L

N O

S W E D E N

F I N

TROMSÖ TO
MURMANSK

Nautical Miles

0 10 20 30 40 50 60

WE BUILD UP PRESSURE

Five Lines

On the evening of July 8, 1942, the Soviet Information Bureau reported: "In the Barents Sea one of our submarines attacked the new German battleship *Tirpitz*, hitting it with two torpedoes and extensively damaging it."

This report took up only five lines in the newspaper. But these five lines had a whole story behind them.

At the time, the burden of the war had shifted to the South. On July 3, the Supreme Command ordered our troops and naval units to abandon Sevastopol, putting an end to an unparalleled, eight months' defense. Furious battles were raging on the Volga and in the Caucasian foothills. But it was obvious that the Germans were not what they had been a year before. It was now beyond them to maintain an offensive along the entire front from the Baltic to the Black Sea.

There was another lull in the North after the spring fighting on land. But at sea the Nazis had to become much more active. Large naval forces—a squadron consisting of the battleship *Tirpitz*, the pocket battleships *Admiral Scheer* and *Lützow*, the heavy cruiser *Admiral Hipper*, the light cruisers *Köln* and *Nürnberg* and more than ten destroyers, a flotilla of torpedo boats and nearly thirty patrol ships and mine sweepers—were being mustered in Norwegian ports. The number of German U-boats increased to forty, and nearly three hundred naval bombers and torpedo carriers were committed. This armada was spearheaded at our external communications. Moreover, the Germans strengthened their anti-submarine defenses—we had already had a taste of it.

We lost two more submarines—M-176 and D-3. Only recently we had rejoiced over the victories scored by Bondarevich in his Midget. Now we had to get used to the thought of never seeing him and his courageous crew again, and also the grand crew of the Northern Fleet's "old lady," which had been the first in the navy to win the title of Guards Submarine and the Order of the Red Banner. They were, without exaggeration, the best crew in the brigade: they were all Communists and all had had superb training.

But the largest losses were, of course, suffered by Allied convoys, and the reason for this was not that the enemy had become stronger or more energetic.

Very indicative in this respect was the story of convoy PQ-17. It has been dealt with quite thoroughly, but it is well worth going into again.

PQ-17 sailed from Iceland on June 17. It consisted of thirty-six transports flying the flags of the Soviet Union, the U.S.A., Great Britain and Panama, and twenty-one escort vessels. Moreover, the convoy had two powerful covering groups of U.S. and British warships. The immediate support task force consisted of the cruisers *London, Norfolk, Wichita*

U.S.S. Washington

and *Tuscaloosa*, and the outer task force had the aircraft
carrier *Victorious*, the battleships *Duke of York* and *Washington*,
the cruisers *Cumberland* and *Nigeria* and nine destroyers.
This was sufficient cover to beat back the German northern
squadron.

Under this escort the convoy had to proceed to Medvezhy
Island, from where ships of the Soviet Northern Fleet would
take over.

We energetically prepared for the assignment. As always,
submarines were deployed in the distant approaches to ward
off surface ships. But the events that our former Allies try to
forget unfolded long before the convoy reached our zone.

At about 03.00 hours on July 4, the first wave of German
torpedo carriers attacked the convoy. Though many aircraft
were involved, the attack was not very skilfully executed with
the result that only one transport was sunk. It probably
would not have required much effort to save the ship, but
none of the crews wanted to tempt fate. Besides, the British
Admiralty considered it right to finish off damaged vessels so
as not to reduce the speed of a convoy and thereby expose it
to unnecessary danger from aircraft and submarines.

The crew was taken off the torpedoed vessel, which was
then sunk by escort ships.

The convoy was again attacked by aircraft at about 18.30
hours. Twenty-four German torpedo carriers took part in this
attack. Once more the result was meager. Two Allied transports and the Soviet motor vessel *Azerbaijan* were hit. As in
the early case, the first two vessels were sunk by escort ships.
On the *Azerbaijan* the crew patched up the holes, extinguished the fire and the ship took up her position in the
convoy.

In the meantime *Tirpitz, Admiral Scheer* and a number of
destroyers were on their way to intercept the convoy. British
intelligence reported that large enemy warships had left their
Norwegian bases. This report was received by the British
Admiralty. The decision that it took was not dictated by
concern for the safety of the convoy or by considerations of
military honor. At 23.00 hours the convoy commander was
ordered by the Admiralty to send the convoy destroyers to
strengthen the screen for the aircraft carrier and to deconcentrate the transports with instructions to sail to Soviet ports on
their own.

Thus, the convoy was dispersed before it reached our zone

of operations. Moreover, the Soviet Northern Fleet Command was not even informed of this more than strange decision and therefore could not take timely steps to protect the undefended convoy.

Two groups of transports headed for Novaya Zemlya. Other ships, sailing singly, made for Kola Bay and the neck of the White Sea. But this was a futile attempt. The ships were easy prey for Nazi U-boats and aircraft, and many of them never reached their destination.

What had been the military expediency of this decision of the British Naval Command? Undisguised fear of losing combat units in an engagement with the Nazi squadron? Or an attempt to build up the greatest numerical superiority at all costs, even at the cost of a convoy, to whose fate the Lords of the Admiralty were evidently completely indifferent? Or, lastly, that the convoy was doomed from the very beginning, that it was used as bait for the German squadron, which the British planned to lure farther out to sea and attack with superior forces?

Without knowing the real, secret reasons of the British Staff it is useless to try to hazard guesses. The curtain might have been lifted by the actions of the British had the Nazi squadron attacked the convoy. But no such attack took place. And that, too, was not fortuitous.

Vice-Admiral Friedrich Ruge of the Federal German Republic, who was a rear-admiral in the Nazi navy, touches on this point in his comprehensive and highly tendentious *War at Sea, 1939-45*. He writes: "It is worth noting how powerful the effect was of solely the news that these German warships (*Tirpitz, Admiral Scheer* and eight destroyers—*I.K.*) had appeared. As a matter of fact, they returned to their base very soon afterward, because the exact location of the British aircraft carrier was not established, and, as a consequence of this, our aircraft had no opportunity of attacking it. Hitler allowed the surface ships to engage in battle only on condition that the aircraft carrier was put out of action first."

But Friedrich Ruge had no desire whatever to stick to facts, which, understandably, do not afford him any pleasure. What really happened was as follows.

On July 5, K-21, which was patrolling an area near Ingö Island, received a radiogram from the Fleet Commander-in-Chief stating that a Nazi squadron was at sea. The radiogram ordered all submarines to hunt it down and attack it.

Lunin had been on patrol for a fairly long time—K-21 had left Polyarnoye on June 18. The continuous polar day, the quiet sea, and the aircraft that kept diving from behind clouds made it a difficult patrol. On the day after the submarine left her base, one of these aircraft gave her some anxious minutes. Lieutenant Martynov, who was officer-of-the-watch, delayed ordering an emergency dive. Two bombs exploded about thirty meters away from K-21 and machine-gun bullets swept across her casing, damaging her trimming system. Water began penetrating into the first trimming and the quick-diving tank. The submarine might as well have returned to her base. But nobody wanted to hear of such an inglorious end to the patrol. Engineering Officer Vladimir Braman, as on other occasions, found a way out of this seemingly hopeless situation. He suggested filling both damaged tanks with water, emptying one of the for'ard torpedo tubes and compensating this by adding water to the bow trimming tank. When that was done the submarine behaved well under water.

The hunt for the enemy yielded nothing, and on June 27 Lunin was ordered to a new area to act as cover for PQ-17. In that area he was informed that the German squadron had put out to sea.

The submarine recharged her batteries and at 16.06 hours proceeded submerged on a course of 182 degrees. At 16.33 hours hydrophone operator Smetanin heard the noise of propellers to starboard of the bow. Lunin ordered the submarine into an attack course and readied all his torpedo tubes for action. At 17.12 hours two destroyers were sighted through the periscope. They were moving in formation in the van of the squadron. Six minutes later Lunin saw the masts of large ships. In another five minutes he could recognize the *Tirpitz* and *Admiral Scheer* surrounded by escorting destroyers.

Lunin selected the *Tirpitz* as his main target. Commissioned in 1939, it was one of Germany's newest warships. Its artillery, consisting of eight 380 mm, twelve 150 mm, fifteen 105 mm and sixteen 37 mm guns, commanded respect. It displaced fifty-three tons and had a top speed of thirty knots.

The timidity of the British in the face of this formidable adversary could be understood. About a year before, when they had the numerical superiority, they hunted the *Bismarck* down in the North Atlantic. It was in the same class as the *Tirpitz* and sold its life dearly. The British battle cruiser *Hood* engaged it in an artillery duel and within five minutes received a direct hit in its magazine and was blown out of existence. The *Bismarck* inflicted enormous damage on the *Prince of Wales* as well, but was sunk after receiving several score of heavy shells and at least half a dozen torpedoes in its side.

The *Tirpitz* was the *Bismarck*'s sister ship. Nikolai Lunin was well aware that even his most successful salvo would not sink the battleship. But by disabling it, by forcing it out of action he would remove a terrible threat to the Allied convoy. Moreover, this would for a long time deprive the Nazi surface forces in the North of their main strike force and thereby somewhat alter the entire situation in our theater. In the circumstances, his decision to attack the battleship was absolutely correct.

To make sure of hitting the *Tirpitz*, the submarine had to dive under the escorting destroyers. Lunin began maneuvering for an attack. The squadron was performing an anti-submarine zigzag, and Lunin had to wait for his opportunity. Despite the risk of detection he raised his periscope fifteen times in order to correct his course.

At 17.36 hours the ships turned 90 degrees to port. K-21 found herself on a counter-course with the battleship. Lunin swerved to starboard in order to go into an attack course and fire his bow torpedoes at the *Tirpitz*.

The tension in the submarine mounted. Everybody realized the importance of what was happening. None of our submarines had had to break through such a powerful screen and, consequently, none of them had faced such overwhelming danger. Besides, none of them had had the chance of attacking a large warship. In this situation everything was new and unusual. The men could hardly believe that everything was turning out so well.

The battleship's course angle reached 55 degrees. Lunin had three minutes in which to fire his torpedoes. The men's hearts beat wildly. Then, as Lunin raised the periscope and put his eye to it his expression changed. Signal flags were fluttering on the battleship's yard—it was a detail that could only have been discerned by a trained eye such as Lunin's. The signals could only mean that a new course had been ordered. The problem was to guess it.

"I only hope they don't turn to port," Nikolai muttered. A turn to portside would have wrecked the attack. He raised his periscope again and could not help smiling. The squadron had turned to starboard. The submarine still had a chance of striking a blow. But the battleship's course angle of 5-7 degrees had become much too sharp despite the fact that it was now nearer to the submarine. Lunin did not risk starting a long sweep for another angle of fire, for the squadron might again take up a new course. Instead he started changing the reciprocal position of the ships by the shortest means, lining the battleship up for a stern salvo.

True, the stern had four and not six torpedo tubes, as in the bow, but the situation forced him into this tactical loss.

At 18.01 hours the submarine fired four torpedoes at the *Tirpitz* at intervals of four seconds from a distance of seventeen cable-lengths. Lunin dived as soon as the torpedoes were fired, sharply veering the submarine off her course. The hydrophone operator clearly heard the propellers of the destroyers churning the water overhead.

Tirpitz

In two minutes fifteen seconds the men in all the compartments distinctly heard two explosions. There were sighs of relief.

The escort did not discover the submarine after the attack. Sixteen minutes passed before three dull rumbles were heard somewhere in the distance.

At 19.09 hours, when K-21 rose to periscope depth, there was nothing to be seen on the horizon. Lunin ordered Chief Wireless Operator Gorbunoy to report the attack on the *Tirpitz* to the Commander-in-Chief.

On the next day Soviet reconnaissance aircraft spotted the enemy squadron near the Norwegian coast. It had given up its intention of striking at the convoy and was returning home. Soon, according to British intelligence reports, the *Tirpitz* was docked for repairs. . . .

No matter what orders of Hitler Friedrich Ruge now cites, it was clear to us at the time that the commander of the German squadron could not go into battle after the battleship had been torpedoed and there was the threat of other torpedo strikes.

K-21 accomplished what the British either hesitated or did not wish to do: she blocked the road for the enemy's main forces, compelling them to turn back and thereby saving PQ-17 from complete disaster.

Lunin's attack was most carefully analyzed by the Brigade Command. His action was recognized as having been correct and as having conformed with the situation. All of us paid tribute to his courage and self-control. Shortly after this K-21 was decorated with the Order of the Red Banner.

These were the events behind the terse communique issued by the Soviet Information Bureau.*

A New Captain

Many submarines took part in the operation to cover PQ-17. I was in one of them, P-422, which had a new Captain in Vidayev.

In June when I returned from a patrol with Shuisky, I learned with surprise that while we had been away Malyshev

*As the result of postwar re-evaluations Western naval historians are unable to substantiate this claim.

had been relieved of his command of P-422 and court-martialed for cowardice.

To this day I really cannot understand what happened to him. On a patrol in January, when I had been with him, he had displayed courage in hunting and attacking the enemy, and there had not been a shade of confusion in his actions when the submarine dropped like a stone to the accompaniment of exploding depth charges.

He had been on patrol several times after that and each time he had returned with his torpedoes unspent although he had had ample opportunity to use them. Senior Political Instructor Dubik, the submarine's Commissar, who knew the captain well, could not deny that the latter's action in the face of the enemy bore the stamp of excessive, inexplicable caution.

In June, Malyshev went on patrol with a new Commissar, Senior Political Instructor Tabenkin. A radiogram was soon received from Tabenkin requesting the submarine's recall in view of the captain's palpable cowardice.

What happened was that when the submarine's gyrocompass went out of commission, Malyshev, who had been divisional navigator, undertook personally to repair it. But after the repairs the compass became useless.

I was told that at the court-martial Malyshev admitted having had deliberately damaged the compass, fearing to carry on with his patrol. I did not get all the details, for before I returned from patrol the building in which prisoners were held was hit during an enemy air-raid. Malyshev was killed.

What was the explanation for what had happened? The accusation brought against Malyshev might have been hasty or insufficiently founded. But he had unquestionably given grounds for it. I have no cause to doubt the opinion of men who were struck by his excessive caution, or timidity, or indecision, or cowardice—the essence here was in objective actions and not in a subjective interpretation of these actions.

All I can surmise is that the fierce bombing during the patrol in January, when the submarine was a hair's breadth away from destruction, had broken Malyshev morally. The loss of M-175 and then of other submarines had been the final psychological jolt making him lose his nerve.

. . . Thus, Vidayev, who had been in the reserve after the loss of P-421 and had been pining for the sea in his various capacities in the brigade, was given a ship.

We left Polyarnoye on July 6, after Lunin's attack on the *Tirpitz*, when, to all intents and purposes, the task given to our submarines had been carried out. The patrol was therefore unsuccessful. We did not meet enemy warships. On the other hand we were harassed by aircraft. Time and again we had to crash-dive to avoid attack from the air.

On that patrol there was only one episode worth mentioning. The submarine was sailing on the surface in good, clear weather, and the situation at sea was calm, when suddenly, the officer-of-the-watch cried out from the bridge, "Request Divisional Commander and the captain to come up on the bridge!"

In the navy this sort of "request" is categorical. Ship's Rules provide for only one formula for calling the captain to the bridge, and its wording is: "Request captain on the bridge." Naturally, this formula is not used to ask the captain to admire the scenery. "Request captain on the bridge" meant that the officer-of-the-watch was unable either to orient himself in the situation independently or to prevent disaster. In any case, the formula remains the same, the only difference being in the intonation of the voice. Naturally, upon hearing this "request" the captain rushes to the bridge, fearing the worst.

Vidayev and I acted accordingly—we wasted no time getting to the bridge.

"Comrade Divisional Commander," the officer-of-the-watch reported excitedly, "a Midget surfaced about ten cablelengths away on starboard course 90 and at once dived."

"A Midget in the Norwegian Sea?" I said unbelievingly. "How could it have got here? You must have imagined it."

"No. It blew its middle tank, then refilled it. I even saw the fountain."

Just then the look-out reported a mysterious submarine surfacing on starboard course 45. We watched it, and I soon identified it. The "submarine" was nothing more nor less than a whale. We had never encountered these giants in the Norwegian Sea. Hitherto we had seen only grampuses, which were their kin.

We watched the whale diving and surfacing. Then, as though tiring of this game, it increased speed, outstripping us and disappearing.

We returned to the base after an absence of twenty-one days.

Fyodor Vidayev quickly settled into his command of P-422. Officially, this was simple, entailing only the signing of an order. But there was another side to it. A captain had to merge with his crew. There have been cases of captains running their submarines efficiently but enjoying neither the respect nor the affection of their men. Usually, this was the case when the captain was self-centered, unjust or simply calloused.

It was different when a captain was really attentive to his men and had their interests at heart. Vidayev was exactly that sort of person. He was stern and exacting but did not let this overshadow generosity. The men felt it at once and responded accordingly.

It was not Vidayev's fault that his patrol in his new submarine gave no results. He had amply demonstrated his competence, while P-421's record of victories had shown that he was skilled in attack. In August, therefore, he went on patrol independently. On that patrol he justified our confidence in him.

The submarine's hydroplanes jammed during the very first attack, with the result that she dived much too deep to allow the periscope to be used. The trim was evened out, but it was too late to take the submarine to her attack level. Only a few seconds were left before the submarine would get into her firing position and here Vidayev decided to fire blind, from a depth of fifteen meters, by his computations in time. This was something not every submarine captain would have decided upon.

He fired four torpedoes at intervals of seven seconds from a distance which his computations showed to be eleven cable-lengths. But he could not establish the results of his attack. The transports and the vessels escorting them were sailing much too close to each other.

This happened on August 23 near Cape Kibergnes.

On the next day, Pitersky, who was officer-of-the-watch, saw two transports with an escort of four vessels. They were not very far away, and though the attack was hurried it was extremely accurate. A transport of about eight thousand tons was hit by three of the four torpedoes fired at it and it sank quickly. However, immediately after the salvo was fired the stern hydroplanes again failed. Warrant Officer Zavyalov went over to manual control. In the meantime the patrol ships located the submarine and depth charges began to explode.

In this difficult situation Vidayev followed Fisanovich's example and sought the cover of the shore batteries at Rybachy. Only the port electric motor worked. The pursuers hung on for a long time. Sweat poured down Zavyalov's body from the physical exertion at the manual controls. The engine room crew were magnificent. But the depth charges kept raining down. When the pursuit was finally called off, it was found that a total of a hundred and seventy-seven depth charges had been dropped. However, as in many previous cases, the first series caused the greatest trouble. The rest harmlessly exploded far from the submarine.

In September P-422 made a kill on its assignment to provide PQ-18 with cover.

"As soon as we surfaced," Vidayev later related, "Pitersky, who was on duty, reported that there was a patrol ship about thirty cable-lengths away from us on starboard 160. We dived and fired our stern tubes when we came to within five cable-lengths of the enemy. You had to be blind to miss at that range. We got both torpedoes into the ship's side and it sank at once. That's the whole story."

He said nothing about himself, about what he felt and experienced during the long half minute of waiting for an explosion to tell him that he had hit his target.

The aftertaste left by what happened to Malyshev was allayed when P-422 acquired a real, fighting captain. I was happy for Vidayev's sake. He loved submarines and the sea, and he did his work seriously, without ostentation.

An Explosion Inside a Submarine

"We were finishing recharging our batteries," Nikolai Zlokazov related. "I was near the torpedo tubes in the first compartment. As always, when we were on patrol, the door to the second compartment was wedged. Suddenly, there was a muffled but powerful explosion. The submarine trembled. I was thrown against the torpedo tubes. The light failed, and smoke began to fill the compartment.

"Through the smoke and the half-open door I saw a bluish flame in the second compartment. I heard men groaning and then there was silence. I cried out, but nobody answered. I ran to the door, there was no time to think.

"The door had been torn off the wedge lock. It occurred to

me that it had to be battened down at all costs. The wing nuts had come loose and it was pitch dark. But I managed to batten the door down all the same. After that I got Petty Officer Yegorov on the voice pipe in the seventh compartment and reported that I had battened down the door but was choking with the smoke. He ordered me to open the lower lid of the hatch. I did as he said and lost consciousness. . . ."

Torpedoman Zlokazov was serving in P-421 when the war broke out and he was with the submarine until it was sunk. After the loss of the submarine he was lucky, getting posted to P-402, which was commanded by Nikolai Stolbov.

During a patrol in July, a torpedo fired by Zlokazov sank a large transport. Several days after that P-402 encountered a U-5-class German submarine. The U-boat was sighted on the surface, not very far away. K-402 started what submariners call a psychological attack. This meant that the captain at once steered a battle course and the orders "Stand by" and "Fire" followed each other in quick succession. Here everything depended upon the torpedomen. Zlokazov did his work faultlessly and the U-boat was destroyed.

In August the crew confidently set out on a routine patrol. Nothing untoward happened. On August 13, the day after the submarine pulled out from the base, the batteries were recharged in the region of Tana Fjord, some twenty-five miles from the shore.

The recharging proceeded normally. The batteries were bled with the aid of the vent from the battery shaft in the fifth compartment: water had flooded the battery bleeding shaft and it had had to be closed. But that did not trouble anybody because this alternative had been used many times.

At 01.30 hours, Electrician Byzov, who was on duty in the control room, checked the storage batteries and the hydrogen content in the shafts and the mains. There was very little hydrogen in the air, and there was no threat of fire-damp.

At the same time, Petty Officer 2nd Class Alexeyev received a report from the fifth compartment that there was a strong smell of oxygen. He felt the compartments should be ventilated, but to do that they would have to stop bleeding the batteries. That was against the regulations. A negligible amount of hydrogen had collected in the shafts. Alexeyev argued that half an hour would make no difference. Believing himself right, he asked Lieutenant Zakharov, who was officer-of-the-watch on the bridge, for permission to ventilate the compartments.

The lieutenant did not go into the matter and gave his permission, relying on the Petty Officer's experience.

A little over twenty minutes passed.

At 01.58 hours the submarine was shaken by an explosion in the second and third compartments.

All the men who could rise to their feet rushed to their battle stations. The voice pipes and ventilation mains were immediately sealed.

The Gunnery Officer Bolshakov and Engineer Officer Kukushkin ran from the diesel compartment to the control room. Together with Alexeyev and Byzov they tried to open the door to the third compartment, where the captain was. But the door was warped. The second and third compartments remained silent.

This meant that the captain, the first lieutenant, the Commissar and the navigator were either dead or badly injured. They had been in the third compartment with the torpedo officer and the doctor. Somebody had to take over.

That somebody proved to be Warrant Officer Yegorov, who was secretary of the submarine's Party organization. He was the first to take a grip on himself.

"I'm taking over as submarine commissar," he announced to the men. "I suggest that Engineer-Lieutenant-Captain Bolshakov take over command of the submarine. You agree with me, Comrade Engineer-Lieutenant-Captain?"

Bolshakov raised no objections, and there and then it was decided to appoint Navigator Electrician Alexandrov the submarine's Navigator. He had finished a navigation school before the war and had had sufficient training to act as navigator.

There was more order when all the duties had been allocated. The first step was to find out what had happened to the men in the second and third compartments. Then the damage to the submarine had to be assessed, and, if necessary, steps taken to save the ship and the men.

Acting on orders from Bolshakov, two sailors climbed to the stern of the deck and opened the top lid of the hatchway into the first compartment. The lower lid had already been opened by Zlokazov. The torpedoman was unconscious. The stream of fresh air brought him round somewhat, and he was carried semiconscious to the deck.

A repair team wearing masks went into the compartment.

The men opened the door first to the second and then to the third compartment. Their flashlights revealed a horrible picture of mangled corpses and scattered heaps of partition and bunk fragments. One of the men fainted.

Half of the crew, including the captain, had been killed. Darkness reigned in the compartments and there was an acrid smell of smoke and chlorine. The submarine could only proceed surfaced—there was no power for sailing submerged. The most terrible thing was that there was no power even to start the diesel engines and operate the transmitters and the gyrocompass.

It was only about twenty-five miles to the enemy shore. The sea was quiet and visibility was excellent: it was August, the best month in the Barents Sea. The survivors had to work swiftly if they wanted to save themselves.

The engines were finally started through the efforts of Electrician Chief Petty Officer Semyonov and engine-room petty officers 2nd Class Chernovtsev and Novak. Putting together all the portable batteries in the submarine they got enough power to start the engines.

With the aid of the magnetic compass, which had begun to lie outrageously after the accident, Alexandrov somehow managed to plot a course to the base. Zlokazov was stationed at the manual controls in the seventh compartment. Incidentally, he remained at that post for a full twenty-four hours. The orders to the helm were passed on from the bridge by word of mouth by men strung out in the compartments.

An enemy aircraft was sighted early in the morning. The guns were manned but the aircraft did not see the submarine and disappeared beyond the horizon. The sun was rising ever higher and Alexandrov took his bearings with a sextant.

However, navigation without a log, by a faulty magnetic compass, could not be very accurate. Toward nightfall the men saw land to starboard of their course. They took it for Rybachy. But suddenly an aircraft appeared in the sky. Once again the guns were manned. The aircraft was obviously reducing height, and it became clear that it was landing at an aerodrome.

Bolshakov and Zakharov, who did not leave the bridge for a minute, realized that it was not Rybachy but a sector of the Norwegian coast. Soon they identified the port of Vardö. The submarine turned to port in the direction of Tysp-Navolok beacon.

The beacon soon came into sight. When the observation post near Tysp-Navolok appeared on the beam, the submarine reported its plight by semaphore. At the entrance into Kola Bay P-402 was met by ships, with the Brigade Commander on board one of them.

The disabled Pike thus ended her tragic patrol. She was saved thanks to the initiative and determination of the Party organization secretary, the leadership and firmness of the surviving officers, and the courage and staunchness of the surviving ratings.

At the same time, this incident was a bitter but instructive lesson to us. It showed what a seemingly innocent infraction of the regulations could lead to. There had been such infractions before, but they had never led to disaster, and that had lulled the seamen into a false sense of security. This time, however, it had been fatal. The commission of inquiry found that the submarine carried old batteries and that when they were recharged they intensively discharged hydrogen. In the course of the last twenty minutes the concentration of hydrogen in the battery shafts was higher than the permissible level. Somebody in the third compartment had evidently turned a switch and the resultant spark had been enough to explode the batteries. This was an unjustified, dreadful loss. Captain 3rd Rank Stolbov had had the experience of ten operational patrols and eight kills. With him perished eighteen other courageous, battle-steeled submariners. They were killed not in battle but as a result of an absurd accident, which might never have happened. That was the most horrible part of it.

P-402 was put in dry dock. The crew were brought up to full strength, and the new commander was Captain 3rd Rank Alexander Kautsky, who had sailed as first lieutenant under Shuisky.

Political Workers

The institution of military commissars was abolished both in the army and the navy in October. The submarines that had had commissars now had political workers who held the rank of officers.

I would say that in the submarine service this change was

less marked than in the army. We had always had a single command in submarines. The Commissar had no authority to interfere in the running of a ship. On patrol, let alone during an attack, the captain was completely independent in his decisions. The Commissar's duties rarely ranged beyond the political education of the crew, explaining to the men how important it was to fulfil combat assignments and the captain's orders to the best of their ability.

In submarines, therefore, the replacement of commissars by political deputies did not inaugurate any substantial change. Their prestige and their relations with the men remained unchanged. Captains, as a rule, had got on well with the commissars, and this became all the more the case now.

It is worth noting that when the post of political deputy was abolished the captains were the first to raise a howl. They keenly felt the drop in the level of the work with the men. With time, this obvious error was rectified.

No matter how smoothly the political machine is reorganized you unexpectedly find problems that can hardly be correctly settled on the spot. Naturally, our captains and political deputies found themselves saddled with quite a few problems. This was foreseen in Moscow, and Army Commissar 2nd Rank Ivan Rogov, Chief of the Central Political Department of the Navy, came to the Northern Fleet in November to sort them out. He paid our brigade a visit as well.

It was his second meeting with Northern submariners. We had been greatly impressed by him when he first visited us in June.

Prior to that we had only heard about him from officers transferred to the North from Moscow or from people who came to us on business. Most people spoke of him with respect but with an undertone that was not very flattering for a Party worker, "He's so strict that he's apt to be unfair," "It's best to steer clear of him." In short, "Ivan the Terrible." That nickname stuck.

In the wardroom at the shore base we had frequently heard fearful stories about how stern he was. But we soon forgot about them. The distance from a submarine captain or a Divisional Commander to him was enormous. We were not worried about meeting his eye, feeling that for this there were the Fleet Commander-in-Chief, the Member of the Military Council, the Chief of the Political Department and the

Brigade Commander. As far as we were concerned, he was an abstract entity.

On June 2, when Shuisky and I had started out on patrol in P-403, we were ordered to stop in Olenya Inlet, where we were checking our trimming tanks. The semaphore signal was signed by the Fleet Staff officer-on-duty. Shuisky and I wondered what it could mean.

We soon saw a launch coming in our direction. On the deck Alexander Nikolayev, the Member of the Military Council, was talking to somebody. When the launch came alongside we recognized Nikolayev's companion. He was Ivan Rogov.

In conformity with regulations, the captain, deputy and I met them on deck. Rogov at once said he wanted to go inside the submarine and talk to the men. We accompanied him.

He impressed us as short-spoken and stern, as a person who listened rather than spoke himself. For all that he managed to comport himself simply, without instilling fear or the desire to keep silent. From the very beginning he set the correct tone in his conversation with the men. One felt that he was on ground that was familiar to him, that he knew what he wanted and was not asking questions simply for form. He did not use a pseudo-seaman's language, and everybody took a liking to him. His brief questions touched the very essence of things and induced similarly brief and businesslike replies.

Elucidating much of what concerned our requirements and difficulties both in combat and everyday life, he settled some of the problems on the spot. What he could not settle immediately was written down by Nikolayev to enable him to look into the matter later.

Rogov did not stay long, and when the launch moved off, Shuisky was silent for a long time and then said thoughtfully, "I wish we had more Terribles like him."

We returned to the base in ten days. Rogov had gone back to Moscow. But in the brigade we spoke of his visit for a long time. He had visited many of the submarines, including Fisanovich's M-172. In D-3 he said that he was displeased that the petty officers and ratings had so few decorations.

"This submarine has sunk many ships, and the men have only one medal each. That won't do," he said. "When an enemy ship is sunk it is the work of the entire crew, with everybody sharing the risk. We must not stint awards for men like these."

Such was our first acquaintanceship with Rogov. Unquestionably, he ranked among clever and striking Party workers, among splendid organizers who were always in the thick of life and had the knack of leadership.

Rogov helped us to settle everything that we were vague about as regards the abolition of the institution of military commissars.

In the brigade the reorganization was accompanied by some new appointments. Brigade Commissar Kozlov and Chief of the Political Department Baikov were given new assignments. Captain 2nd Rank Rudolph Radun became the new Political Department Chief and Deputy to the Brigade Commander. There were a number of internal readjustments: some of the Political Department instructors were appointed Political Deputies in submarines, and some of the former Commissars were transferred to the Political Department and the Political Administration.

The new Political Department Chief was only thirty. But we knew he was experienced. Besides, we were pleased over his appointment because he was a submariner, "one of us." That being the case, we could expect him to settle into his job smoothly.

Radun began his career in the navy as a navigator electrician in a submarine. Capable, well-educated and showing promise of becoming a good organizer, the lad was soon assigned to political work. He was elected a deputy to the Tenth Congress of the Young Communist League. At the Fleet Central Political Administration he was put in charge of Y.C.L. activities.

Our expectations were justified. Rudolph went off to a start enthusiastically, showing energy and initiative. He was seldom to be seen in his office, spending most of his time talking to sailors or to workers and team leaders refitting or repairing submarines, or going to sea with crews on practice runs. He was eager to go on a war patrol but his work kept him tied to the shore.

The new Political Department adopted the best traditions of its predecessor. One was the maxim: "Work with all and each and everyone." This meant combining collective education with work with individuals. Undertakings on a brigade scale were avoided. Besides, there could be no question of such undertakings under wartime conditions. The crew of a submarine was the unit for which lectures, reports and meetings were arranged.

The brigade radio station was used by the Political Department to popularize innovations.

The war had given prominence to men who were adept at their jobs. Each had his own method. Moreover, each war patrol had its own features, and therefore the men involved in it could teach others something that they never knew before.

All this was of great practical interest to submariners, and the Political Department invited officers and ratings to speak of their experience before the microphone, of attacks and enemy bombings, of the behavior of machinery and weapons, of ways and means of repairing damaged instruments and mechanisms.

Of course, innovations were popularized by other means as well: by leaflets devoted to men who had distinguished themselves, or by reports and lectures on specialized subjects for officers and ratings.

The talks covered our own experience and the changes that we had noted in the enemy's tactics.

The Political Department thoughtfully approached every aspect of raising the level of the submariners' political, tactical and special knowledge.

Every instructor at the Political Department had the experience of several operational patrols. Alexander Babushkin, Pavel Petrov, Vasily Smirnov and other instructors frequently went to sea to help political workers and captains.

Our Political Service was a powerful, sensitive, fighting instrument of the Party.

A Myth Is Smashed

Early in October 2nd Division received two Leninets-class submarines. They were L-20 and L-22 and they came fresh from the slips. The finishing touches were put on them at the base before they were given over to their crews.

For the brigade this was an extremely valuable acquisition, for the submarines were designed mainly as mine layers. They carried a large number of mines and the mine-laying apparatus in their stern was much more reliable than the one carried by the Katyushas. They could also be used for torpedo attacks. They had six torpedo tubes in the bow and a considerable operational range.

Lenitets L-Class (U.S.S.R.)

These submarines partially relieved the Katyushas of their mine-laying duties, allowing them to be used more for patrols along the Germans' distant communications, which was what they had been designed for.

L-20 was commanded by Captain 3rd Rank Victor Tamman. Like many of our captains, he had sailed in merchant ships for many years, rising to ship's master. After he was conscripted into the navy he went through a period of training and was posted to a submarine. For some years now he had been a submarine captain.

The commander of L-22 was our old friend Captain 3rd Rank Valentin Afonin, who had sailed with us in P-421's last patrol. He had not only studied the theater, but had been of great assistance in our fight to keep P-421 afloat. If we discount the tragedy-laden situation, it may be said that that patrol had been good training for Afonin and had enabled him to acquire a sound knowledge of the nature of the war in the North.

Khomyakov's Division, which had lost D-3, now had four submarines. L-22 was the first to go into combat. In the period from October to the New Year she carried out three missions, laying her mines in the appointed area and at the required depth. On these missions she had no opportunity of using her torpedoes.

L-20 likewise became operational in October and was likewise used for laying mines.

From intelligence reports, we later learned that several enemy transports and warships were blown up by the mines laid by these two submarines.

At approximately the same time, the brigade received two new Midgets. One of them, M-119, was commanded by Lieutenant Captain Konstantin Kolosov, and the other, M-121, by Lieutenant-Captain Vasily Kozhakin. They partially filled in the gaps in Morozov's division. I say partially, because by that autumn the division had lost three submarines. One of them was M-173, which had had a new captain in Valeryan Terekhin. M-173 was lost almost at the same time as K-2, which was commanded by Vasily Utkin. K-2 was the submarine that inaugurated the tradition of firing a salute in honor of each victory. . . .

The two new Midgets quickly took their place as combat units. After one operational patrol each, with Morozov as Instructor Commander, both Kozhakin and Kolosov received the right of independent command. But luck was against Kozhakin. M-121 set sail on November 7 and never returned.

Kotelnikov and I did not get reinforcements. Each of us had four Katyushas and Pikes. Naturally, we were not very happy about it. "We're growing older and rising in rank," I sometimes thought as I gazed at the two broad new stripes that appeared on our sleeves in October, "but we're not getting any more submarines." But this disappointment could not eclipse the upsurge of elation that gripped all of us during that extremely tempestuous autumn. On all the fronts the tide was turning in our favor. Happy news came from the Volga, the Northern Caucasus and Velikiye Luki.

We eagerly looked forward to the regular talks on the political situation. By now we were no longer tormented by the thought that we'd hear over the radio of another town lost to the enemy. In those days what we wanted from the political talks was some explanation of what was happening, an explanation that would disperse our dazed bewilderment. Now we looked for news that would give us a fuller picture of our obviously mounting successes.

As soon as a submarine surfaced after a long period under water, the attention of the entire crew would be focused on the wireless, where the petty officer with black earphones on his head would start tuning in and writing down the latest news. The men felt that the scale of the new developments was much greater than the last year's offensive near Moscow, that a real turning point was imminent.

In the submarine compartments and in the shore base barracks there was only one theme of conversation:

"It's starting. . . ."

"We'll drive them all the way to Berlin!"

"Farther! To the Bay of Biscay!"

The seamen knew what was what.

The New Year brought with it bright hopes. We assessed the situation in our theater soberly and dispassionately, and found that we had no grounds for our last year's pessimistic evaluation.

True, at sea the Germans had even greater numerical superiority than before. During the summer the number of Nazi surface ships in Norway's northern ports had reached its peak. These forces were spearheaded chiefly against our external communications. But as the PQ-17 affair showed, they were nothing but "bogey forces." However, even this, combined with the more than strange behavior of the British Naval Command, had been sufficient for the convoy to suffer huge losses from torpedo-carriers and U-boats. As far as we were concerned, the most striking thing was not so much the losses but the Allied decision to stop sending convoys to the Soviet Union on the plea that the risk was too great.

Risks are inevitable in war. But the British decision was motivated not by military but by political reasons.

The enemy attempted to disrupt our internal communications. U-boats appeared in the throat of the White Sea, in the Kara Sea and along the shores of Novaya Zemlya. But they had very little success. The pocket battleship *Admiral Scheer* appeared in the Kara Sea, where it sank the ice-breaker *Sibiryakov*, which resisted heroically. After that it tried to destroy the winter camp on Dixon Island, but was driven off by the 152 mm battery. That was the only attempt made by the Germans to use large surface vessels against our internal communications. It was an obviously adventurist endeavor. Our omission was that we failed to strike at the raider with submarines and aircraft.

The main thing was that the enemy's strength was beginning to peter out. We could feel it. Many years later in *A History of the Second World War*, former Wehrmacht

Armiral Scheer

Lieutenant-General Kurt Tippelskirch said about the actions of the German Navy in the North: "The successes of that summer (1942—*I.K.*) were the culminating point of the war against enemy shipping in that area."

The Germans failed to tie down the Northern Fleet, to prevent it from giving the maritime flank of our troops operational and tactical cover. This was borne out by the successful landing of a reconnaissance party near Motovsky Bay, by the actions of our surface ships, which screened the landing, and by our submarine offensive, which sapped the fighting capacity of the Lapland group's northern wing.

At the outbreak of the war, the Nazis had clearly under-estimated the potential of the Soviet submarine fleet. With their usual haughtiness they did not take it seriously, with the result that they found themselves unprepared against it. For six months we sank transports and warships without losing a single submarine. Naturally, the enemy took counter-measures, building up his forces. But we, too, quickly gained the combat experience we needed.

It is a fact that if at the outbreak of the war the Nazi anti-submarine defenses had been as strong as in 1942, we would have suffered enormous casualties, while the enemy's losses would have been considerably smaller. The Germans had the experience and the technical facilities for organizing such a defense as soon as war started.

Now they had extensive minefields screening the busiest sectors of their communications. Most of our lost submarines had in all likelihood been destroyed by mines. Enemy ships ceased to put out to sea singly, receiving powerful sea and air cover. Convoys usually followed a zigzag anti-submarine course. Frequently, they had double screens. Yet our submarines broke through the enemy cover, attacked and sank transports and, as a rule, safely eluded pursuit.

If we discount the false motives that prevented us from assessing the enemy positively in anything, it must be admitted that before the war and in its early stages we had a very high opinion of German submariners. A quarter of a century before the war the Germans had been the first to see the tremendous potentialities of a submarine fleet and developed it with unprecedented speed. They had the most extensive experience in fighting a submarine war. Naturally, the Nazi submarine fleet inherited the experience and traditions of those years. There was a lot of fiendish cruelty, but some of these traditions merited respect for their enterprise and daring. When the Second World War started we heard of German submariners lording it in the Atlantic, of their wolf packs, of German U-boats terrorizing convoys. Some of this was exaggerated, but nobody could afford to underestimate such an enemy.

We expected the German submariners to give us a lot of trouble. But our worst fears proved to be unfounded. In summer there were forty German U-boats in Norway. But they achieved much less than our twenty submarines. That was not all. From the very outset of the war we had sudden encounters with enemy submarines, particularly in 1942. In these encounters the enemy did not display superior vigilance, tactics, or speed in making decisions. In some cases our submarines successfully evaded being attacked by them, and in others they attacked the enemy themselves. Victories over German U-boats were scored by Starikov and Stolbov, while Bondarevich's duel contributed a vivid page to the brigade's combat chronicle.

Some of our submarines were sunk by German U-boats. But a comparison of all data showed that this number did not exceed the number of U-boats sunk by us.

What conclusions did we draw from all this?

Firstly, the assertion that the Nazi submarine fleet was superior proved to be as much a myth as the invincibility of the German Wehrmacht. The officers and crews were well-trained, but it was clearly an exaggeration to say that they were outstanding. Naturally, we arrived at this assessment on the basis of our own experience. Secondly, because that assessment was possible we could say that our own training had improved considerably. We not only overtook the enemy in submarine warfare but surpassed him in a number of aspects. This was a satisfying conclusion.

As yet we did not have radar, and we did not have the radio communication that we desired. This limited our possibilities, and affected combat control and cooperation between the submarines and between them and other services. In spite of this we were able to report to the Motherland that her efforts in building up a submarine fleet had not been in vain.

New Year Gifts

The wind ruled supreme over the wintry, night-enveloped sea. It drove huge waves shoreward, shook prickly snow out of the clouds and lashed it savagely across the black, foaming water. From time to time, the faltering light of the Aurora Borealis showed in the sky. A dreary, chilling scene met the eyes of the men on the bridge of a submarine.

Some fifteen minutes had elapsed since the submarine had surfaced. At periscope depth, in the light and relative warmth of their ship, the crew had ushered in the New Year. There had been no chime of bells, no dancing and no music. The electric motors had hummed monotonously and the watch had been at their stations. In spite of everything one could sense a holiday atmosphere. There were many reasons for it. The Nazis were securely trapped in the Stalingrad cauldron, and it was now a matter of days before the siege of Leningrad would be broken. Nobody now doubted that there would be other, sweeping victories.

As for the submarine itself, it had successfully laid a mine field on December 29.

The crew had had their bit of fun, too. A tiny fir tree, taken from the base by the provident torpedomen, had been set up in the first compartment. It was decorated simply, and bore two banners, with the legends: "1943, Happy New Year" and "We'll Open Our Battle Score in the New Year."

At midnight Senior Lieutenant Nikolai Yamshchikov reported to the Captain, "It's time!"

Captain 3rd Rank Victor Tamman raised his glass and proposed a toast to the New Year.

Glasses clinked and the ration of 100 grams of vodka was downed.

Tamman made the round of all the compartments, shaking hands with the men and wishing them all the best for the New Year.

The minutes of celebration passed, and L-20 surfaced and continued her search. After the laying of the mine field, this was her second assignment on this patrol.

At 03.11 hours, in the uncertain light of Aurora Borealis, Signalman Ivan Mazurov made out a convoy stealing along the shore. Orders for a torpedo attack were given at once, and the submarine made for the convoy.

Within five minutes the submarine was near enough to the convoy to enable the captain to see the ships clearly. Three transports were moving in line ahead formation. They had an escort of several patrol ships and torpedo launches. The biggest of these transports displaced about ten thousand tons and Tamman selected it for his target. The attack proceeded swiftly. At 03.21 hours the submarine was already on a battle course. And four minutes later it fired four torpedoes at short intervals.

Soon the men on the bridge saw a flash of light illumining the transport near the mainmast, and a huge pillar of black smoke rising into the air. A terrifying rumble rolled across the waves, and was followed by an explosion, which, however, did not drown the rumble.

At 03.28 hours the submarine dived and turned away from the attack area, expecting to be pursued. But there was no pursuit. At 04.07 hours L-20 surfaced. About five cable-lengths away from her, two launches, their searchlights sweeping the sea, were picking up survivors from the torpedoed transport.

Soon afterward the submarine's editor put out an issue of the wall newspaper with an article headed "New Year Gift." It stated that in the New Year, the Nazi transport had lived for only three hours and twenty-one minutes.

On January 5, L-20 carried out her third assignment, landing a reconnaissance group on the enemy coast, and a week later returning to base. The transport sunk by her was the brigade's first victory in 1943.

On her next patrol, in January and February, L-20 carried out two successful torpedo attacks, in the first of which she sank a transport and a patrol ship with a single salvo.

Our second New Year gift was presented to us by M-171. She returned on January 7 from her—just think of it—eighteenth patrol since the beginning of the war. True, her victory was not as full and spectacular as that of the *Leninets*. Starikov, now Guards Captain 2nd Rank, had hit a transport with one torpedo. Frequently, this "helping" was not enough to sink a large transport. The escort vessels had made it impossible for Starikov to find out what happened to the torpedoed transport. This was only a partial victory, but even a damaged transport was a good contribution to the brigade's battle score.

M-172 had similarly bad luck. Fisanovich hit a patrol ship which unexpectedly came between him and the transport he was attacking. Everybody in the submarine heard the explosion but it had not been possible to make sure if the ship had been sunk. It, too, was considered as having been damaged.

P-404, on the other hand, had better luck. Vladimir Ivanov attacked transports on January 17 and 22 and sank both his targets. Incidentally, luck, of course, is not the word for it. A Pike's salvo of four bow torpedoes is much more effective than a Midget's two. In order to make sure of sinking a ship, it has to be hit with at least two torpedoes. Consequently, under similar conditions, a Midget has to take sniper shots while a Pike can afford to fire less accurately and yet have every chance of sending the enemy to the bottom.

In winter it was much more difficult to fire accurately. Most of the attacks were carried out on the surface, where the waves kept thrusting a submarine off her course. This was all the more true of a Midget, which was indeed a small ship. She had only one propeller shaft with the result that she was more unsteady on course. More often than not, torpedoes fired singly from the surface missed the target. For that reason, Midgets seldom fired surfaced. In the case of a Pike, direct hits with two out of a salvo of four torpedoes were regarded as a good result, while if the distance was great the result was considered splendid.

Ivanov fired twice in blusterous weather from a fairly long distance—approximately fifteen cable-lengths. And each time he scored direct hits with both torpedoes.

At this point I must mention the scrupulosity of our submarine captains in assessing the results of their attacks. It was hard, sometimes extremely hard, to tell exactly what happened to a torpedoed ship. There had been incredible cases when nobody, not even the hydrophone operator, heard an explosion, yet through the periscope it could clearly be seen that the torpedoed transport was sinking. This, of course, was due to the way sound spreads in water. But most frequently, the reverse happened. Everybody heard the explosion, but nobody saw its results, either because escort vessels gave chase, or a snowfall reduced visibility.

Here the hydrophone operator helped out. He reported whether an attacked ship's propellers could be heard. However, since a convoy consisted of many ships, a hydrophone operator could go wrong, and an allowance for error had to be made even when he was sure that the noise of a ship's propellers had ceased. A torpedoed vessel might remain afloat and, after repairing the damage, return home under its own power. Moreover, it might be towed to the nearest base. It was quite another matter when the hydrophone operator could report sounds of a ship actually sinking. However, this was a rare case because of the then imperfect design of the sonar equipment.

It was the rule that if what happened to a torpedoed ship could not be observed of if no trustworthy data showing that a ship had been sunk were available our captains reported that the result of an attack was doubtful. Personal conviction, if not backed by facts, was not taken into consideration.

Naturally, errors, although they were unintentional, could not be avoided, because subjective element would inevitably creep in.

THE PEOPLE ARE
THE FOUNTAIN OF HEROISM

A Crew Consisting
of Nine Nationalities

In a Pike I like to be in the sixth compartment. It is warmer
and cozier (if, in general, the word "cozy" can be applied to
submarines) than any other compartment. The men off duty
gather there much more frequently than in the other
compartments. I even preferred to sleep there—in the bunk
of the engineering officer—if, of course, he was not using it
himself.

During a patrol, I remember going to the sixth compartment and finding a young sailor named Ramazanov telling his
mates about his native Daghestan.

"What nationality are you?" somebody asked. "There are a
lot of nationalities in your Republic."

"I'm a Lakh," Ramazanov said with a smile, and added,
"How many nationalities do we have on board?"

"Nine," Coxswain Dobrodomov replied.

Nine nationalities in a ship's company of forty-five!

The other submarines in the brigade could boast of a
similarly large national composition, and we had never had a
case of hostility or misunderstanding, or a barrier to friendship.

This brings to mind the lament of a British officer, who was
a representative of the Allied Command. He told me that
when he was in command of a platoon, his main worry was
that half the men were from Wales. He said Welshmen were

stubborn, spoke an unintelligible language, and that it was impossible to make sailors out of them.

I told the Englishman that I could not understand this sort of difficulty. We had men of many nationalities serving in our submarines and all of them were perfectly well aware of what was expected of them in the navy, and each of them did his duty. We respected the national customs of other people, and if anybody spoke poor Russian his mates came to his assistance, acting as teachers.

P-402 started out on patrol on January 17. Before setting sail, the new Captain Alexander Kautsky and I were briefed by Brigade Commander Nikolai Vinogradov. With Chief of the Political Department Rudolph Radun present, Vinogradov outlined the situation in our theater and gave us data on the enemy's movement, and the location of mine fields and the bases of surface ships and submarines in Norway. The rest was contained in sealed instructions, which however did not include warm words and kind wishes which are so necessary to men going on patrol.

Vinogradov and Radun filled the gap.

It was snowing and frosty when we arrived in our patrol area in the morning of January 18. At night we sailed on the surface, and when the impenetrable darkness was driven away by the gray twilight of day we dived. Most of the time we had abominable visibility. When it did not snow there were dense fogs—one found weather like this only within the Arctic Circle.

Kautsky was handling the submarine with confidence. It was as I had expected. He had served only a short term as first lieutenant before becoming captain. In his case this had not been accidental. He was the type of man who would have done his job well in any capacity. Submarines, however, were his vocation. He had been an engine room artificer in D-3. After he re-enlisted he was sent to a naval school and voluntarily returned to submarines upon his graduation from that school.

One could give many instances of men striving to become officers, dreaming of the day when they would be officers, believing that this was their life's vocation. Yet when finally they got their commission and appointment they found the work beyond them. Kautsky, I felt, was not one of these.

I had known and served with him for many years. In his

capacity of divisional torpedo officer he had time and again pressed for active service and had acted as first lieutenant on patrols. This did not enter the round of his direct duties, but he did it willingly.

I would say he was a commander both by vocation and by his qualities as a man.

Difficulties crop up during every patrol. On this patrol we sailed by dead reckoning for several days running, having no opportunity to determine our position by navigational means or by the stars. We could not tell how much error there was in our compass, and we doubted the accuracy with which we laid our course. The echo-sounder was all we could depend upon. As long as it showed that the depth was over a hundred meters we could sail without anxiety. If it was less than a hundred meters we had to be on our guard. In this area the coast inclined steeply into the sea, and where it was less than a hundred meters deep there was the danger of running into an underwater reef.

We hugged the coast, making sure that there was always a hundred meters of water under us. This placed a terrific strain on the navigator and on the captain.

Katusky did not let his anxiety get the better of him. He kept his eye on the mood of his crew, half of whom were newcomers. Some came from other submarines, but most were from the shore base or from the Training Depot. Once they settled into their jobs and became used to each other things would be easy.

On January 22, which was our fourth day at sea, we decided to recharge our batteries. The sea lay under a heavy blanket of fog. Twice the hydrophone operator reported the proximity of launches, but they could not be seen through the periscope. When we surfaced, we felt we would be safer if there was more distance between us and the shore. The fog gave us plenty of cover, but there was always the danger of the noise of the diesels or of a spark giving us away. Besides, we had had some trouble with the hydraulic clutch of our starboard diesel, and to repair it we had to have a greater margin of safety.

We reached our battery-recharging area in the second half of the day. By 23.00 hours we repaired the clutch. Despite the lack of tools the job was skilfully done by Chief Engine-Room Artificer Mikheyev, Petty Officer Chernyavtsev and engine-room artificers Gorozhankin and Lysenko.

Toward 05.00 hours we were back along the enemy coast, getting there, I would say, in time. At 08.33 hours we saw the outlines of ships through the slow-falling snow. They were two transports, two mine sweepers and two launches of the same class as our MO submarine chasers. The distance to the convoy was about twenty cable-lengths.

Things moved swiftly: the battle alarm was sounded, the diesels were stopped and we switched to our electric motors. Kautsky went into a battle course and fired four torpedoes from a distance of eight cable-lengths at 08.43 hours. Two of them hit one of the transports. It displaced approximately six thousand tons. When it began to sink heavy snow obliterated our vision. We would not have been able to watch the results even if we had wanted to, because we had to dive to evade possible attack.

Acting on my advice, Kautsky headed toward a locality where we had every reason to believe that the enemy had a mine field. Our calculation, which proved to be justified, was that the enemy would not risk searching for us there. Until 11.00 hours we heard the mine sweepers and launches scouring the area of attack, but we could not say whether they were looking for us or picking up survivors of the torpedoed vessel. . . .

The days followed one another with little to break the monotony. Either it would become colder and vapor would start rising from the sea, or it would grow warmer and snow would alternate with fog. We saw some fishing boats. They did not see us and we left them alone. We went deep into Varanger Fjord, but it was deserted.

Finally, on January 28, we spotted three patrol ships steaming in line. They were only fifteen cable-lengths away, and the course angle was just right for an attack. Had we attacked them we probably would have been successful. But we were attacked ourselves. Much as it was undesirable, the enemy hydrophone operators naturally heard us, and soon the first two depth charges were fired. They exploded uncomfortably close to us.

Kautsky at once steered the submarine out of the danger zone, and all the other depth charges exploded farther away. Then we heard new sounds, which we did not like either: the enemy was now firing diving shells. But they went harmlessly past us.

We were pursued for about an hour, during which the

enemy dropped forty depth charges. This was a fairly large dose of psychological training for men on their first war patrol.

The crew changed perceptibly in the short space of our first ten days at sea. This was due largely to the early success we had scored. It gave them greater confidence in themselves and this, in turn, made for greater efficiency. And now, after we had given the enemy the slip they felt they were quite effectually secure. It is important for a fighting man, particularly a submariner, to believe that the blows he delivers are fatal for the enemy and that it is quite possible to evade the enemy's blows.

The test on our nerves continued into the next day. An explosion thundered out near the submarine at noon. Yet the hydrophone operator failed to hear any noise in the vicinity, and our periscope showed that there was nothing on the horizon. It, therefore, could only mean that an aircraft had dropped a bomb.

But that was only a prelude. At 18.00 hours the hydrophone operator reported the noise of a destroyer's propellers to starboard. Depth charges began exploding almost at the same time. The explosions now drew nearer and now receded.

I suggested taking a look to see who was practicing with depth charges.

But it was too dark and foggy to see anything through the periscope.

There was another explosion. This time it was closer to us.

"Manual controls," Kautsky ordered.

This was a necessary precaution during a depth-charge attack, because the electrical controls could fail if a bomb exploded very close to the submarine. If that happened the submarine would either plunge deeper or rise to the surface in full view of the enemy. Bitter experience had taught us to forestall that unpleasantness.

There was a special sort of thick silence in the submarine. The men, their faces stone stern, were standing by with emergency repair tools. The bombing was affecting the nerves even of those who had been through such an ordeal before. Every nerve, every muscle was tensed. After each explosion our strained hearing listened for the splash of water in the boat or for an alarmed cry from the next compartment reporting a hole in the casing.

But the silence in the submarine was not broken. The only

sounds were the rhythmical clicking of the instruments and the monotonous hum of the main electric motors.

Kautsky issued his orders in an undertone as he steered us away from danger. From time to time he stopped the submarine to confuse the enemy hydrophone operator.

Our hydrophone operator was the only man on board who knew whether the destroyer was close or far away. He could even hear the depth charges falling into the water and sinking to their explosion depth. He certainly had to have iron nerves.

Kautsky took his bearings from the hydrophone operator's reports and maneuvered accordingly. As soon as there was an explosion we increased speed because the noise cut all acoustic contact with us.

The minutes dragged on. At last, after discharging his ninety-seventh depth charge the enemy left us in peace. The noise of the ship's propellers receded in the distance. We had been under attack for a little over half an hour, but it seemed an age.

We had passed yet another test.

Nothing more occurred until February 2. On that day we had some luck again. At about 13.00 hours the officer-of-the-watch at the periscope saw two transports with an escort of two patrol ships and two other vessels. They were about three and a half miles away from us, and the course angle was very favorable.

"All right, Captain, take a shot at them," I said, giving the periscope over to Kautsky.

Of medium height, thickset and broadboned, he bent toward the eyepiece. He issued a string of curt orders. We were rapidly nearing our point of fire.

"Aft tubes, stand by!"

Then, about a minute later:

"Aft tubes fire!"

From a distance of twelve cable-lengths the torpedoes raced in the direction of the leading transport. It began to sink, hit by the two torpedoes.

We were attacked four minutes after the torpedoed transport began to sink. We dived and headed toward the enemy mine field.

There were thirteen explosions. Then another eight. After that the explosions of the depth charges became hardly audible. Our tactics had again justified itself. The Germans hesitated to enter their own mine field. They circled in the vicinity, dropping depth bombs either as a preventive measure or to clear their conscience. It hurt to lose a transport of eight thousand tons.

The chase was called off two hours later.

On the next day we were signalled home. We were elated over the bag we were taking home with us. The enemy had lost two large vessels, and all of the hundred and ninety-seven depth charges had missed their mark. It was an undoubted success for Alexander Kautsky. The young captain had demonstrated tactical maturity and will power. It was also an undoubted success for the young crew, which had passed a gruelling test with flying colors. There were only a few veterans in P-402, and it was a credit to them that the new men had settled into their work so quickly.

Alexander Kautsky had earned the right to go on war patrols independently.

At the Flag Command Post

P-402 entered Yekaterininskaya Harbor in triumph. In reply to our two-gun salute, the ships riding at anchor or lying alongside the piers raised flag signals congratulating us on our victory. Sailors lined up on the decks of the destroyers in the established ritual of welcome for a submarine returning from an operational patrol.

At the pier we were met by Member of the Military Council Nikolayev, Brigade Commander Vinogradov and Chief of the Political Department Radun. Kautsky and I briefly reported the results of the patrol. There was no time for a leisurely talk. K-3 and K-22 were waiting to set sail on the eastern side of the pier. Vinogradov was going in K-3 with Malofeyev, and Kotelnikov and Radun were going with Captain 3rd Rank Kulbakin, the new commander of K-22.

We had toyed with the idea of submarines patrolling in pairs: together they could destroy an entire convoy. That idea was now being put to the test.

Victor Kotelnikov and I spoke for a few minutes before he went to K-22. The tide was in, and the Katyusha towered over the pier. Victor lightly ran up the steep gangway and went to the bridge. Radun was the last to go on board.

The submarine moved off with Kotelnikov and Radun standing side by side on the bridge. We waved to each other. Somewhat apart from them stood Senior Lieutenant Alexander Matsevich, the *Krassy Flot* correspondent, who had been on many patrols. His accounts were truthful, exciting, ungarnished and written with a knowledge of the subject. War correspondents like him were respected in the navy.

K-22 swung into position behind K-3, on whose bow stood Vinogradov and Divisional Navigator Semyonov. Soon both submarines disappeared behind the nearest cape.

I remained standing on the pier, thinking over what Radun had hastily said as he had hurried away. His words were: "Captain 2nd Rank Boldyrev will report to you. I've left him in charge." I was not sure what this meant. Why should the Acting Chief of the Political Department have to report to me? If anything, I should report to him. I felt Radun had confused something in his hurry.

The train of my thoughts was snapped by Kautsky, who invited me to join him for dinner in his wardroom.

When we arrived, Karpunin and Skorokhvatov were already at the table.

"Congratulations on your new appointment," they said, rising.

"Explain what you mean?" I demanded.

"Don't you know? Then the pleasure will be all the greater to inform you that you have been appointed Brigade Commander."

Nobody had spoken to me about it beforehand. I could not account for this sudden promotion. Would I cope with it? I had been quite happy as Divisional Commander, training submarine captains and acting as their mentor on patrol. It was a job I knew and liked. But it was a totally different thing to direct a brigade from the Flag Command Post, to settle operational problems, to be in charge of an entire brigade. Had I sufficient experience and knowledge? I had never handled a job of this magnitude, and had not finished an academy. . . .

"What's Vinogradov's new job?" I asked.

"Chief of the Fleet Submarine Branch, with the rank of Rear Admiral," Karpunin explained. "I'm being transferred to Supreme Headquarters in Moscow."

Some time later I was received by the Fleet Commander-in-Chief Arseny Golovko. He said he was sure I would be equal to my new job, that earthenware was not made by the gods, and gave me a lot of useful advice.

"Bear in mind," he said in conclusion, "that the brigade will grow. We'll fill in the losses. The time will come when we'll have air cover. Get used to that idea."

I turned my division over to Captain 2nd Rank Vladimir Ivanov, a veteran Pike Captain.

I moved, lock, stock and barrel, to the Brigade Flag Command Post. It was sturdily built and well protected against bombs and shells of any caliber. It had rooms for the Brigade Commander, the Chief-of-Staff, the operational officer-on-duty, and a canteen.

My office was simply furnished: a writing desk, a few chairs, a divan and an iron army cot. It was all that was really wanted. But I did not like sleeping in it. I could not get used to the damp, heavy air underground. True, it was not much more comfortable in a submarine. But there you feel you are in a ship, on the sea. When you're not sailing, however, you feel you want some of the comforts of life on shore. Every time I got the opportunity, I spent the night in the shore base's surface premises.

I had a small and well-organized staff. Each member of the staff had been on patrol in every class of submarine in the brigade; they had gone to sea only in those submarines where their presence and assistance had been most needed. On shore they had their hands full systematizing and introducing advanced experience, arranging classes for officers, petty officers and ratings, and directing training in study rooms.

I had had contact with all staff specialists in my former capacity of Divisional Commander. I had sailed with some of them on operational patrols. In short, they were not only friends and wardroom mates, but men whose qualities I knew quite well. With a staff such as this it was easier to settle into my new job.

Our divisions were getting new submarines. In the old days I would have been happy to see Morozov and Khomyakov get reinforcements to enable them to operate on a larger scale. Now the situation was different—there was little to be happy about. With them I had to see to the refitting of the submarines, to the training of the crews. It was now my worry to appoint officers to take charge of this training and to break new captains into their work.

Vinogradov had done all this easily and simply—at least that was the impression one got as an onlooker. In my case, every problem bred scores of new problems, and the day was never long enough to allow me to wade through all of them.

"Don't take it all so close to heart," Skorokhvatov used to say when I had a particularly thorny problem on my hands. "If you do, you won't have enough heart. In such cases Vinogradov used to...."

This advice from my Chief-of-Staff never failed to take a load off my mind, for I would see that things were not as hopeless as I thought, provided I concentrated on my main objective. I was extremely grateful to him for this unobtrusive, tactful prompting.

Nikolai Vinogradov, too, was extremely helpful. This assistance was of great value to me, because the first few weeks as Brigade Commander brought me more worry and anxiety than I had bargained for.

Reinforcements from the Pacific

On January 24, 2nd Division received our first reinforcement from the Pacific—S-51 commanded by Captain 3rd Rank Ivan Kucherenko. The appearance of that submarine was preceded by a whole series of events.

Back in 1942, by decision of the Government, the Pacific Fleet had turned four Es-class and two Leninets-class submarines over to the Northern Fleet. These ships formed a unit commanded by Captain 1st Rank Alexander Tripolsky. A veteran Baltic frogman, he served in submarines, then completed officers' training courses, after which he was captain of L-55. She was an English submarine and had fought in the Civil War in the Baltic on the side of the whiteguards. In 1919, after an unsuccessful attempt to attack our ships in Kopor Bay, she was sunk by the destroyer *Azard*.

Nine years later she was raised from the seabed by salvage vessels, repaired and commissioned in the Soviet Navy under her old name, L-55, to remind the imperialists of the futility of their efforts to strangle the Soviet Republic. From L-55 Tripolsky was transferred as Captain to S-1, in which he fought against the White Finns and was decorated with the title of Hero of the Soviet Union. When the Nazis attacked the Soviet Union he was in command of a Submarine Division in the Baltic Fleet. But he saw little of the war, because soon afterward he was put in command of a Division in the Pacific Fleet.

The six submarines that were to sail from the Far East to the North across six seas and three oceans were put under his command.

L-15 and L-16 were the first to start on that long and arduous journey. On September 27 they set sail, heading for Dutch Harbor, the U.S. Naval Station on East Amaknak Island in the Pacific. On October 6, they were followed by S-51, S-54, S-55 and S-56.

From Dutch Harbor L-15 and L-16 headed for San Francisco. Our men were troubled by the fact that there had been a lot of talk at the U.S. Naval Station about the date of their departure and about their route. In wartime this information is usually kept secret.

A storm raged for several days, but the submarines proceeded surfaced, keeping on course in strict formation. L-16 was in the lead. On October 11, the wind finally subsided and the sea calmed down.

That morning the captain, the officer-of-the-watch Lieutenant Zhuiko, and Signaller Smolnikov were on the bridge of L-15. The second stage of their passage was drawing to a close: San Francisco was only a few miles away. Suddenly, at 11.15 hours the men on the bridge heard three loud explosions. At the same time, smoke enveloped L-16. The wireless operator received a message in open text from L-16. It said: "We're sinking from..." The message broke off there.

The smoke dispersed and the submarine disappeared from view within a matter of seconds. Smolnikov spotted the periscope of an unidentified submarine. There was no doubt that it had sent L-16 to the bottom. Artillery fire was opened at the periscope and it disappeared under water.

Whose submarine had dealt us this cruel and foul blow?* It had definitely not been a Nazi U-boat. Only U.S. submarines and the Japanese, who were fighting the U.S.A., sailed in these waters. Consequently, it could have been either a

---

*Japanese Captain Tagami's submarine I-25 is now thought to have been responsible for this attack.

submarine belonging to our ally, the U.S.A., or a submarine belonging to Japan, which was a neutral as far as we were concerned.

It might possibly have been an unintentional error. Either the Americans thought our boat was Japanese or the Japanese thought she was American. However that may be, the error could not be classed as a pure accident. The responsibility for the safety of our submarines on that passage devolved on the U.S. Navy. The carelessness and indiscretion of the Americans, on the one hand, and the defective system of notification and the slipshod measures to ensure the safety of the passage, on the other, had created the prerequisites for that error (or, perhaps, it was not an error after all).

L-15 entered San Francisco harbor alone.

The second group of submarines, with Tripolsky on board S-51, arrived in Dutch Harbor on October 23. Five days later the group secretly sailed for San Francisco with an escort of two U.S. destroyers, arriving there on November 2. A week later, with L-15, the entire group headed for Panama, reaching the Caribbean Sea on the far side of the Panama Canal on December 2. From there their route lay across the Atlantic to the port of Halifax in Canada.

This ten-day journey proved to be the most difficult stage of the passage. A hurricane fell upon the submarines, causing damage which the seamen repaired at considerable risk to their lives. Moreover, German U-boats were active in the Atlantic and a sharp look-out had to be kept for them.

From Halifax the group sailed to Iceland. From there their roads parted. Almost all the submarines required repairs and they were sent to different ports in Iceland and Britain. L-15 went into dry-dock at Greenock, Scotland. S-54 sailed to Portsmouth, S-55 to Rosyth, while S-56 remained in Reykjavik.

S-51 was the only submarine in the group that could continue the journey from Iceland directly to Polyarnoye. She arrived safely on January 24 after covering a distance of more than sixteen thousand miles.

Some of the details of this extremely difficult and dangerous passage were given to me by Ivan Kucherenko.

Massive and rough-looking, he made a good impression on me. He was firm and outspoken in his judgments. Speaking for the entire crew of S-51, he pressed me to send them into action as soon as possible.

"The refitting must be speeded up," he said. "We didn't

come here for a rest cure. We'd like you to send us on patrol as quickly as possible."

"The refitting won't hold you up," I told him. "But before I can let you go out you'll have to train a bit at Kildin Reach."

"What for?" Kucherenko said, bristling. "Didn't we have enough training crossing three oceans? We're ready for patrol this very minute."

"I admit your passage was an achievement, but it's not enough," I said, cooling him down. "You won't get very far if you don't get used to our sea. We'll send you into action after you show us what you can do with your torpedoes, particularly at night."

In the end Kucherenko agreed that training would not hurt things.

His desire for immediate action did him credit, while his somewhat overflowing confidence could be easily appreciated: not every submariner accomplishes a voyage around the world.

A Hazardous Experiment

On February 10, Lunin set a course for the Lopp Sea. K-21 had three assignments. The first was to lay a mine field in enemy waters, the second to land a reconnaissance group on the enemy coast, and the third to harass German shipping.

Brigade Command used to be more or less dependent on Fleet Command in the combat utilization of submarines. Before a submarine was sent out permission had to be obtained from the Fleet Commander-in-Chief or his Chief-of-Staff. Even at sea, submarines were in direct wireless communication with them. That system had now been changed, becoming less cumbersome.

Combat patrols were planned directly in the brigade and the Fleet Commander and Headquarters were kept abreast of these plans. As a rule, no objections were raised, but sometimes, acting on new intelligence reports, Headquarters advised us to select a new area for a submarine. At sea a submarine took its orders from the brigade.

Naturally, this gave the Brigade Commander a free hand and allowed him scope for initiative, for developing new tactics. On the other hand, this involved incomparably greater responsibility.

We saw Lunin off with our minds troubled about K-3 and

K-22. How would the experiment come off? Anxiety was wearing me to shreds.

As I have already said, the two submarines were trying out joint action in one and the same area. We had pictured something of the kind for a long time. Lone wolf tactics had ceased to satisfy us. At the time we did not have the means to enable submarines to receive wireless signals when submerged. This meant that if Headquarters was informed of the movements of an enemy convoy it could not at once send this information to all the submarines at sea. Signals were sent, nonetheless, on the off-chance that some of the submarines were on the surface at the given moment.

In winter, when visibility was poor, there was every chance that submarines operating on their own would fail to detect a convoy creeping stealthily along the shore: we did not have radar. In summer, spring and autumn, when there was daylight, submarines were compelled to move far away from the shore when they had to recharge their batteries. They had to do this to avoid detection. But in doing so they could not see the enemy and therefore could not threaten him in any way. To this must be added the fact that it had become much more difficult to attack convoys because now most of them had two screens. If a submarine took a shot at a transport from a great distance, the chance of hitting it was considerably reduced. And to break through the two screens in order to make sure of a hit meant to risk being sunk before having a chance to fire the torpedoes.

These considerations brought us around to the idea that group action would be much more effective. Submarines could then search for the enemy with a greater degree of success, and in attack, too, they could inflict heavier casualties on the enemy.

We felt that only sister submarines were suitable for action in packs. They had to be fast and highly maneuverable. They had to have reliable communication among themselves. And they had to have sufficient artillery power against mine sweepers and patrol ships. That excluded the Midgets and the Pikes. We had too few Leninets- and S-class submarines in the brigade. The choice, therefore, fell on the Katyushas. We selected K-3 and K-22 to try out our ideas.

The submarines were carefully prepared for the joint patrol. The training was supervised by Vinogradov.

They put out to sea on the day I took over as brigade commander.

The first report, sent by K-3 on the night of February 6, delighted us: the submarines had an encounter with an enemy convoy and sank one transport. A start had been made. We awaited more impressive news. But the next few days passed in silence. We were greatly troubled by it. On February 7, Malofeyev reported that he had lost contact with K-22. The submarine did not reply to our signals either. K-3 sailed to another area where she acted independently. We had further communication from her, but not a word came from Victor Kotelnikov. This silence—alas, so familiar now—resounded painfully in our hearts. But we still hoped for news. It could be that all this anxiety was being caused by nothing more than the failure of the submarine's wireless. That had happened before.

On February 13, the day the submarines were scheduled to return to Polyarnoye, the Fleet Commander-in-Chief, who had kept a close watch on the joint patrol, sent patrol ships to meet the submarines at Kildin. On the next day they entered Yekaterininskaya Harbor escorting K-3. There was only one submarine. She fired two salutes. My eyes filled with tears as I watched the scene.

A commander had to keep himself in control not only in battle. I went to the pier to give my comrades the welcome they deserved. But in my heart of hearts I almost no longer doubted that I would never again see Kotelnikov, Radun, Kulbakin, Matsevich and all the other members of K-22's wonderful crew. . . .

I was present when Nikolai Vinogradov gave the Fleet Commander-in-Chief a report on how the new method of action had been tried out in combat.

The submarines' assignment had been to hunt and destroy enemy shipping jointly. They were not molested by the enemy during the passage to the patrol area and maintained contact with each other. They spent about two days in the assigned area, sailing alternately dived and surfaced.

At 22.40 hours on February 5, Lieutenant-Captain Sobolevsky, who was officer-of-the-watch on K-3, and look-out Zvyagin sighted an enemy convoy. It took the submarine ten minutes to enter a battle course. Evidently, K-22 likewise steered an attack course—contact with her was lost during the maneuvering.

K-3 fired four torpedoes at a transport displacing eight thousand tons. Everybody on the bridge watched it sink. Then as K-3 turned around to attack a patrol ship with her stern torpedoes, a searchlight swept the sea and the beam came to rest on the submarine. The escort vessels opened up with all their guns. K-3 dived and left the attack area without having restored contact with K-22.

On the next morning K-3 arrived at the rendezvous which had been agreed upon in the event contact was lost. But she encountered a destroyer and two patrol ships. This compelled her to dive and leave the area. Nine depth charges were dropped but none of them caused her any harm.

The two submarines met, after all, in the course of the day. Kotelnikov said that he had been unable to attack the convoy because K-3 had been in the way. When K-3 began her escape maneuver, a torpedo fired by one of the escort vessels sped past K-22. Vinogradov, however, thought that K-3 had deviated from her course and that it had been one of her torpedoes. After that K-22 came under artillery fire. She dived and began eluding pursuit. The enemy soon gave up the chase.

After coming together, both submarines recharged their batteries and continued their joint search until 19.00 hours, February 7. K-3 had no further communication from K-22.

On the next day it turned out that K-3's underwater sound signal system had failed. The system was repaired, but that was no longer important. K-3 went to the prearranged rendezvous several times, but K-22 failed to appear. Shore contact with Kotelnikov ceased at approximately the same time. Vinogradov lost all hope of meeting K-22 and decided to act in accordance with his alternative variant, namely, independently. The submarine began patrolling the northern part of the area assigned to her.

In the morning of February 12, near Cape Seibines, she attacked a convoy of two transports and seven warships. Six torpedoes were fired at a transport of about ten thousand tons. Two of the torpedoes found their mark and through the periscope our men watched the transport begin to sink.

The submarine was chased. The enemy dropped thirty-two depth charges, but K-3 escaped. On the following day she turned homeward.

Thus, on this attempt, our idea of using two submarines together failed the test of combat. However, the reason for this was not that the idea itself was unsound. The whole thing boiled down to reliable underwater communication. Our system of communication was unreliable. Consequently, we could not recommend any further joint patrols until a new system was developed.

Other shortcomings were brought to light—the captain's attention was divided between looking for his target and keeping his submarine in formation. Without a reliable system of underwater communication, joint patrols would not yield better results than a search by submarines acting single. Lastly, when one of the submarines was bombed, both had to maneuver to safety because it was extremely difficult to tell which of the two was being attacked.

We, therefore, debated the possibility of utilizing two submarines in one patrol area under a different principle: while one recharged her batteries the other could carry on with the search. Smooth organization could exclude the danger of the submarines accidentally colliding, while the assigned sector of the enemy's lane would be under constant observation. These tactics could be particularly useful during the polar day, when submarines could not recharge their batteries near the coast for fear of being seen by the enemy.

We also discussed the possibility of joint action by submarines and aircraft.

Several more days passed, and our last, feeble spark of hope that K-22 would show up was extinguished. This loss was as heavy as the sinking of K-23 with Kerim on board. Kotelnikov had been as vivid and as important a figure among the submariners as Kerim. He had watched the Northern Fleet grow from a flotilla. A veteran seaman, he had won fame long before the war for his part in the rescue of the Papanin Expedition in the high latitudes. During his short term as Divisional Commander he had shown that he would have handled the job splendidly. There was no doubt in my mind that after one or two more patrols Victor would have won the Gold Star of Hero of the Soviet Union. The Fleet Commander-in-Chief had his name at the top of his list of recommendations for that decoration.

His death was a particularly heavy loss to me personally. I had lost a close friend. Ours had been a long friendship, which both of us had valued. How had one to measure such a loss? I cannot find the words to describe it. . . .

The only thing that somewhat distracted us from our sad

thoughts about K-22 was Lunin's report at the Military Council on February 22, the day after he returned from patrol.

The patrol began with trouble. As the submarine was approaching the Norwegian coast and surfaced her power plant in the fifth compartment short-circuited and burst into flames. The fire alarm was sounded and the men began to fight the fire. It was found that the oil and water pumps were damaged, and the diesel engines could not be started. The submarine had to use both electric motors.

The power subplant had to be immediately disconnected. Petty Officer 1st Class Kokonin, the engine room chief, correctly assessed the situation, put on the first sheepskin coat he could lay his hands on and rushed into the fire. That was the only way he could get to the panel. He cut off the switch and lost consciousness. In the meantime, other men battened down the external vents in the fifth compartment and tried to put out the flames with felt and fire extinguishers. These attempts failed. The men's clothes smoldered on them and many of them suffered burns. However, they went on fighting the fire until the Captain ordered them to leave the compartment and seal it so that the lack of oxygen would in itself put out the fire.

The submarine was drifting helplessly. An acrid, stinking smoke spread through the compartments. Some of the men from the fifth compartment were unconscious and had to be carried out. The Katyusha could not dive. Lunin was determined to fight to the end if the enemy appeared, and therefore the guns were manned and the torpedo tubes were readied for action. As a special emergency measure he ordered explosive cartridges to be placed beneath one of the reserve torpedoes and wrote out three wireless messages: "Fire has broken out, am unable to move," "Am engaged in artillery battle," "Am sinking but not surrendering."

The fire in the sealed compartment continued to rage for some time, the temperature reaching 150° C. The captain was worried that the solar oil tank might blow up.

At last the fire began to sputter and go out. The doors were opened and the affected compartment was aired. The damage was considerable: the power subplant and part of the cables running to the stern compartments were completely burned down; all the auxiliary mechanisms of the main diesels, the starboard lighting and the entire signal system in the stern compartments were out of commission, and damage was suffered by many other installations and systems. The crew at once got down to work. There could be no question of returning to the base.

Within eighteen hours it became possible to start the main diesels and the submarine proceeded with her combat assignment. She safely negotiated an enemy mine field at a great depth, and on February 18 mined the area around Arnoy Island. Soon afterward she landed the reconnaissance group, an operation which was considered among the most difficult because of the secrecy, speed and courage it required: a submarine had to surface near an unfamiliar sector of the coast, while if danger loomed she could not submerge at once because that would cut short the landing. Any carelessness on the part of the captain could cost the scouts their lives.

The landing was accomplished successfully, and hardly had it been completed than the wireless operator received a message stating that our troops had liberated Kharkov. The crew were eager to mark that victory with a victory of their own, but not a single convoy came their way. Lunin then took the daring step of entering Vogen Bay, where, intelligence reports stated, the enemy had a base for submarine chasers. Lunin planned torpedoing the wharves along which the chasers were tied up and, on the way back, if the opportunity arose, to sink the patrol ship that had been noticed sailing in the fjord at night with all its lights ablaze.

At about 12.30 hours on February 20 the main ballast tank was blown, the gun crews ordered to their stations, and the submarine, her two diesels pounding away, headed for the entrance to the fjord. Abeam of Lekei Island the submarine was spotted by a signal and observation post: it flashed the signal "A" to the strange vessel with its morse lamp. For a fleeting moment there was some confusion on the bridge, but Lunin once again demonstrated his resourcefulness.

"Reply 'NXT,'" he said to the signalman as though it were the sort of thing he did every day.

The morse lamp started blinking and the reply "NXT," which meant nothing, was sent to the post. While at the post they were trying to sort out the meaning of these symbols the submarine disappeared into the darkness of the night at full speed. When they crossed the fjord and approached its western shore, another post showed curiosity in the unexpected visitors.

"Send 'ZL'," Lunin ordered. "Let them rack their brains over it."

But at the post they did not rack their brains and refrained from further questioning: the signal "ZL" fully satisfied the Germans. One could understand what the signalmen there must have felt. If he raised a rumpus about call signals he could not understand he might be hauled over the carpet, accused of not knowing the morse code properly, not knowing the list of call signals, forgetting some point of the instructions and mistaking a German U-boat for an enemy submarine, and told that his place was not at a signal post but in the guard-house or, still worse, at the firing lines. . . .

The inquisitiveness of the third observation post at the approaches to Vogen Bay was similarly satisfied.

The pier loomed out of the darkness deep in the bay. Alongside were launches and motorboats—their masts could be seen clearly against the background of the coast. Four torpedoes were fired at the pier from a distance of twelve cable-lengths. Half a minute later a deafening explosion reverberated in the bay. Fragments of launches and the pier shot skyward in the bright flash.

The submarine swung around and moved to the exit from the fjord at half speed. Just then snow began to fall and the hope of meeting the patrol ship faded. To make up for it, the outlines of a submarine were seen moving on a head-on course. Lunin ordered full speed, meaning to ram the U-boat. But it dived in time.

By-passing an area where a mine field had been reported, K-21 dived and headed for home. In the evening of the next day the Fleet Commander-in-Chief and I welcomed her at the pier in Polyarnoye. She fired a one-gun salute.

What had been the harvest reaped by K-21? The men who were on the bridge at the time related that there had been many launches and motorboats at the pier in Vogen Bay at the time of the attack. The salvo had been aimed at that part of the pier where they were clustered. There were grounds for believing that at least five launches were destroyed.

Although we looked for new tactics, we could not complain of the old, tried methods: our intrepid captains applied them resourcefully, inflicting telling losses on the enemy.

Y.C.L. Midgets

Morozov's Division received reinforcements in the shape of five Midgets: M-104, M-105, M-106, M-107 and M-108. Among them were our first Y.C.L. submarines. The Y.C.L. assisted the Navy by collecting money for the building of submarines. This undertaking was supported by people who had long ago passed Y.C.L. age. The money was collected quite rapidly, and now we had the submarines.

The first Soviet submarines were named *Decembrist*, *Narodovolets* and *Krasnogvardeyets*. The first of the Pike series was called Pike and her sisters also had fish names. Then the submarines were made nameless, leaving them only with a letter to designate the series and also a number symbol. I really never knew the reason for it: either there was the fear that there would not be enough names because a large submarine fleet was planned, or there were other considerations. But now it was decided to revive the former tradition and christen the Midgets built on money collected by Y.C.L. members. This was of great educational value.

The new submarines had not yet been christened. The naval ensign had not been raised on them. They were still undergoing trials. But we already had the names for them. M-104 was to be known as *Yaroslavsky Komsomolets*, M-105 as *Chelyabinsky Komsomolets*, M-106 as *Leninsky Komsomol* and M-107 as *Novosibirsky Komsomolets*.

We were glad to see the Midgets quickly taking their place in our ranks. Despite their limited combat potentialities and despite the fact that they were used only in the inner zone, submarines of that class had notched up an impressive score. Starikov and Fisanovich, for example, had the largest bag of hits, leaving behind the captains of many of the larger submarines.

On Red Army and Navy Day we had an unusual ceremony. Sailors were lined up on the deck of one of the Midgets, and among them, on the right flank, were people in civilian clothes: one man and three women. They were representatives from Yaroslavl Region who had come for the ensign-hoisting ceremony on *Yaroslavsky Komsomolets*. They were Mikhail Zybin, Secretary of the Rybinsk Town Committee of the Y.C.L., Anfisa Shchukina, who worked at a collective farm, Antonina Malysheva, an agronomist, and Alexandra Soboleva, worker at a rubber plant.

"Raise ensign and dress ship!" Lieutenant-Captain Fyodor Lukyanov, the submarine's commander, ordered. The band struck up *The Internationale*. When the last strains of that stately, immortal melody died away, the workers' representatives officially turned the submarine over to the Northern Fleet.

On the next day the Yaroslavl Region representatives were given a few hours' ride in the submarine.

This meeting with representatives from Yaroslavl Region was remembered for a long time not only by the heroes of the day—the crew of M-104—but also by all the other submariners present. From the educational standpoint it was worth a score of talks and lectures on the bond between the armed forces and the people, on the unity between them. It made a deeper impression than any words could make.

The other Y.C.L. submarines were soon commissioned in much the same way.

Close contact was maintained between the submarines and the men who made them. When *Yaroslavsky Komsomolets* made her first kill she sent Yaroslavl Region a message informing them of it. Soon afterward the Region and the Northern Fleet submariners exchanged delegations.

It is neither possible nor necessary to list all the victories scored by the Midgets in the winter of 1942 and spring of 1943, for the only difference between them was the time, place and some external circumstances. But some were notable and these I would like to mention.

First and foremost, there was the March patrol of Guards M-171 under a new captain. Why a new captain? Because Starikov became captain of K-1, replacing Avgustinovich, who had been posted to the Fleet Submarine Branch. The new captain of the hard-hitting submarine was Lieutenant-Captain Georgi Kovalenko, namesake of the commander of a lost Pike. Prior to his appointment he was First Lieutenant in P-422.

On his first patrol Kovalenko had Nikolai Morozov as his Instructor Commander. On the day after putting out to sea, when the submarine was cruising at periscope depth the captain saw four patrol ships in formation. Kovalenko believed that they would be followed by transports, and Morozov agreed with him. The submarine dived to thirty meters.

Indeed, the noise of more propellers was soon heard. Then something hit the conning tower. Everybody stood stock still, expecting a devastating explosion. But there was no explosion, and the men heard splashes as though some objects were being thrown into the water. Shortly afterward a steel cable rattled against the starboard side. The sound of it was so unexpected that the men's hearts began beating wildly. Within a minute the rattling grew into a loud gnashing. The submarine listed 12 degrees to port.

"We've been caught in a sweep," Morozov guessed.

Soon there was quiet. The noise of propellers faded. The submarine rose to periscope depth and then surfaced. Considerable damage was found on the deck and the conning tower guard. The aerial had been snapped off; the mast signal light had been cut clean off; and there was a deep dent in the conning tower guard. There was now no doubt at all that a mine sweeper had caught the submarine in its sweep, believing it to be a mine. But the submarine's mass and impetus had torn the sweep.

There had been several tense moments, but on the whole it had been a curious experience. The damage did not prevent the submarine from carrying on with her assignment, and it was repaired when the submarine returned to the base.

Another memorable incident was recorded, this time by M-174, which had built up an enviable battle score under Captain 3rd Rank Nikolai Yegorov. With him in command M-174 became a guards submarine. In January 1943 Yegorov was sent to the Naval Academy and his place was taken by Lieutenant-Captain Ivan Sukhorenko, first lieutenant and veteran of P-404.

On March 23 he sailed on his fourth patrol in M-174. On the next day he began by-passing a mine field barring the way to a lane used by German convoys in coastal waters. M-174 followed a corridor that had been reconnoitered by our submarines. As was usual in such cases, the crew were at their battle stations. When, according to computations, the mine field was left behind, the crew were ordered to dinner.

Leading Seaman Mikhail Bayev was pouring out hot borsch in his tiny galley in the first compartment. He was a torpedoman, but a Midget did not carry a regular cook, and that job was done by somebody who could cook. Usually, the choice fell on some torpedoman, because the battle station of torpedomen was in the first compartment. This made it easier to combine the two duties.

With two plates of borsch he went to the second compartment, without taking any precautions—dived, a submarine did not roll. He had already placed one foot over the high threshold when there was a terrific explosion. The plates flew out of his hands and Bayev himself was thrown against a pressurized air tank.

The first thing that his senses became aware of when he recovered was the sound of water rushing into the submarine. He could see nothing in the semidarkness. Instinctively rather than consciously he ran to the door and closed it tight. Now he was alone in the compartment, isolated from everybody, and the fate of the entire crew was in his hands.

In the dim light of the single tiny lamp that was still burning, he saw the hole that was letting in the water. He reported this through the voice pipe and turned to face the danger. The water hit him in a cross shower—it was pouring into the submarine not only through a hole in the side but also through a safety valve, the lids of the torpedo tubes and the cracks in the bulkhead.

Knee-deep in the icy water the sailor fought the blind element single-handedly, without noticing the cold or experiencing fear in his loneliness. His mind was on saving the submarine, his comrades and himself. He grabbed the emergency tools and worked as he was taught to during drills in keeping submarines afloat. He made headway and this gave him confidence that he would avert disaster.

Soon the water was only slowly seeping through the planking and tow. The pump was turned on and the water level in the compartment began to fall. Finally it became possible to open the door. Bayev had triumphed.

The first compartment was not the only place where men fought to keep the submarine afloat. The mine which had blown a hole in the submarine's casing had inflicted a lot of other harm. The hydroplane helms were disabled and to prevent the submarine from sinking, the middle tank had to be blown and the submarine thereby ensured with the possibility of surfacing. This was extremely hazardous because it was not more than five miles to the shore. The situation was somewhat alleviated by the rough sea, in which it was not easy to spot a submarine from the shore.

When the immediate danger of sinking had been averted,

the mutilated submarine was examined. The mine blast had torn away the tip of the outer casing up to the ninth frame. The main ballast tank was punctured. The lower plating of the bow tip was bent, pressing down on the front covers of the torpedo tubes and denting the torpedo charging compartments. In short, it was easier to list what had not been damaged than what had. Yet the submarine retained her buoyancy. That was what mattered.

With a bow trim the submarine turned homeward. The struggle to keep her afloat never ceased throughout the run, which took about twelve hours.

The entire crew displayed supreme courage, but the sternest test, of course, had been passed by Mikhail Bayev.

Bayev was one of those people who dreamt of performing an exploit. In the grim month of June 1941, when naval detachments were hastily formed to help the land forces, he wrote in his application to the Brigade Commander: "My father taught me to be brave and my mother gave me a cool head and endurance. I taught myself to scorn death. I hate the Nazis with all my heart and shall destroy them, wherever I see them." He thought service in a submarine was much too serene, quiet and safe. He made every effort to be sent to the firing lines, but this was denied to him. The submarine was being prepared for action and every trained man was needed.

But the time came when the sailor had to perform an exploit, even if it was not a very spectacular one. He performed it simply, modestly and efficiently, showing that the grandiloquent words in his application were not simply words, that if necessary he was prepared to do more than ready torpedo tubes for firing and cook delicious borsch.

The Northern Fleet Grows

As far as we were concerned, International Women's Day did not turn out to have anything in common with the gentle sex. Two Esses, which had been in dry-dock in foreign ports after their passage from the Pacific, arrived on that day.

They came singly. The first to appear in Yekaterininskaya Harbor was S-56 commanded by Grigory Shchedrin. She came in the morning.

It was our custom to meet each new submarine in a surface ship in the region of Teriberka and accompany her to Kildin

Salma. There the officer sent to meet the submarine would board her and act as "pilot" all the way to Polyarnoye.

This custom derived not only from the laws of hospitality. Kildin Salma was an extremely narrow strait and not every captain could get through if he was unfamiliar with it. But the main thing was that German U-boats had begun to appear in the approaches to Kola Bay. To safeguard our submarines against them an officer was needed who knew the enemy's habits, and also at least one surface vessel to act as an escort.

Shchedrin was met by Captain 3rd Rank Semyonov, the new brigade flag navigator, who had taken over from Aladjanov when the latter became fleet flag navigator.

After lunch I went to meet S-55 on the *Kuibyshev*. At Teriberka we saw the submarine, which had just surfaced. We exchanged signals, hoisted flags welcoming the submarine and together set a course for home. At Salma a launch took me from the destroyer to the submarine. I was warmly welcomed by the commander, Captain 3rd Rank Lev Sushkin, whom I liked at first sight. I congratulated him on his arrival in the Northern Fleet.

I had already heard from Kucherenko that Sushkin was a first-class submariner. Indeed, my first impression of him was that he had a great deal of experience, and one could see that he enjoyed the respect of his men.

Captain 2nd Rank Ivan Palilov, an old friend of mine, appeared on the bridge as soon as we passed through the narrowest point of the strait. He had served in the North since the summer of 1933. In 1937 he went to Spain as a volunteer. I did not see him after his return and never suspected that he was on board.

He brought us regards from the Naval Attache in the U.S.A. Ivan Yegorichev and from the entire Soviet colony in the United States. There was no end to his questions. He wanted to know everything at once: who of his old mates were in the North, what Polyarnoye was like, how we lived and fought.

"We'll be there soon and you'll see everything for yourself," I told him.

At the pier the submarine was met by the Fleet Commander-in-Chief, the Member of the Military Council and the Chief of the Submarine Branch. This addition to the Northern Fleet had put everybody in a good mood. It was particularly gratifying that both captains reported to the Commander-in-Chief that the submarines would be ready for combat duty as soon as the mechanisms were inspected and the stocks replenished.

In the evening Alexander Tripolsky, who came in S-56, gave me the details of the passage, describing the submarines, the officers and the crews. It was interesting to listen to him. He gave a comprehensive assessment of everybody he mentioned and tried to be as fair as possible. In conclusion he noted that the men were itching for action.

These were welcome reinforcements, and soon the other submarines, which were completing repairs in Britain, would be arriving. New Midgets and Esses were expected in the near future. All this posed me with the problem of changing the brigade's organizational pattern.

After Kotelnikov's death, command of 1st Division was taken over by Mikhail Khomyakov. He had sailed in all classes of submarines before the war, and knew his Katyushas well. But by this time we only had two Katyushas left. K-3 did not outlive K-22 for long. Kuzma Malofeyev and his tried crew went on their last war patrol in spring. K-3's grave was somewhere in the Norwegian Sea. 1st Division was acutely in need of reinforcements and we gave it L-class submarines, which were closer than any others to the Katyushas.

2nd Division consisted of S-class submarines. Captain 1st Rank Tripolsky replaced Khomyakov as Divisional Commander. But when all the Pacific Esses arrived and we were informed that we would be getting more of these submarines it was found that there would be too many ships in one division. We therefore formed another division, the 5th, of S-class submarines and Captain 2nd Rank Pavel Yegorov, a namesake of the former captain of M-174, became its commander.

Yegorov was no novice in the Northern Fleet. He arrived from the Baltic in the summer of 1939 as captain of P-421. He fought in the war against Finland, and in the summer of the next year entered the Naval Academy. In the summer of 1941 he graduated from the Academy and returned to the North, where he was appointed to staff work. But he did not take root at Headquarters and insisted on a transfer to a submarine. In the end, his request was satisfied, and in the autumn he was appointed captain of S-101.

The submarine did not have a distinguished battle record. On the contrary, she even earned the nickname "bombcatcher," which was by no means conducive to high morale. In September 1941, during her first passage from the shipyard to Polyarnoye, she was bombed by our own aircraft, due to some confusion in identification signals. Although there was no direct hit, the attack was so "successful" that the submarine had to return to the shipyard for repairs. She arrived in Polyarnoye only in mid-December.

On combat patrol she was dogged by depth charges and aircraft bombs. In April 1942, while providing cover for an Allied convoy, she drew so close to its course that the escort vessels bombed her. Luckily, the bombing was inaccurate and no grave damage was inflicted.

A month later, in the region of Tana Fjord, when she was laying a battle course to attack a convoy, Torpedoman Troitsky fired a torpedo without waiting for orders. The submarine was immediately attacked by escort vessels. The chase was called off nearly twenty-seven hours later, when many of the crew were beginning to lose consciousness from the shortage of oxygen and the high content of hydrogen in the submarine.

In the course of five patrols the submarine sank only one transport, and nearly one thousand two hundred depth charges were fired at her. This run of bad luck was taken keenly to heart by the crew, and it was decided to appoint a new captain. Yegorov got the job.

In March, during his first operational patrol, he attacked two convoys, sinking a transport each time. This greatly heartened the crew. The submarine, of course, was depth-charged, and pretty heavily, too, especially after her second attack. But she evaded her pursuers skilfully. The crew had developed an immunity to bombings, and the enemy attacks made little impression on them.

The next patrol brought another victory. Then followed a patrol during which the submarine attacked five ships. She sank a transport of seven thousand tons and a mine sweeper of eight hundred tons. The other vessels were damaged. The figure 6 appeared in the heart of the star painted on S-101's conning tower.

Such was Captain 2nd Rank Yegorov, commander of the new, 5th Division. He turned his submarine over to his First Lieutenant-Captain Yevgeny Trofimov.

Vladimir Ivanov continued commanding 3rd Division. In P-404 he was succeeded by Lieutenant-Captain Grigory Makarenkov. All of the division's four remaining Pikes were now commanded by captains who had received their appointments during the war. Incidentally, in Shuisky's case I'm stretching it a little when I say he became a Captain during the war. It was a job that he had held before the war. Our shipyards were not building any more Pikes. Ivanov's Division was, nonetheless, expecting reinforcements. We knew that a modified version of the Midget was in the slips. The new submarines would carry two diesels and four torpedo tubes and would have a larger range. Moreover, they would be faster. We planned to use them in the same division as Pikes, because they resembled the latter rather than the Midgets we now had.

4th Division had grown and would receive further reinforcements. Morozov had more than he could handle breaking in the new captains, and the answer to that problem was to form a 6th Division. Captain 2nd Rank Israel Fisanovich was put in command of the new division of Midgets. We could not wish for anybody better for that post. He knew these submarines like the back of his hand and, besides, he was a clever, subtle tactician with a flair for coaching.

At the shore base in a large, bright room that looked like a classroom, a sheet of Whatman paper showing the situation at sea hung next to the blackboard. The diagrams on the paper had been expertly drawn by Zubrilkin, navigator in P-422. The submarine's captain, Fyodor Vidayev, stood at the diagram with a pointer in his hand.

At the black desks sat submarine captains, first lieutenants, Political Deputies, Divisional Commanders, Staff Officers and Officers from the Political Department. Vidayev was analyzing the results of his latest patrol.

Usually a submarine returning home was met at the pier by the Fleet Commander-in-Chief and the Brigade Commander. There and then, on the pier, the captain would report the results of the patrol.

"You'll report in detail the day after tomorrow," the Fleet Commander-in-Chief would say. "And now I want you to rest."

But it was not so simple for a submarine captain to rest. He had to give his Division and Brigade commanders a full, day-to-day description of all that had happened during the patrol. This would usually take the form of an animated talk during which arguments and clashes of opinion would arise. The patrol would be examined and all the i's dotted and t's crossed. At the appointed time the three of them would go to the Fleet Commander-in-Chief and each give him his opinion.

Arseny Golovko took these analyses very seriously. He went into all details, sometimes finding things in them for which we'd be taken to task. But he never allowed the main thing to be clouded over by details. He was always fair in his end assessment.

These analyses with the Fleet Commander-in-Chief were extremely useful training. And in order to spread this training to as large a number of officers as possible it was decided to conduct the analyses in the presence of a large audience of officers, chiefly submarine officers. All noteworthy patrols were analyzed in this fashion. In 1942 this practice became rooted in the brigade.

Now Vidayev was giving officers a report—this formula was coming more and more into use—on his patrol. He and all the other officers were wearing yellow shoulder straps. They had been introduced in the navy during the previous month and we still had to get used to them.

Vidayev was no orator. Properly speaking, that was not required of him. The important thing was not pretty words but business. And business was what the diagrams eloquently spoke of. With explanations, even the most laconic, they reproduced the entire picture of attacks.

"At 14.50 hours on February 20," Vidayev said, "hydrophone operator Zhuchkov heard propellers. We steered a course according to acoustic bearings. At 15.03 hours we saw masts through our periscope. At 15.21 hours a convoy—a transport and three patrol ships—came into view. Then astern of the transport we saw the fourth patrol ship and another transport. While we were getting ready to attack we saw more and more ships. Altogether we counted fifteen vessels—warships and transports.

"We selected the leading transport for our target. It was the largest and the most convenient to attack. At 16.15 hours we fired four torpedoes from a distance of ten cable-lengths. Two of the torpedoes found their mark and the transport, displacing about eight thousand tons, sank. We were pursued by two patrol ships and three submarine chasers. But they dropped only eleven depth charges. . . ."

Vidayev gave a similarly brief description of his second attack, which took place on February 27. During that attack, as well, he took his bearings by sound. The target was a patrol ship of about eight hundred tons. A minute before the salvo was fired the captain clearly saw that it was flying the

Nazi naval ensign. The submarine fired from a distance of seven cable-lengths, and three of the four torpedoes struck and sank the patrol ship. Torpedo boats gave chase. They dropped only four depth charges which exploded dangerously close to the submarine. After that P-422 bypassed a deeply-lying mine field and steered a course for home, arriving in Polyarnoye on March 1.

Among the audience were Kucherenko, Sushkin and Shchedrin, commanders of the submarines that had come from the Pacific. They listened closely to what Vidayev was saying, because for them this training was of particular value: eager as they were to see action they had not yet been on patrol. But S-51 was still undergoing repairs, and I had told Sushkin and Shchedrin, "I want you to look around, to get used to our theater. You need training before I can let you go on patrol."

Like Kucherenko, they had at first felt hurt.

"Haven't we had enough training? Why all this formality? We're only wasting time."

But order was order. Before permitting a submarine to go on operational patrols we had to be sure that she was not going for nothing, that the captain could be entrusted with the lives of fifty sailors.

The Vidayev report gave the Pacific captains many new angles. Shortly afterward I sailed in our slow depot ship *Umba* to Kildin Reach to watch Sushkin and Shchedrin take their submarines through their paces. The practice attacks came off well. Indeed, they knew their business and it was decided to send the submarines on patrol.

The submarines followed each other to sea with an interval of three days, S-55 leaving on March 28 and S-56 on March 31.

S-55 was the first to open her battle score. And she did it impressively. On the day after pulling out from the base she attacked two transports. They were sailing close to each other. Two torpedoes hit the leading vessel, which displaced about eight thousand tons, and one torpedo sank the second ship, which was a transport of about two thousand tons. The submarine was pursued for eighteen hours, being bombed continuously for seven hours. But of the hundred and seven depth charges that were dropped, not one harmed her.

Shchedrin opened his score on April 10. The transport

attacked by him with stern tubes was sliced in half, the bow half keeling over to starboard and the stern half to port. The captain photographed this spectacle through the periscope. Four days later S-56 again fired her stern torpedoes, one of which hit the target. But there was no possibility of observing the results of the attack.

On her way home S-56 was attacked by a German U-boat. Had it not been for the vigilance of Divisional Navigator Palastrov, who was officer-of-the-watch, this first patrol would have been the last.

The submarine returned to the base on April 19. Reporting the results, Shchedrin said, "We feel we've paid our 'entrance fee' to the Northern Fleet."

Indeed, the two submarines passed their initiation with flying colors. The crews were accorded a gala reception which included a dinner in which suckling pigs figured in the menu. Lately, the tradition of suckling pig dinners had been somewhat amended.

Victories had become too frequent and habitual to be marked with a dinner each time. For that reason a dinner was given when a submarine returned with her first victory, or scored victories in several patrols consecutively, or if the victory coincided with the anniversary of the hoisting of the submarine's ensign.

Sushkin and Shchedrin showed that their successes were not accidental. On her next patrol S-55 attacked a large convoy on April 29. Sushkin broke through the escort screen and sank a large transport with four torpedoes, which he fired from a distance of five cable-lengths. The submarine was fiercely depth-charged. A total of eighty-five depth charges were dropped and there were some narrow escapes. Both the outer and inner casings were damaged. The magnificent work of hydrophone operator Belkov and the skilful maneuvering saved the ship. S-55 limped home where she was repaired.

In May Shchedrin repeated Sushkin's best effort. With a salvo of four torpedoes he hit two ships—a transport and a tanker. Later, intelligence reported that both ships had been sunk. The Pacific submariners liked sinking two ships with a single salvo. This was becoming their style. In June Shchedrin once again fired at two targets simultaneously. They were a transport and a patrol ship, and both vessels were hit. A few days later, during the same patrol, S-56 sank a patrol ship with a salvo from her stern tubes.

On the way home she collided under water with some unseen obstacle. Judging by the sounds the obstacle was a sunken vessel. S-56 was caught between its mast and shrouds. It took a long time to get out of this trap.

The third Pacific submarine, S-51, went into action in May. On that first patrol she hit a transport with a salvo of three torpedoes from her bow tubes. In June she started her patrol by sinking a transport, and then, four days later, Kucherenko fired a salvo at a mine sweeper and a transport simultaneously. Both targets were sunk. The convoy had consisted of only these ships, and Kucherenko had made short work of it with a single salvo.

The other Pacific submarines—S-54 and L-15—were committed later, in July. During her very first patrol S-54, commanded by Dmitri Bratishko, sank a transport. Vasily Komarov, Captain of L-15, successfully fulfilled his assignment of laying a mine field. We were extremely pleased with the reinforcements received from the Pacific Fleet.

EXPLOITS AND GLORY

The Soviet Character

The strains of martial music floated across Yekaterininskaya Harbor at 08.00 hours on July 25. Seamen wearing dress uniforms and Orders and medals were lined up on the decks of the ships, which were flying their dress flags.

The Northern Fleet was marking a double festival: its own tenth anniversary and Navy Day.

The following decree was read on each of the submarines in the base, in front of the men lined up on the decks:

"For exemplary fulfilment of combat assignments of the High Command in the struggle against the German invaders and for displaying gallantry and courage, the Northern Fleet Submarine Brigade is decorated with the Order of the Red Banner.

"*M. Kalinin*. President of the Presidium of the Supreme Soviet of the U.S.S.R.

"*A. Gorkin*. Secretary of the Presidium of the Supreme Soviet of the U.S.S.R.

"The Kremlin, Moscow. July 24, 1943."

The cheers rolled across the decks and faded in a distant echo in the hills.

P-403 and P-404 were awarded the Order of the Red Banner, and M-172, P-402 and P-422 were named guards submarines.

Submariners were not the only ones to receive honors. The destroyer *Valerian Kuibyshev*, the Submarine-Chaser Division commanded by Captain 3rd Rank Zyuzin, the mine sweeper MS-32, Major Kosmachev's Separate Coast Artillery

Division, and the 12th Marine Brigade received the Order of the Red Banner. *Gremyachy* was a named guards destroyer.

To think that we had come to this area only ten years ago! It had looked wild and desolate. How our hearts were wrung at the very mention of Leningrad, Kronstadt and the Baltic, which we had regarded as our home. And how improbable it had seemed to us that a bitter war would be fought in these virtually unpeopled places, where man had to grapple with nature almost daily.

Ten years! It was a short span of time compared with the history of the Baltic Fleet, which was founded by Peter the Great, or with the history of the fleet in the Black Sea, whose waves once bore the ships of admirals Grigory Spiridov and Fyodor Ushakov. But what a long time it was judging by what had been accomplished in the North and how our fleet had grown. We now had submarines of various classes. Despite losses, our submarine brigade was numerically stronger than before the war. Our aircraft had won supremacy in the air. Our coastal artillery was an unassailable defensive force. And we were fighting a war over a vaster area than the Baltic or the Black Sea.

This was the first time since the outbreak of the war that Navy Day was being marked on such a large scale. One could understand it. Victory was not yet near, but it was in sight. We had triumphed on the Volga. A battle of almost the same scale was being fought at Kursk. The unparalleled tank battles were clearly showing that we would win. Things were going well for us there, where the main destiny of the war was being decided, and here, on the northernmost flank. We had much to celebrate.

A concert in Naval House was followed by a banquet. Congratulations poured in. However, there was no peace of mind: we could not help remembering friends who had not returned from sea.

P-422 did not survive to receive the award she had earned. Contact with her broke off ten days before the Decree was signed. She had put out to sea on July 1.

There had been an incongruous coincidence when Vidayev took over P-421, which likewise did not live to receive a battle decoration. But at that time the submarine herself was lost but the crew were saved. Now matters were a thousand times worse. Neither the submarine nor the crew had returned. Nobody knew what had happened to them.

I shall always remember Fyodor Vidayev telling his friends with his usual optimism and shy smile, "I'll make just one more run and then go on leave. The Fleet Commander-in-Chief has promised to let me go. I must see my son."

Shortly before that patrol he had finally resumed correspondence with his wife, whom he had been unable to contact for a long time. He had seen very little of his small son. That meeting would now never take place.

Shuisky and Kautsky were eating their hearts out with grief. They had been inseparable from Vidayev, and they had made a fine trio. Despite their different characters, they were brought together by their honest, scrupulously conscientious attitude to their work, by their love of the sea. I do not wish to say that other officers did not have these qualities. But in Shuisky, Kautsky and Vidayev they were expressed strikingly, and this made its imprint on their personalities. They were modest men by nature and by their way of thinking. But their deeds in battle could not be called modest.

Vidayev won the reputation of being a tenacious hunter and courageous officer. When he spotted a target he did everything possible and impossible to prevent it from escaping him. No matter how heavily escorted a target was he would break through to deliver a salvo from close range, from a distance of four or five cable-lengths, in order to make sure of a hit. In this way he had attacked a huge transport in April and then again in May, when his attack was followed by a three-hour chase in which the enemy dropped three hundred and fifty depth charges.

All submarine captains were interested in Vidayev's attacks, which bore the stamp of a striking talent. Everything he did proved to be reasonable and acceptable in the given situation. His ability to take his bearings by sound for an attack in bad visibility was cited as an example.

During one of his attacks, he saw that a patrol ship escorting his target had turned directly toward the submarine. It was hard to say whether it had detected the submarine or had, by coincidence, changed course in the execution of a zigzag. However that may be, the ship drew nearer to the submarine. Very little time remained before the torpedoes would be fired. Vidayev stuck to his attack course.

The patrol ship suddenly veered away, and within the next few moments the submarine shuddered as the torpedoes were fired. Later Fyodor explained his action:

"I was almost certain that the patrol ship was accidentally coming in our direction. Even if it intended to ram us we would have had time to fire our torpedoes."

That was Vidayev all over.

His crew were like him to a man. "If nails were made of them, they'd be the toughest nails in the world," Tikhonov once wrote, as though having the crew of P-422 in mind.

The sailors loved their Captain. He was extremely popular in the Brigade. And the Fleet Commander-in-Chief, too, liked him.

On the day P-422 set out on her last patrol, Arseny Golovko presented Vidayev with his third Order of the Red Banner. This short military ceremony took place on the submarine. The men beamed with joy as they watched their Captain receive the decoration.

When Golovko returned to the pier he said:

"Sailors would follow an officer like him through thick and thin. He's unassuming, selfless and gifted. Since he took over P-422, the submarine's battle score has risen from four to eleven. He'll be a Hero before long."

When I felt there was no longer any hope of seeing P-422 again, I reported to Golovko, Nikolayev and Vinogradov that Vidayev would not return. . . .

In Polyarnoye, near Yekaterininskaya Harbor, stands a small monument designed by naval artist Alexei Koltsov. It is a bust of Fyodor Vidayev in uniform, a token of the respect and affection that he enjoyed among Northern Fleet submariners.

Much, very much could be written about each one of the men who went down with Guards P-422. About First Lieutenant Nikolai Belayev, who as Navigator had saved P-403 from being rammed; about Engineering Officer Alexei Bolshakov, who brought P-402 back to the base after she was disabled by an explosion; about Navigator Electrician Stephan Chernousov, who wrote his will in a letter to his parents:

"My dears, I am fighting for my country and I want to hit the accursed cannibals as hard as I can. My life is devoted to the struggle for the happiness of my people. I may be killed in this struggle. If that happens, I want you to know that your Stepan served his country, that he fought Nazism and sacrificed his life for a righteous cause, for the people, for the Party. . . ."

But in speaking of those who deserved the greatest credit, mention must be made of the youngest.

In the Brigade we had many ship's boys. Among them were Stanislav and Yura Miroshnichenko, sons of the Flag Deputy Engineering Officer (who later became officers), and Valentin Khrulev, son of the Captain of M-105 (he re-enlisted as Warrant Officer). Most of the boys worked in the ship-repair workshops. But some of them learned other trades. Mitya Komlin, for example, became a wireless operator.

All of them, without exception, dreamed of going on a war patrol. It required an effort to hold them back. Mitya, too, wanted to go to sea. To win that right he learned a trade in less than six months. But he was allowed only as far as Kildin Reach in the *Umba*, or in submarines polishing up on some training task.

At the close of June, Flag Signals Officer Bolonkin reported to me that Mitya had become a good wireless operator, that he knew his way about submarines and was begging to be allowed to go on an operational patrol. We had already had cases of ship's boys stealing out to sea after permission to do so had been withheld. They would hide where there was the least chance of being discovered. Possibly, in some cases they were helped by one or two of the sailors. And when the submarine would be far out at sea the stowaway would emerge from his hiding place. The Captain could do nothing about it—he couldn't very well return to the base because of him.

Mitya had evidently made up his mind to do something of the kind. With an aching heart I gave him permission to sail in P-422.

The lad was delighted, as though he were being given leave to see his parents. Who knew what destiny had in store for him. . . .

An Unsung Song

For us the month of October began with Headquarters moving to a new command post, whose building had started when war broke out. It was a large and spacious building. I had two whole rooms to myself—an office and a bedroom.

But that unimportant event was by no means what made October a memorable month for us. I mentioned that detail simply because in that new building we received both good and sad news, of which there was quite enough for one month.

Vasily Khrulev, Captain of *Chelyabinsky Komsomolets*, reported:

"We were proceeding surfaced when at 00.20 hours on October 4 we sighted four mine sweeper launches sailing in formation. We dived under them, and Demyanenko, my hydrophone operator, reported that he heard the propellers of large vessels. We set a course for them. At 00.50 hours we surfaced and found a quite large convoy silhouetted about fifteen cable-lengths away. There were four transports, two patrol ships and four torpedo boats. I went into a battle course, and at 01.15 hours fired a salvo from six cable-lengths. You should have seen the fireworks," Khrulev could not help grinning. "There was a huge pillar of water and smoke. The transport sank quickly. We dived and made in the direction of the coast. The Nazis looked for us in the open sea, where, of course, they did not find us. That about sums it up."

Sushkin's S-55 went on patrol again on September 30, after completing her repairs. In the morning of October 12, hydrophone operator Belkov heard the propellers of many ships. The submarine drew closer to them and despite the poor visibility the captain made out a convoy of two transports, five patrol ships and two mine sweepers. Sushkin steered an attack course and five minutes before the torpedoes were to be fired he suddenly saw a patrol ship coming swiftly in his direction. It was so close that it blanketed the view in the periscope.

There was no time to speculate whether it was an attack or the patrol ship had changed course. Sushkin ordered the submarine down to fifteen meters. The patrol ship's propellers swished past overhead. With that danger averted, Sushkin's thoughts returned to the attack, which he had not given up. He had not even changed his course, for all the computations had been completed and the captain had no grounds for doubting them. He had every confidence in his hydrophone operator, and relying on his sound bearings and computations he fired a salvo from his bow tubes.

Hollow rumbles were heard a minute and twenty seconds later—three of the torpedoes had struck home. The chase lasted for about an hour with the enemy dropping forty-nine depth charges with no effect.

Soon afterward intelligence reported that S-55 sank one transport and damaged another.

The news of these victories warmed our hearts. However, there was other news that brought nothing but sadness.

Suddenly I received orders from the Fleet Commander-in-Chief to send K-1 to the Kara Sea.

These orders caught me by surprise. I could not understand the need for them. Both our Katyushas were undergoing repairs. True, K-1 was almost ready for combat duty, but her captain, Valentin Starikov, had gone on leave and had not yet returned. There was no time to recall him.

But why had it been found necessary to send a Katyusha to the Kara Sea? A Pike or even an Es would have been much more suitable.

The Fleet Commander-in-Chief patiently explained that it was felt that our internal communication lines might be attacked by surface raiders and it was therefore found expedient to have in the Kara Sea a large submarine armed with large guns that would enable it, if the necessity arose, to engage in an artillery duel.

Tactically this surmise had no grounds. If a submarine was set the task of covering our own communications against surface forces, only its torpedo strength had to be taken into account. Moreover, if the enemy sent a raider it would be at least a cruiser, and it would be ludicrous to attempt to oppose it with the artillery carried by a submarine exclusively for self-defense in the event it was forced to the surface or for sinking a torpedoed transport. A submarine could successfully fight a patrol ship or small destroyers, but even that was extremely hazardous as was shown by the patrol from which Kerim Gadjiev never returned.

On the other hand, if there was a need for a "submarine with cannon," why did the choice not fall on one of our many Esses? They had a 100 mm gun, like the Katyushas. Lastly, how could a submarine be sent on an operational patrol without her captain?

I said all this perhaps with much too much emotion to the Fleet Commander-in-Chief and was backed up by Vinogradov, who was present.

Arseny Golovko replied in a tired voice:

"I'm as much aware of it as you are. But Moscow insists that we send K-1. I've rung them up twice, but they rejected all my arguments. They insist that the Divisional Commander replace Starikov. Prepare K-1, there's no help for it. Khomyakov will go."

The repairs on K-1 were rounded off and the submarine was hurriedly prepared for her assignment. I saw Mikhail Khomyakov off to sea with a heavy heart. I was worried about the submarine's condition.

That took place in September. In October communication with the submarine broke off and she did not return home. We never knew what happened.

What we did know was that we had lost a large submarine and a fine crew headed by Captain 1st Rank Khomyakov.

October brought us another heavy loss. P-403, which sank six transports, two mine sweepers and a patrol ship in the course of fourteen patrols, did not return to Polyarnoye. With that submarine we lost a superb officer, valiant fighter and wonderful person in Konstantin Shuisky.

Our list of bitter losses that month ended with M-172, which went on her second patrol after a long period in dry-dock. Her commander was Lieutenant-Captain Kunets.

The reader will remember that Kunets had been in command of another *Midget*, but had been unable to show what he was capable of. Under him M-173 did not score a single victory. Even when he clashed with the enemy he had been unable to bring off a torpedo attack. He simply did not have the qualities one expected in a submarine captain. Early in 1942 he was appointed first lieutenant in S-102. It had been the correct thing to do.

Some people labor under a delusion about themselves. Kunets was one of them. He never understood—one could not, of course, blame him for it—that he would never make a good submarine captain. He was firmly convinced that he was cut out for the command of a submarine. He used to say as much to Morozov and to his new captain, Gorodnichy.

When Fisanovich was appointed Divisional Commander, Kunets applied for his place as captain of M-172. He was supported by Morozov and Gorodnichy. Although I knew I was doing the wrong thing, I allowed myself to be persuaded.

He took over the command of the famous Midget, which

was undergoing repairs at the time. I was glad to see that Fisanovich kept an eye on the submarine, visiting it and talking to the men whenever he had the opportunity. I felt that that too would help Kunets.

After the repairs, M-172 went on patrol with Fisanovich as Instructor Commander. It was a fruitless hunt, and in Fisanovich's report there was nothing against the new captain. It was therefore decided to send him on the next patrol independently.

While waiting for the return of his Midget, Fisanovich prepared a small present for her. He not only loved to read poetry but also tried his hand at writing it. This time he wrote lyrics, which he dedicated to the crew of M-172. Composer Yevgeny Zharkovsky, who was serving with us at the time, liked them and wrote the music.

But the song was never sung. M-172 never returned.

I reproached myself for having agreed to Kunets' appointment. Had the submarine been in more reliable hands she might not have perished.

However, when I think of it, these reproaches were somewhat exaggerated. M-174, which sank about a month before, was commanded by Ivan Sukhoruchenko, a courageous and capable officer, who had fully demonstrated his skill as a sailor and submariner when he brought the submarine back to the base after she had hit a mine. Then there were Vidayev, Khomyakov, Malofeyev and Shuisky. Nobody could say that they had lacked skill, resourcefulness and self-control.

In spite of everything I could not help thinking that through some miscalculation I was somehow responsible for the loss of the submarine. Logic and sober reasoning are sometimes helpless in a case like this.

The Third War Year

A frowning, tear-laden autumn hung over Central Russia. It seemed that the sky was returning to the earth all the tears shed by widows and orphans. Winter had already set in in the North. It was the third war winter. But in that year the inconsolable grief of people who had lost dear and loved ones was assuaged more and more by a smile. That year witnessed a great and final turning point in the war. It was clear to everybody that our successes were lasting and irreversible, that the enemy was being driven out of our country. On the scales of human emotions, the joy that this gave outweighed the heavy burden of personal grief.

In this mood we celebrated the November anniversary, which in the North is marked with an extremely short day and a shrieking wind.

In the brigade we carried on with our combat assignments. Winter helped the submariners to operate in greater secrecy, but it hindered the search for the enemy and required redoubled efforts for the struggle with the relentless elements.

It was the first polar winter for the submarines that had come from the Pacific. To L-15 that winter brought the joy of further victories.

On November 22 it attacked a mine layer, which was escorted by two patrol ships. Only one of the six torpedoes that were fired found its mark, but it was enough to sink the mine layer.

In two days, while she was on the surface, the submarine encountered three mine sweepers. Komarov attacked them without diving, sinking one of them with a salvo of three torpedoes. Good as the result was it could have been better if the captain had dived, filled his main ballast tanks and fired in position. Had he done that he might have sunk all three mine sweepers. Although victors are not judged, this slip was underlined when the attack was analyzed.

S-55, on the other hand, had to be considered lost. Lev Sushkin had gone on his first war patrol only eight months before and had been the first of the Pacific captains to open his battle score. He had been the first to sink two transports with a single salvo. It was hard to believe that Lev Sushkin had been unable to extricate himself from danger and that S-55 would never again enter Yekaterininskaya Harbor firing salutes. We waited until the New Year, and even after the Order of the Day declaring that the submarine had perished was published some of us still hoped that all was not lost, that it was simply a delay due to unforeseen circumstances. Our hopes did not materialize. The submarine had indeed perished, and, as always, we never knew how.

That winter our submarines hunted singly and not in pairs, as was frequently the case in spring and summer. The system, under which one submarine carried on the search while another recharged her batteries, had justified itself. True, we had not been able to utilize that system under all circumstances because it required a large number of submarines ready to set sail at a given moment. At times we were short-handed, due to losses and our inadequate repair facilities.

In winter submarines did not have to go far from the shore to recharge their batteries. Batteries were recharged without interrupting the search, which was conducted on the surface under cover of the darkness. In the meantime, we were already planning to organize combined attacks on convoys. Our fleet now had a powerful aircraft branch. Torpedo carriers frequently cruised over the sea hunting the enemy. Together with bombers they attacked enemy naval units.

We now had more torpedo boats, including U.S. and British boats that we had received under Lend-Lease. These boats were organized into a Brigade commanded by Captain 1st Rank Alexander Kuzmin, who was extremely attached to vessels of that class. On inner communication lines in the region of Varanger Fjord the torpedo boats began to compete with Midgets.

I should mention that in 1943 we were already trying to coordinate action with the Torpedo-Boat Brigade. But so far only two or three attempts were made, and in each case we did not have a carefully worked out, centralized plan, acting on the spur of the moment when the situation suddenly became favorable. Another reason was that we did not have air reconnaissance specially assigned for the purpose, and there had been a shortage of torpedo boats—we only began getting reinforcements toward the close of the year. All this made our joint action not as effective as we would have liked. At the end of March, for example, submarines and aircraft attacked three convoys and sank a total of seven transports. Had these attacks been planned more carefully it would have been quite possible to sink each of these convoys entirely.

We had further reinforcements at the end of the year. In November and December we received four Esses (S-14, S-15, S-103 and S-104) and two double-shafted Midgets (M-200 and M-201). The 200th Midget had the formidable and unusual name of *Mest (Revenge)*. There was a story behind that name.

Unexpected as the war had been for us, it was much more unexpected for our children. On that day in June, when anti-aircraft batteries in Murmansk and Polyarnoye opened fire on Nazi bombers, the children of many officers and

civilian workers of the Northern Fleet were in a Young
Pioneer summer camp at Siverskaya Station, Leningrad Region.
From there they were evacuated to the village of Bolshiye
Vogultsi, Kirov Region, which, according to all surmises,
would not be touched by the bloody paw of war.

Lyubov Lobodenko, wife of Regimental Commissar Vasily
Lobodenko, was in charge of the camp.

I knew Vasily well. In the autumn of 1940 he had temporarily performed the duties of Commissar of our brigade. His
permanent job was in the Fleet Political Administration,
where he headed the Instruction Organization Department. I
remember that in the brigade we were sorry that he came to
us only temporarily, for he quickly became popular. When he
returned to his job in the Political Administration, many
submariners kept up their friendship with him.

At the beginning of July Vasily was in a naval task force
that helped to stop the enemy's first offensive on Murmansk.
But his fighting career ended much too soon. On July 20 he
died on the destroyer *Stremitelny*, which was sunk by Nazi
aircraft in the roadstead of Yekaterininskaya Harbor.

In Bolshiye Vogultsi the postman brought sad news, which
echoed with pain in two hearts: Lyubov Lobodenko lost her
husband, and her only son Vilen lost his father.

When the enemy approached the banks of the Volga Lyubov
Lobodenko suggested that all the camp staff, who were naval
wives like her, should collect money for the construction of a
submarine. She made the first contribution—a sum of 2,500
rubles, which she had saved with difficulty from her modest
pay and her son's pension. The women responded enthusiastically, and soon the first 20,000 rubles were deposited in
the State Bank.

Lyubov wrote to the Government requesting that the
money be used for building a submarine with the name
Revenge. At the same time she called upon all women with
husbands in the navy to collect money for the submarine. The
State Bank soon began receiving contributions from widows
and from women with husbands in the navy.

Such was the pre-history of *Revenge*, which became part of
our brigade early in December. Captain 3rd Rank Vasily
Turayev, who had recently come to us from the Baltic,
became her commander.

Turayev had been in command of a submarine for several

years before the war. That alone spoke of his experience. He had been on operational patrols in the Baltic.

Paradoxical as it may sound, in the Baltic submariners had longer patrols than we had in our vast theater. The reason for this was that the most difficult stage of a patrol was to get through the German anti-submarine barrage in the Gulf of Finland. Submarines, therefore, stayed in the Baltic for as long as possible.

In the first wartime autumn, for example, S-12, commanded by Turayev, spent sixty-one days on a single patrol. A submarine that broke through the barrage had to combat nets, depth-charge attacks and mines. She was hunted by aircraft and torpedo boats. She was shelled by surface vessels. But despite all these obstacles, S-12 reached the open sea and in the course of a month sank two transports and damaged another so heavily that in order to escape sinking it had to strand itself on a shoal.

The transfer to a Midget was naturally no promotion for Turayev. It was the result of some not very grave breach of duty. However, he soon showed his worth and in February was put in command of S-104.

Revenge, which had not yet opened her battle score, received a new captain. He was Lieutenant-Captain Vladimir Gladkov, Grigory Shchedrin's First Lieutenant in S-56.

We had some changes in the Brigade toward the end of the year. We had lost three Midgets and another, M-171, was refitted as a mine layer and turned over to 1st Division. As a result, we had to do away with 6th Division. 4th Division was enlarged and remained under Nikolai Morozov. Israel Fisanovich was sent to Britain with a group of other submariners to receive the submarines that were being turned over to us.

The question of transferring ships of the British navy to us arose as a result of events that took place in the distant South of the European Continent. The Mussolini regime in Italy collapsed on September 3, and the government that replaced it signed an armistice with the anti-Hitler coalition. The Germans invaded Italy and were opposed by the Anglo-U.S. forces that had landed near Naples.

These events decided the destiny of the Italian navy. Agreement was reached on dividing it up among the Allies. Under this agreement Britain undertook to lend the Soviet Union ships that were needed now in the North. These ships included submarines. Crews were formed by our various fleets to receive these submarines. One of these crews was headed by Israel Fisanovich.

Nikolai Lunin became the new commander of 1st Division in place of Khomyakov, who was lost at sea in K-1. He turned his submarine over to Captain 3rd Rank Zarmair Arvanov, the officer who two years previously had suggested to Gadjiev that submarines should fire salutes in honor of their victories and was thereby responsible for one of the most popular traditions in the navy. Lieutenant-Captain Vladimir Uzharovsky became First Lieutenant in K-21.

1st Division was dogged by ill luck. It had changed its commander four times since the start of the war. On the other hand, 4th Division continued under Morozov, despite the fact that he went to sea more frequently than any of the other Divisional Commanders. It was just another illustration that many of the things that happen during war are not subject to any laws.

In 1943 the situation in the North changed further in our favor. The enemy's attempt to send the battleship *Scharnhorst* against an Allied convoy ended ignominiously.

The largest German battleship after the *Bismarck* and the *Tirpitz,* the *Scharnhorst* arrived in the North in March and used Alten Fjord as its base. It left the fjord only twice. Its December raid, like many other German naval operations in the North, was nothing more than a piece of adventurism. Also adventurist was the decision of Rear-Admiral Bey, commander of a German squadron, to recall his destroyers when it was found that there was a heavy sea. As a result, when the *Scharnhorst* left Alten Fjord on December 25 to intercept a convoy returning to Britain from Archangel and Murmansk it had no escort whatever. This step lacked elementary military wisdom.

The fact that this sortie was decided upon without careful reconnaissance likewise showed the adventurism of the German Command. Had intelligence been equal to the occasion, the Germans would have known that large British naval forces were in Polyarnoye. They consisted of the battleship *Duke of York,* the cruiser *Jamaica* and four destroyers flying the flag of Admiral Fraser, and a cruiser squadron consisting of *Norfolk,* *Belfast* and *Sheffield.* These squadrons had accompanied the convoy on its way to the Soviet Union and, after a few days in

Scharnhorst

Kola Bay, they put out to sea to cover the convoy's return.

The British, obviously, were posted about the enemy's intentions and were certain that the *Scharnhorst* would be lured into attacking an unarmed convoy, which (as the Germans were led to believe) was proceeding without a heavy escort. In any case, everything happened exactly as the British expected.

In the polar darkness of December 26, the *Scharnhorst* ran into a squadron of cruisers 70 miles southeast of Medvezhy Island. But a snowstorm suddenly arose and the ships lost sight of each other without having had time to do anything. Contact was re-established several hours later. True to itself, the *Scharnhorst* was still heading in the direction of the convoy. An artillery battle ensued. The *Sheffield* received a direct hit and was forced to drop out of the battle. But the British did not leave that unanswered. Later it became known that one of the British shells blinded the battleship by destroying its radar.

That explains why the appearance of the *Duke of York* and its escort came as a surprise for the Germans. Powerful broadsides forced the *Scharnhorst* to reduce speed and turn away. At this point it was engaged by destroyers, and eight torpedoes striking the battleship finally sank it. Of the ship's company of two thousand and twenty-nine only thirty-eight were picked up. There was not a single officer among them. The prisoners said that Rear-Admiral Bey and the battleship's commander Captain 1st Rank Hintze shot themselves. The British casualties were small. They lost twenty-six men.

Thus ended the last major German naval adventure in the North.

Throughout that year the Lapland group sat tight in the hills and cliffs without even thinking of starting an offensive. Evidently, the time was not far distant when we'd begin dislodging it. In the meantime, it existed thanks to the convoys that were bringing it supplies and reinforcements.

In 1943 we concentrated our blows on these convoys and on the convoys that were taking nickel and copper from Norway and Finland to the "Great Reich." The difficulties confronting us mounted. The convoys were getting increasingly greater cover. The grazing of mines against the sides of our submarines was reported more and more frequently—the Germans were laying new mine fields and renewing the old ones. Their sonars had improved, for they began detecting our submarines and bombing them more accurately.

In spite of everything, we went from success to success. That was only natural, for we, too, had become stronger and more experienced.

On the Road to the New

It was a winter of unending patrols and countless attacks. We had been active in the preceding winters as well. But there was something different about this winter. It was full of signs of the new.

In January we undertook an attempt at coordinating three of the Fleet's strike forces: submarines, torpedo aircraft and torpedo boats. It was planned that submarines would attack the enemy's outer communication lines, and that this would be followed by aircraft blows against the approach lanes, with torpedo boats striking the lanes closest to us.

Eight submarines—L-22, S-56, S-102, M-119, S-103, S-104, M-200 and M-201—were sent on mine-laying missions. L-22 and S-103 had the further assignment of keeping a watch on the movement of enemy convoys. By that time our signalmen had developed a sliding antenna that could be raised together with the periscope. This relatively simple device considerably improved communication with submarines. They no longer had to surface to receive radio signals. Incidentally, in winter, during the interminable polar night, submarines spent more time on the surface than dived. We therefore regarded the sliding antenna as a valuable aid in spring and summer.

M-201, commanded by Lieutenant-Captain Balin, who had Divisional Commander Ivanov as Instructor Commander with him, delivered the first blow. In Tana Fjord she attacked a transport riding at anchor. Her first salvo of two torpedoes went wide off the mark. But the new Midget carried four torpedo tubes and she still had the last word. Her second salvo sank the transport.

That took place in the evening of January 19. On the next day S-56 went into action. True, this time luck was against Shchedrin. In the darkness after he had identified patrol ships and was starting to get into a position to attack one of them, he saw the silhouettes of transports. He had to change aim and fire from his stern tubes. At the moment the torpedoes were fired, the submarine was spotted by a patrol ship which tried to contact her with its signal lamp. S-56 dived immediately, the captain preferring not to reply to the inquisitive ship.

Nobody in the submarine heard explosions—the torpedoes must have missed the target. On the other hand, nobody pursued the submarine. Half an hour later Shchedrin surfaced with the intention of overtaking the convoy and taking another shot at it. There was a display of the Aurora Borealis in the sky and it was as light as day. The convoy had gone pretty far, but Shchedrin gave chase nonetheless.

However, he found himself on the boundary of S-102's patrol area before he could carry out his intentions. He could not cross into it because that would jeopardize the actions of his neighbor. Soon, from his bridge Shchedrin saw the trail of tracer bullets being fired from the ships. He concluded that the convoy was being worried by S-102. He stopped his pursuit, informed Polyarnoye of the enemy's location and course, and returned to his area.

S-102, indeed, attacked one of the transports. Captain 3rd Rank Gorodnichy fired four torpedoes, one of which sank the vessel. As he later reported, the escort put up hardly any resistance and did not pursue him. The explanation for this was that S-56's unsuccessful attack had been discovered and the escort's attention had been diverted to the direction from which another attack could be expected.

This same convoy was subsequently attacked by our torpedo carriers and torpedo boats.

On January 22, the Soviet Information Bureau communique stated: "Two enemy transports of six thousand tons each, a patrol ship and a German U-boat have been sunk in the Barents Sea."

On the 28th Shchedrin attacked a large tanker, which was escorted by two patrol ships and several torpedo boats. Once again he had to use his stern tubes, but this time a rolling explosion was heard, and the hydrophone operator reported that he could not hear the tanker's propellers.

On her next patrol in February and March, S-56 was badly mauled. It began with a gale. I pictured to myself the huge waves tossing the submarine, then lifting her on their crests and then dropping her so that it seemed she would never again see the light of day. But there was always another wave that brought her to the surface in a fountain of foam. It was as though a whale were frolicking in the sea.

It is hardly worth mentioning what is experienced in such weather by the men on the bridge and in the submarine. S-56 had a hardy crew that had completed a passage across two oceans and none of them were prone to be seasick. But in the Barents Sea storms are fiercer than in the southern latitudes. The icy cold penetrates to the very marrow of one's bones, while the fogs and snowfalls sometimes last for weeks.

When the elements quietened down the submarine was detected by patrol ships and destroyers close to the enemy shore. They pursued her for more than twenty-six hours, dropping over three hundred depth charges. Just think that figure over! It meant continuous work and colossal nervous strain for more than a day for each member of the crew and particularly for the captain. Death stalked them for more than a day, with a depth charge exploding somewhere in the vicinity every five minutes. One experienced more in a day like that than during a whole lifetime. And you cannot help asking yourself what the limit of human endurance is.

The submarine finally shook off her pursuers and carried on with her patrol. Soon the look-out reported that in the darkness he could see the outlines of two transports and many escort vessels. The submarine was in a disadvantageous position for an attack: she was on the bright side of the horizon. In addition, snow was beginning to fall. Under these conditions the enemy could attack the submarine before she could deliver a blow herself. However, Shchedrin stuck to

H.M.S. Sheffield

our rule of attacking the enemy whenever and wherever possible.

The submarine dived to twenty meters, a depth that placed her out of the danger of being rammed. Sound contact was established with one of the transports. S-56 had a reliable sonars and her hydrophone operators were well trained. Shchedrin decided to attack without the aid of his periscope. When he was five cable-lengths away from the enemy he fired two torpedoes. One of them jammed, but forty-five seconds later there was an explosion and the noise of propellers ceased. Shchedrin had scored a bull's eye.

This was the first purely acoustic attack in the Northern Fleet. It was accomplished at a depth of twenty meters. We had had cases of submarines combining bearings taken by sound with corrections of the attack course by periscope. Sound ensured either the beginning or the completion of an attack.

In this case the periscope had not been used at all. Acoustics had ensured the attack from beginning to end. Besides, the depth of firing was novel—nobody had fired a salvo from twenty meters.

At the base we thoroughly analysed the attack. Captains whose submarines had reliable sonar equipment were told that they could attack blind if they had no opportunity of using their periscopes. It was recommended that all the bow tubes be used for a salvo in order to increase the probability of a hit. As regards firing at a depth of twenty meters, it was recognized as expedient in individual cases.

The news that by a Decree of March 31 the Presidium of the Supreme Soviet of the U.S.S.R. had decorated S-56 with the Order of the Red Banner was welcomed by all of us.

But let us return to the January attempt to coordinate our actions with those of torpedo carriers and torpedo boats. How were we to assess the results? I must admit that we had expected more. Once again reconnaissance had let us down. The submarines assigned to this task could not have done more than they did. Their possibilities were limited. They were slow. Which meant that they could not cover a large area. The distance over which a surface target could be detected did not exceed ten miles, while at night it was even shorter than that. This gave very little time in which to strike at the enemy. Lastly, a submarine engaged in reconnaissance had, like any other submarine, to withdraw to her battery-recharging area and cut short her search. And, like any other submarine, she could be discovered by anti-submarine vessels and forced to dive. In the meantime, a convoy could pass through her area unnoticed.

The result was that the other submarines, as in former cases, had to fall back on their patrol areas and continue the search independently, groping their way through mine fields and exposing themselves to unnecessary risks. With reliable reconnaissance a submarine could lie in wait outside a mine field and break through it only when she is informed that a convoy is moving along the coast.

This reliable reconnaissance could only be ensured by aircraft. Our efforts to get that assistance failed. For that reason, while groping our way to new tactics, we continued fighting in the old fashion. Submarines went on patrol, hunting, finding and sinking enemy vessels.

Our Midgets were extremely active in the period from February to April. It was their last curtain call, for it had been decided to transfer them to the Black Sea Fleet in the spring. The decision was correct and timely, for in the polar seas these submarines and their crews were subject to terrific strain. It was bad both for the men and the ships. We now had quite a few medium-sized submarines that were better adapted to the polar elements, and were expecting reinforcements from Britain. There was, therefore, no reason to keep the Midgets in our theater and deprive our large torpedo-boat flotilla of its "livelihood." The conditions in the Black Sea allowed these submarines to be used with greater effect.

In February M-108 announced a victory with a salute, and in the next month victories were won by *Yaroslavsky Komsomolets*, *Chelyabinsky Komsomolets* and M-119.

On April 1, M-199 scored another victory—the last victory of the old Midgets in the North. In May, under the command of Captain 1st Rank Nikolai Morozov, they sailed for the south. Only M-171 remained in the Brigade. M-201 and *Revenge* likewise remained, but they were called Midgets more from habit than anything else, because they were almost in the same class as the Pikes.

On a cold but sunny spring day I was summoned to the Fleet Commander-in-Chief. When I arrived in his large office, Lieutenant-General Andreyev, commander of the Fleet's Air

Arm, and his Chief-of-Staff, Major-General Preobrazhensky were already there. The talk was about a major air operation and the role to be played in it by reconnaissance. When Andreyev stopped I seized the initiative, "It's about time Air gave us some aircraft for reconnaissance. Look what's happening. In terms of 1941 we're doing a good job, but it's primitive in terms of 1944. Besides, we cannot speak seriously of coordination until we get air reconnaissance."

"I object to that," Andreyev said, bristling. "We can't have aircraft flying back and forth specially for you, submariners. We've got our hands full as it is."

"I think you can, Comrade Andreyev," the Fleet Commander-in-Chief said, interrupting him. "You can because it's what the fleet needs, and very badly too. Let's hear what the submariners have to say. Comrade Kolyshkin, report your considerations."

We reached agreement fairly quickly. Andreyev's objections were neither more nor less than the first reaction of a thrifty master who felt that something he had had a hard time getting was being taken away from him. But this "parochialism" fell before the pressure of common sense and common interests. We found a common language with Air Command, especially as in the final analysis distant reconnaissance was needed by them as much as by us.

We began with class exercises for airmen. Our staffs drew up and specified variants of joint action. They were instructed to work out the details of bilateral exercises in which submarines, aircraft, transports and escort vessels were to take part. Although the war at sea never relaxed for a moment—the situation remained tense and each submarine, aircraft and surface vessel was needed—the exercises were carried out. We were planning something big and that required precise coordination. To avoid landing in a mess we prepared for it with the greatest of care.

The exercises were analyzed comprehensively and it was agreed that they had been useful and successful. Some shortcomings and vulnerable spots were brought to light, and these were eliminated later through the efforts of both staffs.

In May our submarines began operating in a new way against the enemy's communications. They lay in wait in areas demarcated along the external edge of the mine fields. Between the internal boundary of these obstacles and the shore there were corridors that were used by German shipping. The submarines thus formed a screen which hung over the enemy's communication lines instead of blocking it.

In the meantime aircraft patrolled the exits from the fjords and reported the strength, direction and course of convoys. This information was passed on directly to the submarines and Headquarters. For its part Headquarters repeated this information for the benefit of the submarines and planned where and when the torpedo carriers and torpedo boats would strike.

On the basis of this intelligence submarine Captains determined where they would most likely meet the enemy and headed for that point through mine fields. That set the cover in motion, enabling it to converge on the enemy.

Such, in general outline, were the new tactics that we began to employ.

We got quick results. As early as May and the beginning of June, thanks to air reconnaissance, three submarines returned home with victories. M-201 was the first to use reconnaissance intelligence. At 17.25 hours on May 25, when the periscope was raised the submarine received a signal from Polyarnoye giving the position of a convoy and instructing her to proceed to the point where the convoy was expected. Lieutenant-Captain Balin took the shortest route to the "rendezvous."

At 03.49 hours on May 26 he fired two torpedoes at a transport whose bow was hidden by the stern of a patrol ship. He did not have the opportunity of seeing the results, but intelligence later reported that the patrol ship was sunk and the transport damaged.

Nechayev in S-103 was the next to report success. In the morning of May 29 he went to the area where a convoy was expected, but found no sign of the enemy. Meanwhile, two mine sweepers were slowly making their way across the calm sea in the vicinity. Nechayev did not risk waiting any longer, for after the convoy was discovered by reconnaissance it might have changed its course. He turned his attention on the two mine sweepers and sank both of them with a salvo of four torpedoes.

S-104, commanded by Turayev, was directed to a convoy in which the transports were sailing in close formation with their escorts. Turayev aimed at several targets simultaneously, and the four torpedoes fired by him sank one transport and two mine sweepers. It was Turayev's first kill in the North, and it established a dazzling record.

In August we reaped a bumper harvest. Nechayev's S-103 had two encounters with the enemy. The first ended with the sinking of a tanker. In the second Nechayev sank a transport and a patrol ship.

S-15 likewise reported sinking a transport with two torpedoes.

The vessels transferred to us in advance of our share of the Italian Fleet arrived from Britain in August.

A battleship and eight destroyers flying the Soviet naval ensign appeared in Kola Bay early in the month, and these were followed singly by submarines.

I had already mentioned that Fisanovich and Tripolsky were sent to Britain to receive the submarines. They were followed by complete crews for four submarines. The ceremony of transferring these submarines to the Soviet Union was held at Rosyth on May 30. Our ensigns were raised on them, and the command of the new Division was taken over by Alexander Tripolsky. Submarines of this class were given the index V and were correspondingly named V-1, V-2, V-3 and V-4.

They were neither new nor of improved design. Though reminiscent of our Pikes, there were many essential differences in the design. They had, after all, been built in a country whose long-standing ship-building traditions differed

V-3 (ex-H.M.S. Ursula)

from ours. For that reason our men had a difficult task in front of them to learn to handle these submarines efficiently.

That was what the British, too, thought, and they were vastly surprised when our crews quickly grew accustomed to the new submarines. Rumor in Rosyth had it that the Russians had brought engineers dressed in sailors' uniforms.

It is not worth the effort to prove how absurd that rumor was. The crews consisted of petty officers and ratings. Naturally, all had been selected for their knowhow and combat experience. For example, Chief Petty Officer Rashevsky, who was in charge of the wireless office in V-3, had served in the Baltic, accomplished two war patrols in S-13 and two in P-309, and had taken part in sinking six transports. All the other men had had approximately the same "engineering" training.

The most capable officers were slected for the command of the new submarines. Among them were three Heroes of the Soviet Union. The reader knows two of them—Fisanovich and Tripolsky. The third was Captain 3rd Rank Yaroslav Iosseliani, who was First Lieutenant in a Midget in the Black Sea when the war broke out. Later he became captain, sinking thirteen vessels—from self-propelled barges to transports and warships.

Captain 3rd Rank Isaac Kabo was captain of P-309 in the Baltic, where he sent five transports to the bottom. I've already mentioned that in the Baltic patrols were no holiday spree. Each began and ended with a passage through mine fields in the Gulf of Finland. Many submarines never got through these obstacles.

In his last patrol in P-309, Kabo covered two thousand one hundred and five miles on the surface and one thousand and forty-three miles under water. This was a feat in itself, considering that a Pike's surface speed did not exceed thirteen knots, while under water she had to move as slowly as possible in order to save on electric power.

V-1 under Israel Fisanovich was the first to sail for the Soviet Union. But she never got to Kola Bay. Nobody ever knew what had happened. It was impossible to measure our grief, for in that submarine, which was not of very great value to us, was a crew that could be justly called the flower of the North Sea submariners. Israel Fisanovich, charming and gifted, had been a favorite with all the veterans in the brigade. In the intervals between operational patrols he had kept a diary which gave the history of his Midget in fairly good literary style. The diary had many interesting digressions generalizing the experience of the submarine war in the North and observations on tactics. Had Fisanovich lived he might have reached a very high rank or become a leading naval tactician.

But it was no use speculating on that. The important thing was what he had accomplished. He had done much more than other people could do in their lifetime. It was not surprising that like many other intrepid soldiers he did not live to see final victory. A real soldier never fights shy of difficulties and dangers. And for that reason, more frequently than anybody else, dies with his boots on, in the fulfilment of his duty.

Thus, the first submarine to appear in Yekaterininskaya Harbor was not V-1 but V-2. She was brought by Alexander Tripolsky. Her commander, Captain 3rd Rank Panov, fell ill and had to be sent to a hospital in Britain. His place was taken by Lieutenant-Captain Alexei Shchekin, who had been First Lieutenant in M-171. V-3 commanded by Kabo came in next, and was followed by V-4 with Iosseliani in command.

Although these submarines were manned by experienced crews and officers we did not make an exception from our general rule for them. Each submarine had to pass the test of day and night attacks, while officers from other theaters had to acquaint themselves with the features of our theater and of operations along enemy shores.

These submarines were assigned to 3rd Division, which continued under Vladimir Ivanov. Tripolsky was posted to a new job in the Far East. Generally speaking, the war in the North was ending, and it was clear that there would be a lot to do for our Pacific Fleet.

WON IN BATTLE

Our Last Salvoes

Nineteen forty-four has entered the chronicle of war as a year of crushing strategic blows which cleared the Soviet Union of the Nazi invaders. The last of these blows, which ended the campaign of that victorious year, was struck in the North by troops of the Karelian Front in cooperation with the Northern Fleet. The biggest operation on this sector was the Petsamo-Kirkenes offensive, which was started on October 7.

The enemy Lapland group felt that they would be the next to face the pressure of Soviet troops. They therefore fortified their defenses in depth. Hitler ordered them to hang on to Kirkenes and Petsamo at all costs, for that region was where Germany was getting her nickel, a key strategic raw material.

Finland withdrew from the war on September 4. She undertook to clear her territory of Nazi troops by September 15. But this was only a symbolic commitment. The Germans had no intention of leaving voluntarily. All the defense installations manned by Finns were taken over by Germans. Finland simply did not have the forces to seriously prevent this.

The Germans prepared for battle at sea as well. They had a formidable force in the Nord group in North Norway. The battleship *Tirpitz* was lurking in one of the fjords. Destroyers, of which there were at least a dozen, were transferred from Alten Fjord to Tana Fjord, which was close to Soviet communications. Nord also had about eighty patrol ships, mine sweepers, and submarine chasers, and several score of fast landing barges and other auxiliary vessels. Its Air Arm consisted of about two hundred aircraft.

Archangel (ex-H.M.S. Royal Sovereign)

The presence of these forces determined the place of the Northern Fleet in the coming operation. Every available ship was committed, including the new squadron consisting of the *Archangel* (an old battleship that we had received), the cruiser *Murmansk* and other warships. The squadron was commanded by Captain 1st Rank Vitaly Fokin, a veteran of the Northern Fleet.

The artillery of 14th Army opened up in the morning of October 7. On the next day the Fleet Commander-in-Chief and his campaign Staff moved to Ozerko, in Pummanki Inlet on Rybachy Peninsula. The commanders of all the units taking part in the operation, except the squadron of surface ships and the Submarine Brigade, likewise moved their Headquarters to Ozerko.

To speak of the fleet's participation in the seizure of Petsamo and Kirkenes means first and foremost mentioning the valorous feats of the 63rd and 12th Marine Brigades, the crews of the launches that landed units of the 63rd Brigade on an exposed section of the enemy shore, reconnaissance groups led by Ivan Barchenko-Yemelyanov and Victor Leonov, who captured two shore batteries, the launches commanded by Alexander Shabalin, who took a task force through the heavily fortified Petsamo-Vuono corridor all the way to the wharves of Liinahamari. . . .

But all these episodes are well known and have been described in detail. I did not participate in these events directly and therefore cannot give any personal impressions. Throughout almost the entire operation I was at my command post. I think it would be appropriate to mention the tasks that our submarines had in this period, the role that they played in the operation and how they coped with their assignments.

The preparations for the operation were started a month in advance. Early in September we held a conference of officers at the Brigade in the presence of Vice-Admiral Nikolayev, Member of the Military Council.

At that conference we heard the first official statement that there would be a major offensive in the North and that the fleet, including the Submarine Brigade, would play a conspicuous part in it. True, the date of the offensive was not mentioned, but it was obvious that we would not have to wait long.

On September 8 a directive from the Fleet Military Council outlined the tasks confronting our fleet. It had to prepare to avert the attempts of enemy surface ships and U-boats to hinder the landing of troops, and prevent German warships from supporting their land units and hampering our own shipping. It was also important to deprive the enemy of the means of sending reinforcements, disrupt his sea-borne supplies, stop him receiving strategic materials from North Norway and Finland and prevent him from evacuating troops pinned to the beaches after a successful operation by our forces. Nobody doubted that the operation would be successful. In addition to destroying the enemy at sea our fleet had to land task forces and support Army units operating in the coastal regions.

Submarines cooperating with torpedo carrying aircraft and torpedo boats had the assignment of paralyzing the enemy's sea communications and blockading his ports and bases long before the Soviet offensive was started. The Nazis expected more vigorous action on our part and prepared for it, increasing their transportation by sea.

* * *

For us this operation began toward the end of September. We sent our submarines out singly, as soon as they were ready. L-20 acted as mine layer, and S-14, S-51, S-56, S-101, S-102, S-104, V-2, V-4 and M-171 were sent out to lay mines and attack shipping.

S-15 likewise set out on a patrol of more than twenty days. Her assignment was to cover the northern flank of a U.S.S.R.-bound convoy against possible German raiders. It was an extremely arduous patrol, for the submarine had to sail as far as the edge of the icefield.

Gales and snowstorms raged throughout October. It was wicked sailing in such a weather, and, besides, the Germans resisted fiercely. They strengthened and renewed their mine fields. Their convoys were provided with powerful escorts. Each convoy was protected by as many as six warships. Despite everything, our successes mounted.

S-56, commanded by Grigory Shchedrin, who was now Captain 2nd Rank, was the first to go into battle and the first to return victorious. She sank a transport of about four thousand tons and a mine sweeper of eight hundred tons.

After October 7, when the offensive got under way both on land and at sea, our submarines reported victorious almost every day.

On October 10, Kolosov in S-51 increased the battle score that he had started in a Midget. Drawing close to a convoy following an anti-submarine zigzag he fired four trackless torpedoes (which we had by this time) at a fairly large transport. A destroyer suddenly appeared in the path of the torpedoes. It received two of them in its side and sank quickly. One of the other torpedoes hit the transport. Fire broke out on the vessel and it lost speed. But Kolosov was unable to stay to see if it would sink.

On the next day command post received further gratifying news. Shchekin, who had gone on his first war patrol in V-2, sent a transport to the bottom, hitting it with three of a salvo of four torpedoes. On the day after that he reported putting two of four torpedoes into a heavily guarded transport. He had had to fire from a great distance.

That day—October 12—we received other victory reports. One of them came from Kovalenko in M-171. In the morning the sound of propellers was heard after the submarine had successfully laid a mine field. Kovalenko took his bearings by that sound and about fifteen minutes later saw a convoy consisting of two groups of vessels. The first was hugging the shore so that it could hardly be seen. The second, a transport and three patrol ships, was farther out seaward. Kovalenko decided to attack the second group.

When the salvo was fired the patrol ship bringing up the rear was in the same range as the transport. One of the torpedoes found a mark, but it was impossible to tell which of the vessels was hit.

The submarine returned to the base, and went to sea again as soon as she replenished her stock of torpedoes.

Aircraft and torpedo boats fought side by side with our submarines. In that period we achieved the closest possible coordination. A striking example of this was the action by S-104 on that same October 12.

At about 13.00 hours Turayev closed in on a convoy, which had just been attacked by torpedo carriers. The enemy had had no time to recover and the submarine was able to come close enough to strike at a transport and a patrol ship simultaneously. Both vessels were sunk. The transport evidently had troops on board, because some of the escort vessels stopped to pick up survivors.

The other ships would most certainly have given chase if they had not been attacked again by aircraft, which sank several more patrol ships.

Three days later, shortly after midnight, S-104's officer-of-the-watch spotted a convoy creeping stealthily eastward. Turayev, too, was on the bridge. The convoy was only a short distance away and the submarine had to attack it at once, with its stern tubes. However, the entire salvo went wide off the mark.

But Turayev hung on, deciding to overtake the convoy and repeat the attack. The submarine was not seen and forty minutes later it got into a battle course. However, as soon as the order to stand by was given, one of the torpedoes tore out of its tube. Before the transport reached the salvo course and Turayev was able to give the command to fire the air was shaken by a violent explosion. The ship must have carried munitions because it went down like a stone.

This case was carefully gone into, at first in the submarine at sea, and then at Brigade Headquarters. The torpedomen could not be blamed for it. Without going into technical details, it may be said that this was an exceptional case— nothing of the kind had ever happened in the North—but it could be explained. The torpedo hit the target because the salvo distance was extremely short. Had the submarine fired the full salvo at intervals, as the captain had intended, this particular torpedo would probably have harmlessly shot past the transport. The others, judging by the computations, would have found the mark. However, the end result was what mattered.

On the day S-104 scored that freak hit, the Soviet Information Bureau reported: "Troops of the Karelian Front breached the powerful German defenses northwest of Murmansk and today, October 15, with the cooperation of warships and task units of the Northern Fleet captured the town of Petsamo (Pechenga), an important naval base and powerful strongpoint of the Germans in the Far North."

It was inspiring news for the Northern Fleet, including the submariners who were at sea. They hunted for the enemy with even greater zeal than before, and regarded an encounter with the enemy as the greatest happiness. In those days victories were won even by crews that had been dogged by bad luck. The offensive was continuing and they made every effort to contribute to it. Ahead of us were Kirkenes, the cliffs and the tundra in the north of Norway.

S-14, commanded by Captain 3rd Rank Victor Kalanin, was one of these unlucky submarines. Kalanin knew his job thoroughly and he had a well-trained crew, but in the course of six patrols in the period from January to October, S-14 torpedoed only one enemy vessel—in July. But even in that attack it was not known if the vessel sank. In short, the submarine saw a great deal of the sea but the results were extremely modest. Properly speaking, nobody could be blamed for it. It was simply a case of bad luck.

S-14 started out on her seventh war patrol on October 13, and three days later encountered three mine sweepers sailing in jagged formation near Porsanger Fjord. They were sweeping the area. The situation allowed the submarine to attack the entire group, and here Kalanin showed what he could do. Maneuvering skilfully, he fired four torpedoes at intervals of ten seconds from a distance of six cable-lengths. The mine sweeper in the lead and the one following it broke in half and began to sink. The third mine sweeper evaded the torpedoes.

On the next day, October 17, M-171 reported yet another kill. This time, firing from the surface, she sank a transport with two torpedoes.

Yaroslav Iosseliani and the Black Sea crew in V-4 gave a good account of themselves on their very first patrol. The submarine set sail on the day Pechenga was captured. On the night of October 18, while she was recharging her batteries the hydrophone operator reported the noise of propellers. Iosseliani stopped the recharging, ordered the men to battle stations and closed in on the invisible target. Soon the outlines of a tanker of about three thousand tons were made out in the darkness. Dived, the submarine fired three torpedoes from a distance of five cable-lengths. One of the torpedoes failed to leave its tube because of some technical fault, while the other two missed the target.

Iosseliani repeated the attack, firing two torpedoes from a short distance. The torpedoes missed again. Possibly the tanker had noticed the torpedoes and had had time to get out of their way. It seemed that all chance of victory had slipped away. But Iosseliani refused to accept defeat. Although the tanker was moving away at top speed he went after it. In the end, with both her diesels madly pounding away, the submarine got into position for a third salvo. This time the tanker was hit and sank quickly.

Two days later V-4 took up a position in the shadow of cliffs and lay in wait. Very soon a convoy appeared and the submarine, leaving her ambush, drew up unnoticed to within only two cable-lengths. Each of the two transports received a torpedo amidships and both began to sink.

The submarine dived and escaped from pursuit fairly quickly.

"These attacks are an example of perseverance, courage and seamanship," said Arseny Golovko in assessing V-4's first patrol.

It should be noted that to a large extent Iosseliani owed his success to Mikhail Semyonov, our flag navigator, who was on board with him. Having been on twenty war patrols he knew the conditions in our theater and all of the enemy's wiles, and he gave the captain a great deal of useful shrewd advice, which the latter ably utilized.

In the morning of October 20, S-14, too, sank a transport, which had been sighted by aircraft. This was the "luckless" submarine's second kill in four days.

S-101 was the last to join in the Petsamo-Kirkenes operation. She was commanded by Lieutenant-Captain Nikolai Zinovyev, former first lieutenant in S-15 who succeeded to the command when Troumov was transferred to Fleet Headquarters. Both the new captain and his crew impatiently waited for the hour when they could cast off and join the submarines on war patrol. But repairs delayed them.

On October 25, the day Kirkenes was captured, S-101 finally left Yekaterininskaya Harbor. She hunted for six days before meeting two destroyers and a patrol ship. Three trackless torpedoes raced out of her tubes and two minutes later they hit the destroyer.

That happened in the morning. Then, at about 15.00 hours S-101 spotted a solitary enemy mine sweeper in the same area. When she began drawing close to the target another mine sweeper came into sight. Zinovyev fired at the first mine sweeper, but before the torpedoes reached their target several patrol ships appeared from around Cape Nordkin.

Hit by torpedoes, the mine sweeper began to sink. The other ships started a chase which lasted nearly twenty-four hours. The enemy dropped a hundred and forty-seven depth charges, and the submarine sustained heavy damage. But thanks to the courage and skill of her young captain, she finally made good her escape.

Thus, the two salvoes fired by S-101 completed our brigade's combat patrols in the Petsamo-Kirkenes offensive. The offensive ended on November 1, but our land forces continued to advance in Norway.

Our submarines, torpedo-carrying aircraft and torpedo boats carried out their assignment of blockading the enemy's bases and ports. Not more than a fourth of the total number of German ships reached their destination. The heaviest losses were sustained by transports, on whose destruction the efforts of our submarines, aircraft and torpedo boats were concentrated. In the period from October 7 to 31, the Nazis lost thirty-nine transports and fifteen warships; twenty-six vessels were damaged.

Our submarines accounted for fifteen transports and warships, not counting the vessels damaged by them. The brigade did not lose a single submarine. This was a notable and tangible success.

Peace Enters Our Home

S-101's last salvoes in the Petsamo-Kirkenes operation proved to be the last combat salvoes of our brigade. North Norway was liberated and that obviated the need for convoys in our operational zone. The enemy lost his polar bases and surface ships. Our submarines found themselves "unemployed" or, to be more exact, without their main work, because war was still raging and German U-boats kept appearing in the Barents Sea.

The Northern Fleet devoted the last six months of the war to fighting the enemy submarine threat. For this purpose it used mainly its destroyers, patrol ships, large and small submarine chasers and aircraft. These forces protected Soviet shipping lanes because Allied convoys were still coming to Murmansk and Archangel.

Our brigade also took part in the struggle against U-boats. Two new submarines, S-16 and S-19, which were fitted with radar, were sent on combat patrol in November. We had received these submarines in autumn, but when the battles for Petsamo and Kirkenes started they were not ready for independent action. In their patrols in November neither S-16 nor S-19 encountered the enemy.

In January 1945 two other new submarines went on patrol. These patrols, which likewise yielded no result, brought our brigade's combat activities to a close.

It was obvious to each and everyone that final victory was near. But the war, dogged and savage, was still raging along a huge front stretching from the Danube to the Baltic. We could not afford to be caught unaware. The brigade was held in readiness for sudden patrols to distant regions along the western shore of Norway. Training did not stop in the submarines, and weapons and mechanisms were maintained in full combat readiness.

We could now sum up the results of three and a half years of submarine war in the North. In that period we had traversed a long road not only in technical improvements but in tactics as well. Our views concerning the role and place of submarines in the many-faceted pattern of the Navy were reshaped.

Some pre-war notions about the tasks of submarines now could raise nothing but a smile. We had pictured war at sea as involving primarily artillery and torpedo duels between surface vessels in the zone of shipping lanes. Naval power was computed in terms of the number of such ships. It was believed that submarines would be used chiefly against battleships, cruisers and destroyers.

We had prepared for such attacks in the pre-war years. We

learned to fire at fast-moving targets, i.e., at destroyers and cruisers, and rarely at transports, which did not inspire respect. We never thought of coordinated action, of giving serious consideration to cooperation with other services. And there was much else that we overlooked.

The war brought us a host of surprises. It turned out that aircraft were a formidable threat at sea, that bombers could oppose the fire power of a destroyer. It turned out that the torpedoes carried by destroyers were used incomparably less frequently than their artillery. Lastly, it was found that the principal task of submarines was to harass enemy communications. In the early stage of the war we registered misses, because we had not been trained to fire at slow-moving targets. Attempts to hit a target with a single torpedo brought us many a disappointment until we went over to firing salvoes.

Then we had to work out tactics enabling our submarines to break through a double screen, use sonars to locate the enemy, and enlist the aid of air reconnaissance. It would be hard to list all that the war taught us. The end of the war did not find us weakened or exhausted (which would not have been surprising because we had a skilful and formidable enemy). On the contrary, we were stronger numerically and in tactics. The small but well-organized Soviet submarine fleet with its highly-trained crews fulfilled its assignments satisfactorily.

We were prepared for other, harder assignments if our country thought they were necessary.

Victory came on the wings of spring. We had waited for it daily, hourly and were prepared for it by the entire course of events. Nonetheless it caught us by surprise. Time and again it seemed that the defeated enemy would come to his senses and dot his i's and cross his t's, that at last the Red Banner would be hoisted on the Reichstag putting an end to the bloodshed. But Nazism remained true to its suicidal doctrine to the very end. Even in its death throes it did not spare the lives of thousands of its adherents. In spite of everything the i's were dotted and t's were crossed. By us.

At 02.00 hours on May 9, 1945, this glorious news spread through Polyarnoye with the speed of lightning.

At 08.00 hours all the ships in the harbor and in the roadstead decked themselves out with ensigns and signal flags. The crews were lined up and the Order of the Day of the Supreme Commander-in-Chief to the Red Army and the Red Navy was read out to them. It stated that the German Armed Forces had signed an unconditional surrender.

Ships' crews and shore units were lined up after dinner on the second and third piers. Workers and employees of Polyarnoye and Pala-guba and the families of sailors gathered to watch the ceremony. Among them was a group of British sailors. Never before had so many people assembled in one place in Polyarnoye. Somehow I found it hard to believe that we had so many people in our small naval township.

The bridge of one of the destroyers tied up alongside the third pier was used as a speaker's platform. On it were Admiral Golovko, Fleet Commander-in-Chief, Vice-Admiral Nikolayev, Member of the Military Council, Major-General Torik, Chief of the Political Department, and Rear-Admiral Egerton, Chief of the British Naval Mission in the Soviet Union.

The meeting was opened by the Member of the Military Council. Congratulating everybody on the victory he gave the floor to Admiral Golovko.

"Many of our comrades are not with us today," he said in a voice filled with emotion. "They paid with their lives for this hour of triumph, for victory, for their country, for their people. Their blood shall eternally illumine our banners. This day of triumph, this Day of Victory, is the best monument to them."

People bared their heads and stood in mournful silence as the band played the soul-gripping funeral march. Bitter tears rolled down weather-beaten cheeks. We thought of the friends and relatives we had lost, of the men who met their death deep in the polar seas, on the stony slopes of snow-covered hills, in cold, besieged towns. . . .

The Admiral spoke of the immortal feat of Soviet men and women, of the historical mission of the Soviet people, who had delivered the world from the horrors of the Nazi plague. He spoke of the men who defended our North, where during the very first months of the war the Nazis had to give up their hope of a blitzkrieg in the Soviet Union.

The naval parade held to mark Victory Day on May 13 will always be remembered by those who saw it. Surface ships and submarines rode at anchor in Kola Bay near Murmansk. It was an impressive sight. Such a fleet could no longer be

termed small. It was much larger than the fleet we had before
the war, while its combat experience was incomparably greater.

On that day songs were sung in Polyarnoye and Murmansk
late into the night. People were freed from terrible exhaustion,
from the burden of constant alarm for the destiny of their
country, for the lives of their loved ones and for their own
lives. The nightmare of war was over.

We Had Forged Victory Together

With what is one to compare a war patrol in a submarine?
It is two or three weeks of minute-to-minute unflaging tension,
of constant unseen danger. It requires unceasing attention,
restraint, patience when the enemy is hunted, and self-
control, courage and a cool head when a submarine is pursued.
And in battle it requires the utmost concentration of moral
and physical strength. Although it is usual to regard a naval
battle as transient, it is by no means transient for submariners.
An attack sometimes lasts more than an hour, and if to this we
add the time that a submarine sometimes requires to elude
the enemy we find that it runs to more than twenty-four
hours. Nervous tension relaxes only when a submarine re-
turns to her base. On patrol it alternates with high and
super-high tension. And the main thing is that this tension is
maintained over a long period.

I mention this to explain why so much has been written
about submariners in newspapers, why their names became
well known in the navy, and why some submariners became
nationally famous. It is my view that the honors that were
heaped on submariners were not exaggerated. They conformed
with the spiritual and all other tests that fell to the lot of the
crews manning submarines.

The hundreds of men serving on shore, although their
work was unspectacular, helped submariners to surmount
these tests. They were less exposed to risk, fewer people
knew about them and they received less attention and fewer
awards, but victory at sea would have been impossible without
them. I have in mind those who readied submarines for
patrol, and those who in stern wartime conditions did their
best to provide submariners with all the facilities for rest
and recreation in the intervals between patrols.

I have already spoken of our shore base, and it remains

for me to add that the men there always had their hands full. Repairs and the provision of supplies kept them constantly busy.

The training rooms, where seamen mastered the practical aspects of fighting water and fire, plugging holes and removing the consequences of accidents, and improved their handling of weapons and machinery, worked uninterruptedly. These submariners received the foundation of combat skill, which they later demonstrated so brilliantly at sea.

Many of the men at the shore base were famous in their own rights. Almost all of them had sailed in ships before the war, while some had been in the North from the day the Northern Fleet was organized.

I shall not name any of them because the list is a long one, but I must mention our women.

Girls were assigned to the brigade in the spring of 1942. This caused some astonishment because we were not used to seeing girls in sailors' uniform. Besides, this invasion into our daily life embarrassed many of us and put us on our guard. But we soon got used to the combination of femininity and military uniforms and to the girl-sailors themselves.

The girls proved to be serious and they comported themselves with modesty and dignity. It was what we should have expected. They joined the navy from lofty, patriotic motives and were prepared to brave all difficulties in order to take a direct part in the war.

They were assigned to work as telephone operators, nurses and cooks. They worked at the radio station too, and in the library and at other jobs. They quickly mastered their duties and fulfilled them conscientiously. Some of them won promotion, becoming warrant officers. I believe that all of them dreamed of going on a war patrol in a submarine. At any rate we had any number of applications to that effect. Naturally, service in a ship, particularly in a submarine, made that impossible, and the girls received courteous but firm refusals.

"You're fighting the war here, at the shore base," they were usually told. And they tried to work as though they were at the firing lines.

Most of them were disciplined and there were cases when they were cited as examples to the sailors.

The enlistment of girls into the navy fully justified itself. Thanks to them, we were, for example, able to assign some of the sailors to marine units, which were used where there was an acute shortage of soldiers. Then there was the moral factor, the influence that the girls had on a traditionally male collective, which accepted them as equals.

We also had civilian women working in the various workshops and as waitresses in the canteens. Among them were old-timers to whom we had grown used long ago. They put their hearts into their work.

I must mention the huge contribution that was made to our victory by writers, poets and painters, who gave us a powerful and effective ideological weapon. The subject of the North, the subject of the grim and merciless submarine war inspired many writers, composers and painters. Their works helped us to fight, warmed us when we were up against difficulties, and called upon us to fulfil our duty to the best of our ability. From these works our people learned of the feats of our submariners. Some of the writers and painters I have in mind are well-known for their sea stories or seascapes, others were brought around to the subject of the sea by the war and it did not make much headway in their works. However, almost all of them wrote for our fleet magazines and newspapers, and they gave striking descriptions of the northern sailors.

Writers did not pass the local press by either, contributing thrilling stories, in which men recognized their comrades.

Lyrics writers were extremely popular with our men. In the case of Dmitri Kovalev he was altogether a submariner-poet, for he served in our brigade. In his poems, which appeared regularly in *Boyevoi Kurs*, he dealt mostly with the submarine war. The themes were drawn from events eye-witnessed by him.

Many writers shared the life of submariners over long periods, frequently going on patrol with them. But in this sphere they could not compete with war correspondents, whose job took them on combat patrol more than anybody else.

Songs written by composers Yevgeny Zharkovsky and Boris Terentyev, who served in the North, were our faithful companions during the war. Zharkovsky's *Farewell, Rocky Mountains* with lyrics by Bukin has passed the test of time and is sung in the North and in other fleets to this day.

I had particularly close contact with painters.

About two months before the war, a group of eight painters arrived in the North from Moscow. For some reason the Fleet Political Administration sent them to the Submarine Brigade. Pike Division, which I commanded at the time, was their host. There was a reason for that: the Midgets were too small to enable the painters to work in them, the Katyushas were undergoing repairs, while in my division five of the six submarines were operational.

We treated the painters hospitably, giving them the possibility of going out to sea. They got down to work enthusiastically, their eye being caught by the sullen rocky coast, the unusual hues of the Barents Sea, the fantastic northern sky and, of course, the men who had tamed this hostile nature. Their albums of sketches grew rapidly.

Unfortunately this inspired work did not last long. When the war broke out most of the painters were recalled to Moscow. Naturally, so many battle painters and seascapists could not be left in the North. Only three of them remained behind. They were Alexander Merkulov, Alexei Koltsov and Naum Tseitlin.

They helped to illustrate magazines and newspapers, designed posters, painted, and even did some sculpturing (until the Fleet got its own professional sculptor). To get the themes for their work they went to the firing lines and sailed in warships, sharing the risks with the sailors.

In the second half of 1943 the Northern Fleet received a sculptor in Lev Kerbel, who had just finished a school for sculptors. The Member of the Military Council assigned him to the Submarine Division. We were flattered, of course, to have "our own" sculptor. True, we knew nothing about his professional merits and we did not have a suitable studio for him, but we hoped that he would show his worth. We were not disappointed.

He quickly turned his room into a studio and soon began carving busts of submariners, naval airmen, torpedo-boat men and infantrymen. Connoisseurs spoke well of his work, finding signs of outstanding talent in it.

That winter the idea was put forward of erecting a monument to submariners who lost their lives in the war. It was suggested that the monument should stand on the territory of the shore base. The Fleet Military Council and Political Administration approved the idea and, naturally, Lev Kerbel was given the job.

It was the young sculptor's first big assignment. He drew up the project and chose the site, and then started on the project with the help of a team of sailors. The unveiling took place on June 22, 1944 in the presence of the Fleet Commander-in-Chief, Staff and Political Administration officers, and guests from other units.

Conclusion

This about completes my story of the grim war years, of the fearless, intrepid submariners with whom I had the privilege of serving during the four most difficult years of my life. But before closing I must say a few words about the destiny of some of the men I have described in this book.

Nikolai Vinogradov is now an Admiral and is devoting his energy to training naval personnel. Many of the men who fought in submarines of the Northern Fleet are now instructors at naval schools. They include Hero of the Soviet Union Valentin Starikov, who commanded the legendary M-171, and Engineer-Captain 1st Rank Vladimir Braman, who was Engineering Officer in K-21 and had saved the submarine from a desperate situation. It is gratifying to know that the training of the new generation of naval officers is in the hands of men who have had valuable combat experience and are exponents of glorious battle traditions.

Vice-Admiral Grigory Shchedrin is still serving in the navy. After the war he finished a naval academy, held responsible command posts and became known as a talented commander. His reminiscences In S-56, which give a true story of the Submarine Brigade during the second half of the war, has been read eagerly in the navy.

Ivan Kovalenko, our brigade flag engineering officer, now holds the rank of Engineer Vice-Admiral. It was due to his selfless work that our submarines were maintained in combat readiness and the crews were trained to handle machinery and repair damage.

Mikhail Zakharov, who was an instructor in our Political Department, is now a Vice-Admiral.

Many of my other comrades are still serving in the navy. They include Leonid Gorodnichy, who commanded S-102 throughout the war, Nikolai Yamshchikov, who served in L-20 and then became divisional navigator, Vladimir Uzharovsky, who served in K-21, Ivan Zhuiko, who sailed in L-15 from the Pacific, and Ivan Papylev, who in 1943 went over from political work to combat duty. All of them are now Rear-Admirals.

The years have left their mark on the health of many of my comrades. Rear-Admiral Chernyshev, who headed our Political Department, is now in the Reserve. Engineer-Captain 1st Rank Pyotr Miroshnichenko, who was our brigade flag deputy Engineering Officer, has retired. Despite his illness he does some lecturing and is active as a social worker. Also in the Reserve are Hero of the Soviet Union Rear-Admiral Nikolai Lunin and Rear-Admiral Nikolai Morozov, who had a record of more than twenty war patrols in Midgets. I, too, am now in the Reserve.

I have named only some of the men who deserve to be named and whose names I remember, whom I meet to this day or with whom I am in correspondence. I have had unexpected, accidental meetings with many of them, and these meetings always afforded me the greatest of pleasure.

In March 1961, while I was travelling in a Moscow suburban train, I was suddenly hailed by a man whose face looked familiar. As soon as he began to speak I recognized Warrant Officer 1st Class Lisin, who was helmsman in S-14. He was now skipper of a large motor vessel plying the Volga.

Meetings like these awaken many vivid and bright memories. Besides a lot of bitterness, we had in the war much that we remember with pleasure. First and foremost, this concerns the comradeship that frequently helped us to achieve the impossible.

I feel sad whenever I think that I shall never again see Hero of the Soviet Union Rear-Admiral Ivan Kucherenko, who died in 1959, and Boris Skorokhvatov, who was brigade Chief-of-Staff almost throughout the war. But these are only two of many. Time has inflicted tangible losses upon the ranks of the North Sea submariners, who had passed through the crucible of combat.

Though these men are no longer with us, they live on in the memory of the people. The work of many of them is continued by their children. The name of Kautsky, for example, figures in the list of officers of the submarine fleet. Alexander's wife Vera and two sons lived in Leningrad throughout the siege and the war. She brought up her sons to be worthy of their father's memory. The older boy, Alexander, is now

Captain 2nd Rank and serves in submarines. Igor, the second lad, also served in submarines but was later transferred to shore duty because of ill health. He is an instructor at a naval school and holds the rank of lieutenant-captain.

Some time ago I paid my last visit to the North, and it seemed to me that I was once again in the atmosphere of the war. As I walked along the streets I read their names. Victor Kotelnikov Street. Kerim Gadjiev Street. Israel Fisanovich Street. Fyodor Vidayev Street. Arkady Moiseyev Street. Ivan Gandyukhin Street. As I gazed at the simple plaques on the corners of the houses I felt as though I were meeting my old comrades, as though they were walking by my side. It was pleasant to know that their memory is revered in the town where they had lived and fought. It meant that the traditions laid down by them were revered, that they were held up as examples, and submariners were doing their best to tackle problems in the way they had been tackled by Fisanovich, Vidayev, Gandyukhin. . . .

The best monument to those who perished were the new submarines and surface vessels moored alongside the piers of distant Northern garrisons. The new ships of the qualitatively new fleet have multiplied their combat might many times over. This is due not only to the increase in the number of ships but also to atomic reactors, electronics and accurate and formidable missiles.

A courtesy visit was paid to Sweden in 1961 by the submarine depot ship *Victor Kotelnikov*. Other ships of the Northern Fleet have been named after other wartime commanders: Kerim Gadjiev, Fyodor Vidayev, Nikolai Stolbov. Vasily Veresovoi and Dmitri Galkin.

During the war these names were known not only in the Soviet Union but also in the countries that were our allies. Regrettably, some people in these countries have adopted Hitler's mad idea of a "crusade" against communism. It would be useful if they saw the ships that bear the names of heroes of the Soviet submarine fleet. It would remind them of what our numerically small submarine forces accomplished during the war, and it would help to give them an idea of the fighting potential of our present, numerically large, new submarine fleet, whose strength lies not only in up-to-date technology but also in men who are prepared to lay down their lives for their country.